ECONOMIC FORCES IN FRENCH HISTORY

By the same author

THEORIES OF IMPERIALISM

INDUSTRIALIZATION IN NINETEENTH-CENTURY EUROPE

ECONOMIC FORCES IN FRENCH HISTORY

by

TOM KEMP

Senior Lecturer in Economic History at Hull University

London
DENNIS DOBSON

First published in Great Britain in 1971

by Dobson Books Ltd, 80 Kensington Church Street, London W.8

Printed by Willmer Brothers Limited, Birkenhead

Bound by C. Tinling & Co. Ltd., Prescot

ISBN 0 234 77238 7

Contents

Preface

There are few economic histories of France for the period covered by this book in English or, indeed, in French. Until recent years economic history has not had an established position in the French universities and it still does not compare with the comparatively exalted and independent status which it enjoys in Britain. This undoubtedly accounts for the paucity of general works in French. To explain the lack of such studies in English it suffices to mention the insularity in which the study of the subject in Britain is still locked.

Despite the lack of general studies, however, there has in recent years been an abundance of research of a high calibre both by French historians and economists and by foreign, particularly American, scholars. Liberal use has been made of the results of such research in writing the present work. The American emphasis has been to a large extent upon entrepreneurial history. French scholars, working under the conditions imposed by the peculiarities of the French doctoral thesis, have produced mainly elaborate and detailed studies of particular problems and short periods of time, often within the confines of a restricted geographical area. While the Americans have offered brilliant suggestive ideas of a generalized nature, French scholars have tended to eschew the broad synthesis for the microcosm.

The British contributions to French economic history, few in number, have been mainly notable for their empirical and common sense nature. As a general text Sir John Clapham's *Economic Development of France and Germany* remains the standard work for English-speaking students. Much of the detail of Clapham, as well as the broad outline of the work, remains valid to this day, but since his book was published much interesting work in French economic history has been done on both sides of the Atlantic. There seems to be room, therefore, for a book which seeks to supplement rather than supersede it by making accessible to the student the results of this research and distilling it into a fresh narrative with a different perspective.

The present work, therefore, does not stand alone as an introduction to French economic history; in that respect it is not a textbook. It does not claim, either, to be a work of original scholarship: it is compiled from secondary sources not from new research. As an interpretive account of French economic development it aims to interest the advanced undergraduate or research student, or the general reader interested in French history, in the problems as they seem to be in the light of modern work on economic growth and the lines of enquiry opened up in the economic history of other countries. It would be a fair criticism that it is not sufficiently rigorous or explicit in its treatment of economic growth and that it is essentially a 'qualitative' treatment of the old kind. The reader who ponders this work will, however, find a model of economic growth, though one which cannot, perhaps, be detached from the material which it attempts to order and explain. In any case, this is not the place to embark upon a methodological discussion of the relative merits of the qualitative and the quantitative approach of the kind which is now going on amongst economic historians. In fact there can be no exclusive reliance on pages of prose or upon statistical tables and econometric analysis. If there is very little of the latter this stems in large measure from the author's lack of competence in these fields – but he would add that however important it is to accumulate and process quantitative information, and a strong school under J. Marczewski is doing just that for the French economy, in the last analysis it is through the analysis and interpretation of structural changes and a many-sided approach to the society as a whole that historical studies are most likely to yield fruitful results.

There is no attempt here, then, to compete with the specialists in quantitative history. Certainly the French past offers a rich field for their enquiries. There are enormous areas of French economic history which have not been covered at all by any method. In fact, in the present state of things it may seem pretentious and hazardous to offer a work like the present one which is, in essence, an interpretive essay in economic change and development. Such a synthesis, in view of the state of French economic historiography, is bound to be tentative and perhaps premature. It seems useful, however, to attempt a general outline, filling in the gaps where necessary with an hypothesis which others can then proceed to explore, verify and where necessary discard.

It is on these modest lines, therefore, that this study seeks to fill a gap in the literature. It is far from being a compendium of facts and for a full descriptive treatment other works will have to be consulted. It does not profess to be complete or definitive in any way. In places it re-iterates some well-worn hypotheses, in others it suggests that some of our stereotypes may be overdrawn or of little use. It invites the student to further thought and study. It offers a coherent account of what the author sees as the dominating economic forces in French history before 1914, but it does not strive to give a complete or rounded picture of all aspects of economic change. It may cast some light on the problems of economic and social change in contemporary France by revealing their historical roots.

For the period since 1914, however, only a summary treatment is attempted here. The author is now engaged on a fuller study of the French economy between the wars which will carry the story forward on a more adequate scale.

This study was begun some years ago and continues an interest in French society and history which dates from the last war and which has been heightened by many personal and family ties. Stimulus to continue it was provided in discussions with Professor Herbert Kisch of Michigan State University. Thanks are also due to Professor Grant Reuber in whose department at the University of Western Ontario I spent the session 1965-6 and worked on the second half of this book. No doubt this work owes more than I realise to the students and colleagues in the Department of Economics, University of Hull, with whom I have discussed the problems of economic history over the past twenty years.

CHAPTER I

French Agriculture Before the Revolution

THE AGRARIAN ECONOMY OF THE OLD RÉGIME

THE economy of eighteenth-century France was overwhelmingly agrarian. This in itself would account for the low income per head and sluggish rate of change under the old régime, especially since the actual conduct of agriculture was in the hands of a peasantry which lacked the will or the means to effect important changes in productivity. In this respect France shared the characteristics of the whole of the rest of the world at this time: she was an 'under-developed' or pre-industrial society. Yet these broad categories conceal as much as they reveal. What was significant was not what France had in common with the rest of Europe, indeed most of the settled areas of the world, but the distinguishing features of her economy which made her the most advanced of the Continental countries with a relatively rapid rate of growth. In the agrarian economy some reasons for this may be found, but the main forces of change lay outside the sphere of rural life which was dominated by custom, tradition and long-established habit. An agrarian economy, especially one based on peasant agriculture, was unlikely to develop autonomous forces making for change and growth. The question really was how adaptable it would be to the stimuli and pressures generated by the growing points in trade and industry. In turn, the extent to which these sectors could bring about a major transformation in the whole national economy would depend upon their ability to break through the defensive barriers which rural societies erected against change. For this is was necessary to find allies within. Agrarian change was most rapid, and most conducive to industrial development, where it was assisted by the landowning class turning to commercial methods or by the emergence of new incentives to stimulate increased output from the direct producers, either through the operation of market forces or through policies encouraged or imposed by the state.

The cultivation of the land

The formation of the French agrarian landscape, with all its regional and local variations, had its roots deep in the past.[1] Conditions of climate and soil, the nature of the land and the plough used to till it, the cultural influences which had been dominant in the early stages of settlement and the vicissitudes of wars and price movements accounted for the specific characteristics and variations. It was a pattern still in continuous if almost imperceptible change under the pressure of population growth and new social forces. Retrospectively the signs of an agrarian revolution can be discerned, but its nature and eventual outcome had yet to be determined. The Revolutionary years after 1789 were to be the great crucible for change. The nature of the land settlement which then took place was to have great formative significance for the whole of subsequent economic development.

Most of Northern France falls within the area of Europe in which the open-field type of agriculture prevailed, following a three-field, more rarely a two-field, rotation. Under this type of agriculture the land lay in three great arable fields, divided into strips whose holders were obliged to conform with the routines of cultivation based upon custom and imposed by the collectivity. Thus, although the land was owned or held individually—or more strictly by members of the families which made up the village—and there was no pooling of the cultivated product, husbandry itself was a collective and not an individual operation. It assumed and imposed a high degree of social cohesion on the part of the members of the village group. Not only were their holdings inextricably mixed up in the arable fields, but after harvest they became available for pasture for the animals of the villagers. Around the village lay woodlands, meadows, pastures, commons in which they possessed various customary rights to gather fuel, wood, food, fodder and whatever else nature might yield of economic value. These rights were an essential part of the economy of the open field village, no less important to the cultivators than their arable strips. The rights themselves were regulated according to immemorial custom and were far from being regarded as burdensome restrictions by the peasants themselves.

The replacement of the two-field by a three-field system, where it had taken place, had represented an important step forward in raising the productivity of the land. Since it had been learned that continuous cropping exhausted the fertility of the soil, custom imposed a fallow year. The adoption of a three-field rotation was clearly less wasteful, and indicated that the land was more fertile, or that the technique of cultivation was better than on land where half lay uncultivated each year. On the other hand, even the abandonment of a third of the land to nature represented a waste. True the plants which grew provided nourishment for the village beasts, which in turn provided indispensable manure. It was, indeed, only as crops became available which could do this more efficiently, or provide direct nourishment for the population or raw material for industry, that the extent of the waste could be measured—and then much less by the villagers than by those who brought to husbandry an empirically scientific approach of which the villagers were not capable. There is no doubt that we have here two sharply contrasting attitudes of mind. For the peasant the first necessity was that the land should produce a sufficiency for those who lived on it. This the open fields were able to do, and would do better if part of the peasant's time was not spent cultivating the land of others or part of his product not expropriated by the lord, church and tax-collector. Custom, tradition and the sheer lack of any obvious alternative thus gave this type of agriculture, and all the practices bound up with it, deep roots in a whole society from which it was inseparable. It could only go when this society was destroyed or profoundly re-shaped. In the meantime the open fields, with their collective servitudes, were adopted to a society desperately short of capital, operating at a low level of technique and understanding and having to produce from its own soil practically everything which it consumed.

For successful operation the open field system pre-supposed a certain degree of soil fertility, a certain balance of land and population. It was a complex and delicately balanced system whose flexibility was limited, but which had behind it the proven experience of centuries. In sparsely populated, infertile and newly-settled areas; in mountainous and broken country; on land which was not suitable for the heavy wheeled plough, other forms of land use and field layout necessarily prevailed. Representing a combination of arable with pasture farming it was likely to be less firmly rooted where crops other than cereals prevailed or where pastoral activities assumed a major rôle. Thus even in Northern France the open fields did not hold universal sway. In Brittany and other parts of Western France enclosed fields of irregular size and shape were used for arable farming side-by-side with extensive communal pastures. The individualism found here was thus of a relative kind, which had arisen not from the pull of the market but from the adaptation of thinly scattered communities to a rugged country of poorish soil. This was still a form of group settlement and cultivation, but in scattered hamlets rather than villages. The abundance of pasture made collective grazing on the arable fields unnecessary. Part of the common and waste would be brought into temporary cultivation as occasion warranted and according to the custom of the country. It was only the abundance of available land which permitted individual ownership and enclosure of the permanent arable.

If the great 'champion' country of Northern France was part of a greater band running across the continent, and Brittany represented a Celtic fringe with a régime similar to that to be found in parts of the British Isles, the South had felt more firmly the imprint of the classical Roman pattern. Here the two-field system prevailed, still with outposts extending as far North as parts of Alsace, but giving way in places to the three-field rotation. The greater yield of the latter, where conditions were suitable, account for its spread at the expense of the two-field system. Throughout the Midi proper, however, the two-fields maintained their sway; by routine, perhaps, or simply because a less fertile soil and a more arid climate made any alternative impracticable. At the same time, however, the two-field system in this area was coupled, not with strip-farming, but with irregularly shaped patches generally rectangular in form. This layout was no doubt connected with the use of a lighter plough which could be turned more easily but cut a shallower furrow into the dry soil. In this region there had never been the same need for a closely-knit and regulated communal effort in the processes of husbandry as in the lands of the North. Communal pressures, though important in the past and still tenacious in the eighteenth century, were less pervasive in the areas of irregularly sized holdings in the South. On the other hand the soil was not bountiful and the external stimulus to a faster development of individualism was lacking, at least until the eighteenth century, though the barriers to it were certainly weaker. In some places, where transhumance was practised, the ending of communal practices for pasture was a step taken by the cultivators to defend themselves against the large sheep-raisers whose flocks passed through, and grazed on, their lands.

In most places pride of place was given to the basic cereals needed to feed the population. Green vegetables and root crops were only slowly adopted by the mass of the people who, besides, eat little meat. Some areas were suited for the growing of fruit but unless, like apples it could be turned into cyder, or like olives into oil, the market was limited by the possibilities of conservation and transport. The vine, of course, was cultivated where conditions were favourable or where nature could be assisted by improved techniques of cultivation. The development of specialised vine production was an evident mark of the growth of an exchange economy. Producers were favourable to the free circulation of cereals, as well as wine, since they could then drive ahead with profitable specialisation without regard for the food supply. Likewise, the production of the vine brought many small peasants an invaluable cash addition to their incomes. Despite this, cereals remained the basis of the agriculture, as of the dietary, of the population in the eighteenth century. Inevitably, therefore, agricultural specialisation was held back as almost everywhere some land, perhaps a substantial part, had to be devoted to maintaining the essential food supply. The state played its part by restricting internal trade in grain: a source of contention under the old régime.

The ownership of the land

What distinguished French agriculture in the eighteenth century was that almost everywhere the control of agricultural operations remained in the hands of the peasant cultivators acting through the village communities. Whether as owners or as customary or contractual tenants it was they, and not the lords, who determined how agriculture should be practised. To a large extent, though not invariably, the seigneur was interested in his estate only in so far as he could exact a revenue from the peasants who lived on them. Frequently he was an absentee for the whole or a good part of the year and had become entirely parasitic as far as agriculture was concerned. In many cases he left large areas uncultivated for purposes of the chase or from sheer lack of desire or incentive to do anything else with them.[2] This was the outcome of a long process of development in the status and fortune of the nobility since the fifteenth century which had reduced its powers relatively to those of the Crown while cutting it off from active concern with the problems of estate management. Even the wealthy bourgeois who became ennobled through the purchase of state offices, or the patrician families from the commercial towns, tended to follow the pattern established by the traditional land-owners and not to concern themselves with agriculture.[3] There were, of course, exceptions and signs of change in the course of the eighteenth century. In some areas, such as Normandy, large landed property was stronger relatively to the peasant community and enclosure of land and the leasing of land to larger farmers had been going on from the sixteenth century. But the general rule was for the seigneur to view his estate merely as a source of revenue derived from the customary dues and obligations levied on the dependent peasantry. He might be satisfied to lease these rights for an agreed payment to a 'farmer' who would then exact what he could from the cultivators.

From a purely economic point of view, then, the nobility drew off a surplus from the land and put little or nothing back. It was, as a whole, not familiar with the process of investment as a means of improving the productive capacity of the land. It was not an investing but a spending class. However its spending may be judged, it cannot be claimed that it did as much to further economic growth as judicious investment might have done.[4] On the other hand, more systematic concern with, and investment in, agriculture by the nobility, if delayed until the eighteenth century, would have brought them into a sharp collision with the peasantry. Profitable investment would hardly have been possible without disturbing that collective bundle of rights and individually heriditable titles which the peasants had to the lands over which the jurisdiction and ownership of the nobility nominally extended. To improve the land would have meant exerting rights to the common and waste and ending the practices associated with the open fields which were basic to the existence of the peasant community. It would have involved the interests of the Royal Government which, while bound up with the privileged orders, had no wish to see those privileges extended and might be alarmed at the threat to public order which a blow at the peasantry would entail. Not least it also drew off part of the peasant's income in taxes and *corvées*, while the lords enjoyed fiscal privileges which the events of the 1780's were to show they were unwilling to give up without a struggle which brought into question the foundations of the state.

Sections of the nobility did, in the course of the eighteenth century, move tentatively towards an attack on the agrarian problem. Estates were extended, some urban capital found its way into the land, improving landlords appeared and attempts were made by the Provincial Estates, or by the Government, to facilitate enclosure, a necessary step towards improvment.[5] The pressure of rising prices on the incomes of the nobility, coupled with the growing opportunities for commercial agriculture and specialisation, account for these tendencies. Economists and physiocrats were emphasizing the land as the main or unique source of wealth and income and thus its improvement as a means of increasing them. They placed the improving landowner in the centre of the picture and saw in the ancient communal practices the main obstacle to improvement. Their conception of property followed the absolute right of use and abuse of the Roman law. An outlook was developing, and had already penetrated the ranks of the nobility, especially the *noblesse de robe,* which was profoundly bourgeois in conception. It differed markedly from the old seigneurial view of property which looked back to the Middle Ages, and was definitely alien to that which prevailed in the peasantry. The educated men, mostly landowners or wealthy bourgeois themselves, who formulated and accepted the enlightened ideas of the eighteenth century regarded the peasants in much the same way as any self-confident class of property owners regards those who appear to be unenterprising, slothful and ignorant.[6]

The penetration of the bourgeois view of property, and all that it meant for society, had been taking place slowly for some centuries. In the course of the eighteenth century, however, it gripped many landowners who had formerly been content to move in the old grooves and the *intendants* and other officials of the Royal Government coming on the scene by the mid-century were themselves more open to the ideas of the reformers. Yet individual property, especially agrarian individualism, came into collision with the deeply-rooted practices of the peasant mass, a mass, not of isolated individuals, but of collective groups associated in village communities.[7] There was developing through this period, in essence, a trial of strength between two antagonistic conceptions of property representing conflicting social forces. Yet the lines were by no means clearly drawn and the course of the struggle was accompanied by strange paradoxes.

Bourgeois individualism, sometimes expressed by a nobility which itself had no intention of renouncing its feudal privileges, had to break through the defences of the peasant village if it was to find unequivocal expression in agriculture. The peasants still lived in a pre-capitalist environment; a minority only had an interest in seeing the extension of agrarian capitalism. The whole experience of the peasant was with a society firmly cemented in an inherited complex of rights and obligations relating to the village lands. He was a willing prisoner of his traditional inheritance, by whose standards his view of property rights was determined. He did not understand property in its Roman or modern 'bourgeois' sense. Land was generally held or 'owned' subject to a set of understood limitations on its free use or disposal and the acceptance that others, indeed the whole village community, might have rights over it for which other valued rights were obtained in return over the 'property' of others.

The lack of sustained seigneurial concern with agriculture, whereby most of the nobility became mere rent receivers, enabled the village communities to perpetuate and strengthen themselves. In the past the peasants had vigorously resisted feudal encroachments both by violent revolt and, in more recent times, by firm collective action or by litigation. However low the material conditions of the peasants and however heavy the feudal burdens to which they were subject, the village community provided a living organ for the maintenance of customary prerogatives and opposing new exactions. The power of the community to defend the interests of the peasants, varying from case to case, was at all times conditional. It could be weakened and eventually destroyed from within by the growth of discordant tendencies within the peasantry. It could be threatened with destruction from without by the noble landowners and the state. Its powers, indeed its very existence, at any moment depended upon a balance of forces, the relative strength of the peasantry on the one hand, and those aligned against the old communal ties and practices on the other.

The renewed interest of the nobility in their estates was a major threat to the village community. The nobility had obtained the right to take one third of the commons. In places it was seeking to facilitate the process of enclosure and the division of the commons. At the same time it was seeking new means to increase or add to the already extremely burdensome charges to which the peasantry was subject. Through these efforts ran two contrasting strains. A re-assertion of feudal rights over the land by such means as the re-imposition of old dues which had fallen into desuetude was accompanied by a growing tendency to see the land as a commercial asset. Both threatened the village community. The pressure against the peasantry built up, but so did rural opposition to the exactions of the lay and the ecclesiastical landowners. What the outcome would have been without the Revolution it is impossible to guess.

It does seem clear, however, that the offensive against the communal practices of the peasantry proceeded very unevenly and did not involve the nobility as a whole. The State, or its agents, ready to support the improving landlords from the mid-century by measures favourable to agrarian individualism, drew back when it recognized that the weight of opposition could result in a threat to public order.[8] The attempt to squeeze more out of the peasantry by the old methods which made up the so-called 'feudal reaction' had behind it only the sanction of privilege and the old forms of property embodied in rotting documents secreted in the manor house. It differed fundamentally from the methods used by the enclosing landlords in England and those in France who sought to follow their example. It looked back, not forward, and it explicitly accepted that the peasantry had to remain on the land and continue to control the operations of agriculture. It represented, therefore, a sign of weakness: the French nobility as a whole neither would, nor could, clear their estates and open the way for a rapid development of capitalist agriculture and increase, by the same stroke, the labour available for industry.

The question of who owned the land was really subordinate to the continuously changing balance of forces between nobility and peasantry upon which the privileges of the former and the customary usages of the latter rested.[9] The fact that the noble landowners generally had lost any intimate contact with estate management placed them at a disadvantage from which, in fact, they never recovered. To ask whether it could have been otherwise would entail a lengthy review of French social history up to and including the Revolution which displayed the full power of the village community. Nominally a large part of the land which the peasants regarded as theirs was still the lords' and was subject to varied and often onerous charges. As long as an equilibrium was maintained between feudal owner and village community the peasant 'owned' his holding and could pass it on by inheritance or in other ways. In general the peasant was free to leave the land; it was the land, not the peasant as such, upon which the burden fell. The balance could not have been tilted decisively in the lords' favour without destroying the village community and asserting the rights of strict law against immemorial custom. It could, perhaps, have been done, as it was done in other countries, had the lords had the power to do it and been able to enlist the state on their side—but it was unlikely. The whole of preceding French agrarian history told against it and the Revolution was in line with it. Events from the 1750's showed the inability of the nobility to adapt the old forms of ownership to changing conditions and thus ensure its survival.

In the light of the above, then, it can be said that the peasantry was not only dominant in agriculture, but had also acquired what amounted to *de facto* rights of ownership over a substantial part of the land. On that account it can be said that peasant proprietorship was firmly established before the Revolution, though from a strictly legal point of view it was not full ownership. Peasant property was subject not only to the rights of usage possessed by other members of the village community but also to payments in money and kind. Apart from this the owner could dispose of his holding by sale, gift or lease and pass it on to his heirs. We are speaking here of the plots which had a distant, probably servile, origin, the heriditable tenures on the manorial estates. In addition peasants rented land from the lords, as well as from each other, for money payment, while in places *métayage* was widely used. The question of the economic welfare of the peasant was not entirely bound up with the amount of land he owned. Equally, if not more important, was his ownership of the means to work it successfully, notably a plough team, and of liquid reserves.[10] Where land was available to rent and in close proximity to urban markets, the enterprising agriculturalist was a tenant farmer rather than a peasant owner. There is no doubt, however, that there was also a notable rural proletariat, or near proleteriat, made up of peasants who had no land at all or insufficient to support themselves and their families and only the strength of their own arms.[11] The growth of the rural population, coupled with the custom of dividing land on inheritance, had created, in places, excessively large numbers of small holdings. All this meant a chronic problem of land hunger over a large part of rural France.

The above characteristics must be seen in the light of

the considerable regional variation which made up the agrarian map of the eighteenth century. The extent of peasant, noble and Church land differed very markedly from place to place and considerable differences could even be found within, as well as between, provinces. In some places, moreover, bourgeois families from the towns had established themselves on the land, taking the place, to some extent of the nobility of ancient lineage. According to Lefebvre's studies it appears that the share of the nobility varied from 9 to 44 per cent on a regional basis; that of the clergy from 1 to 20 per cent; that of the peasantry from 22 to 70 per cent[12]. It should be emphasised again that a great part of the noble domains was, in fact, leased out to peasants and that the distinction between these peasants and those regarded as 'proprietors' was not always easy to make. Not only did the peasants own a large part of the land, but a large number of peasants appear as owners of land: *mercellement* was already an established feature of the French agrarian scene. Inevitably this meant that the technique of agriculture was backward and that the surplus above the subsistence needs of the peasants, which, in any case was largely garnered in one form or another by nobility, Church and State, was less than it might have been. On the whole this was a primitive subsistence agriculture; peasant ownership was, if anything, a brake on more rapid development.

No doubt the reasons for the slow rate of change in agriculture are not to be sought exclusively in the agrarian structure. Poor communications, lack of markets, deprived agriculture of the vital outside stimulus which it needed: where this did exist, on the other hand, the old structure underwent change or came under pressure. And, so far as this happened, differentiation within the peasantry proceeded. Those owning draught animals were able to produce a surplus for sale in the market and to employ their less fortunate neighbours who had little or no land. The richer peasants, through their ownership of stock, often benefited correspondingly to a greater degree than the poorer peasants from the old communal practices. At the same time, their possession of reserves gave them important advantages. They did not, like many of the poorer peasants, have to sell grain immediately after harvest, but could hold stocks until prices rose. Besides being employers of labour they might also play the rôle of usurers lending seed or money to those hard hit by private or general adversity. Within the village community, therefore, there was often a clear social distinction into a rural 'bourgeoisie' and a landless proletariat. The solidarity of interest embodied in the opposition to feudal burdens, and to a somewhat lesser extent in the preservation of communal practices, was bound to come under strain after their disappearance.

The crisis of the agrarian economy

The social setting within which the peasantry lived, although it possessed relative stability, was undergoing continuous change. The disintegrating effects of commercialism were visible in the divisions which had appeared within the peasantry itself. A large proportion of the peasants, varying, of course, from place to place, now appeared in the market either as the sellers of commodities or as sellers of labour power, perhaps as both. A peasant economy, which in any case is completely exposed to the fluctuations in the harvest, finds itself doubly vulnerable when it becomes dependent upon the effects of those fluctuations on prices, wages and the demand for labour. Yet it must be remembered that the changes which were undermining village self-sufficiency also made, under favourable conditions, for an improvement on the past, at least in aggregate output. Agricultural improvement, slow as it was, increased the food supply. Without such an increase it is difficult to explain the growth in the population as a whole, as well as the increasing proportion no longer directly engaged in agriculture. As generally happens in a pre-industrial society, increases in food output were in large part eaten up by a growth in the rural population. This manifested itself in eighteenth-century France in some of the ways already referred to: continued division of holdings, growth in the landless proletariat and in the number of peasants having to supplement the family income by some form of wage earning. Part of the population growth was simply squeezed onto the fringes of society where it existed in a state of chronic mendicity—the great social problem of the time.[13]

This situation contained contrasting elements of improvement and deterioration. In the first half of the century there was greater internal peace than in the past, the incidence of wars was less acute, harvests were reasonably good, plagues and epidemics were perhaps less devastating. Under these conditions population and production grew and agrarian society was more settled than it had been in the past. There were no great peasant uprisings in this period, but the village community consolidated itself and built up a resistance to the pretensions of the nobility which was to save the peasantry from destruction. Yet, at the same time, the basis of this society became more precarious, more subject to sharp swings in fortune. Rural overpopulation and land hunger steadily built up to become chronic problems in many areas. They became less easy to bear as changes took place within the village along the lines already sketched. Peasants desperately short of land, or overwhelmed by feudal charges on their plots, cast covetous eyes at the large farms, or land held and worked by the lords or the clergy. The events of 1789 can only be explained as the outcome of a smouldering resentment built up over time and under conditions which differed from those which had prompted peasant revolts in the past. A change in the attitude of large sections of the peasantry can be assumed from its behaviour since, as an inarticulate class, it left few records of its opinions and outlook. If the peasantry was largely impervious to the thinking of the Enlightenment, it was itself the product of changing conditions which threw into relief the capacity of man to alter nature and to turn it to his will and, following this, showed that he need not be the plaything of social forces either. The quest for material progress and security had reached the village, but a village still in the grip of social arrangements which denied it to many, if not to most. The peasant reacted in his own way: for him the land should provide a sufficiency for all, though not necessarily an equal share, and the fruits of the land should belong to those who tilled it. These sentiments were embodied in the practices of the village community and the informal expressions of peasant will: a collective, not an individual, will.[14]

The complex criss-crossing of the forces of change with the custom of centuries produced new disturbances, a new insecurity in peasant life, which have been subjected to sophisticated study by modern historians.[15] We are warned to see the eighteenth century not as a uniform bloc but as a phase of development characterized by 'short term rises and falls, . . . some periods of slow progress, some periods of accelerated progress, and exceptionally some of decline.' A surge of prosperity after the Seven Years War was checked in 1770 to be followed by a further advance which was arrested in 1778 and led into an abnormal decline which ended about 1787. These movements were expressed in the price trends of the main marketable commodities produced by the agrarian sector, namely wine and cereals. The price trend of the latter was broadly upward from the 1730's to 1817: this reflected the dominant rôle of cereals in the food of the populace and the pressure of rising population. For those who had a surplus of cereals to sell, therefore, the period was generally, if not uniformly, favourable. In the face of steadily increasing demand supply proved relatively inelastic and was especially so in the short-run. A shift of income to sellers of grain could therefore be expected to have taken place. But the majority of the small peasants, proprietors or tenants, and obviously those with insufficient land to support themselves and their families, were not sellers of grain and might even be net purchasers, especially when bad years are taken with the good. If the harvest had always drummed out the rhythm of rural life it now did so to the accompaniment of the ominous echoes thrown back into the village from the market place.

A large part of the peasantry had little grain to sell, or none at all, because the surplus had been paid away to lord, tithe-owner, taxgatherer and usurer. The marketable surplus passed through the hands of these people or came from the larger growers. Those who collected their share of the produce in kind benefited particularly from the upward price trend. Farming for the market would also be encouraged. The peasant mass, however, which needed to conserve part of the grain for seed and consumed the rest, gained nothing from rising grain prices and, so far as it bought grain, would be adversely affected. To meet necessary outgoings the peasant might have to sell directly after harvest, when prices stood at their lowest point, and buy in during the spring and early summer when he was waiting for the harvest to ripen. The rising prices stimulated commercial agriculture and benefited the recipients of rents and dues; they also enriched those engaged in trade in farm products. There was growing prosperity, but it was unevenly spread. It contributed to the growth of towns and thus to the prosperity and self-confidence of the urban bourgeoisie. The towns in turn stimulated investment in trade and industry and were the basis for the prosperity of the trade in colonial products. At the other end of the scale there was a growth in rural poverty and mendicity: some deterioration in an already miserably low standard of living.

Eighteenth-century France was able to keep more people alive in the lower layers of society. The peasant family had more mouths to feed, more heirs among whom often exiguous plots of land had to be divided. Younger sons left the village in search of work. The landless proletariat grew. The demand for labour expanded, but not fast enough to prevent the growth in the disposable labour force from exerting a downward pressure on wages. The numbers buying some or all of their food requirements in the market increased and the aggregate demand for grain rose correspondingly, sustaining the upward price trend. The total amount paid out in wages was becoming larger but, as Labrousse has put it, 'the human diviser increased even more rapidly. In the end the "real" share of each individual diminished. This fall in wages stands in marked contrast to the increase in the return on capital during this period'.[16] In short the situation was favourable for capital accumulation and investment, including investment in agriculture, but it aggravated the problems of the wage-earner and the small peasant. Short term increases in the price of cereals could affect them disastrously, driving up the proportion of income which had to be spent on basic bread grains and reducing the income left over for other purchases. Such price increases, resulting from a short-fall in the harvest, would hit the rural wage-earner in a double sense: less labour would be required to bring in the crops and both wage-rates and work done would decline. Even Government intervention in the grain trade could only moderate local price movements and not arrest the general trend.

Over a large part of France wine provided the main cash crop for the peasant cultivators. Wherever it was important it linked the producer closely to the market since he consumed only a small part of his product and depended upon the price realized by his sales to purchase his other requirements. The wine-grower was thus pre-eminently a commodity producer and not a subsistence farmer: he had to sell to live and the price at which he sold determined how well he would live until the next harvest. From a national point of view the vine came second only to cereals in agricultural production and held first place in the exports of agricultural produce. The vine supported a large number of small peasants and many larger producers who employed some hired labour. Any change which affected the wine market had direct effects on large numbers of people; two and a half million, according to Lavoisier.[17] When prices rose peasants and workers flourished, investment was encouraged, potential output was increased. Such a period of expansion and relative prosperity extended from the 1730's until the late 1780's: half a century of growing production and profitable trade in the wine-growing areas and in the towns associated with them, like Bordeaux. All the more serious, therefore, were the effects of the price slide in the wine market which subsequently set in. Profits were struck a severe blow. Fixed money charges, dues, rents, taxes, became a heavier real burden. The demand for labour fell away. The incentive for improvement and the extension of cultivation disappeared. The large producers, specializing in high-grade wines, and the merchants were hit, as well as the mass of small cultivators.

Only a few less important sectors of French agriculture, such as stock-raising, mostly carried on by large farmers, were spared the effects of the depression of prices of the pre-revolutionary decade. Almost everywhere, however, the privileged orders, as receivers of rent in kind or money, of feudal dues and tithes, were able to defend themselves against the price fall as they had benefited during the period of rising prices. The loss involved in the receipt of produce whose prices had fallen could be offset by setting severer conditions for the small farmer or *métayer*. The small tenants held their land more frequently on a *métayage* tenure than for a money rent. With the number of prospective *métayers* tending to outrun the supply of land, the proprietors were able to take full advantage of their strong bargaining position to increase their real share of the produce above the customary half. The amount of land let out to each *métayer* could be reduced, fiscal charges could be shifted to him and the task of extracting the maximum from the land hunger of the peasantry could be left to a 'farmer' who made his own terms with the *métayer* in return for an agreed payment to the landowner.

Down to the Revolution, therefore, French agriculture was in the grip of a growing crisis, a veritable impasse to which no solution seemed likely within the prevailing social relations. The growing real burden on the peasantry, including most of the small 'proprietors', as well as the *métayers* and landless proletariat, account for the explosive outcome of the crisis, which was to be solved violently, from below. The *Cahiers de doléances* of 1789 were to express vividly and angrily the extent and depth of peasant grievance against the practices of the feudal order and the state which sustained it.

Conclusions: the pre-revolutionary agrarian scene

Although agriculture had enjoyed a period of relative prosperity in the half century up to the end of the 1770's it had undergone comparatively little technical improvement. The old methods of husbandry and the old field layouts generally prevailed, with their waste of cultivable land in the fallow year and their restrictions on change and improvement. This was chiefly because the control of agriculture remained with the peasantry, which was still deeply enmeshed in the old communal customs and had neither desire nor incentive to change. New crops and new methods were taken up slowly and then generally only on the larger farms or where landowners, under the influence of the Physiocrats or the English agronomes, took an interest in technical improvement. There were relatively few such improving landowners in France. The central and provincial authorities took some tentative steps towards stimulating enclosure and promoting agrarian change, but rapidly drew back when the social dangers became clear. The main part of the agrarian surplus went into the coffers of the State, the Church and the Nobility: very little found its way back to agriculture or even went into productive investment. In this sense the social structure of the old régime was a positive drag upon more rapid economic growth and ensured that what growth did take place was of a one-sided character.

The French agrarian system before the Revolution may be said to have been a kind of decadent feudal order. It supported a privileged but functionless nobility which sought to maintain or increase its income by imposing still further burdens on the peasantry. At the same time, while the material conditions of the mass of the peasantry deteriorated, a substantial section of it established what were virtually rights of ownership over as much as 40 per cent of the land. The village community, unlike its English counterpart, remained a vigorous organ of the peasantry able to resist the pretensions of the nobility, if not always very successfully. Despite the so-called 'feudal reaction' the social position of the nobility was being steadily undermined even while it maintained or increased its share of the national revenue.

In its existing technical form, as long as agricultural investment was held back and a large part of the product went to sustain the privileged orders, French agriculture could not support a growing population without a deterioration in living standards. In particular there was a continuous increase in the landless or semi-landless rural population which had to work wholly or partly for wages or fall into dependence upon public or private charity. An uneasy, mobile mass of workless and underemployed had been created and was swollen in every period of agrarian underproduction. Inevitably real wages fell. No doubt the amount of wage work grew, but it may well be asked why this ostensibly large pool of labour power did not give rise to more rapid industrial growth in the closing decades of the eighteenth century? The answer, if one can be given, clearly involves an examination of other sectors of the economy.

Notes and further reading

1. M. Bloch, *Les caractères originaux de l'histoire rurale française* (new ed. Paris 1952) is the classic work and has been freely used in this outline. Published in English as *French Rural History: an essay on its basic characteristics* (translated by J. Sondheimer, Oxford 1966).
2. It was this trait which so much irritated Arthur Young. Speaking of the prince of Subise's estate he says, 'whenever you stumble on a Grand Seigneur, even one that was worth millions, you are sure to find his property desert. The duke of Bouillon's and the prince's are two of the greatest properties in France; and all the

signs I have yet seen of their greatness are wastes, *landes,* deserts, fern, ling.—Go to their residence, wherever it may be, and you would probably find them in the midst of a forest, very well peopled with deer, wild boars and wolves. Oh! if I was the legislator of France for a day, I would make such great lords skip again.' *Travels in France* (Bohn library ed. edited by M. Betham-Edwards), pp. 70-71. Also his reflection on the Prince of Condé's forest around Chantilly, said to be 100 miles in circumference—'That is to say, all the inhabitants for that extent are pestered with game, without permission to destroy it, in order to give one man diversion. Ought not these captaineries to be extirpated?', p. 11.

3. Many of the smaller bourgeois who acquired land looked on it as a badge of status or an investment. They preferred to deal with tenants, often *métayers,* rather than to occupy themselves with farming.
4. The tendency to 'pity the plumage and forget the dying bird' has often operated in appraisals of the French nobility. Whether its cultural monuments were as much surpassed by those of the bourgeoisie as its material contribution certainly was must remain a matter of opinion. See, e.g. N. Hampson, *A Social History of the French Revolution* (London 1963), p. 13.
5. The most thorough and perceptive account is M. Bloch, 'La lutte pour l'individualisme agraire dans la France du XVIII siècle', originally published in *Annales d'histoire sociale,* Vol. 2, 1930, and reprinted in *Mélanges Marc Bloch* (Paris 1963).
6. The gulf between the masses and the upper classes was clearly immense as indicated by Young's observations. The idea that the peasant was destined to be the beast of burden and support for society was deeply rooted and accompanied by a feeling of mistrust and contempt. As Lefebvre puts it: 'everywhere, for the bourgeois and the townsmen, as well as for the nobility, he remained an ignorant and uncouth being, destined, following tradition, to maintain the ruling classes, to be the main source for supplying the Royal treasury and to feed the urban population', G. Lefebvre, *La révolution française* (3rd ed. Paris 1963), p. 53. Fear of the 'populace' or the '*canaille*' was extremely widespread, ibid. p. 63.
7. The history of the French peasantry had, for centuries, been one of struggle to preserve and win recognition for the rights embodied in the village community. 'In the eyes of the historian . . .' wrote Bloch, 'agrarian revolt appears to be as inseparably connected with the seigneurial regime as the strike from the big capitalist enterprise', *Les caractères . . .*, p. 175. An accessible study is that of A. Soboul, 'The French Rural Community in the eighteenth and nineteenth centuries', in *Past and Present*, No. 30, 1956. As he sees it the village community 'possessed a certain administrative structure, an economic system founded on the interplay of communal pressures, the limitation of private property and the existence of collectively exploited lands', p. 80. The struggles of the peasantry are dealt with at length in G. Walter, *Histoire*

des paysans de France (Paris 1963). See the comparison between the French and English peasantry in J. L. and B. Hammond in *The Village Labourer* (London 1927), Introduction and pp. 80-1. For the Hammonds the French peasant was 'not a casual figure in a drifting proletariat: he belongs to a community that can withstand the seigneur, dispute his claims at law, resume its rights, recover its possessions, and establish, one day, its independence'. This was certainly true of part of the French peasantry: there was, in addition, a 'drifting proletariat' and antagonistic interests within the village community.

8. M. Bloch, 'La lutte pour l'individualisme agraire . . .'
9. On the question of property see the writings of Bloch and Lefebvre; also F. O. Sargent, 'Feudalism to Family Farms in France', *Agricultural History*, Vol. XXV, No. 4, 1967, and A. L. Davies, 'The Origins of the French Peasant Revolution of 1789', in *History*, Vol. XLIX, No. 165, February, 1964.
10. Hence the classic distinction between the *laboureurs,* having at least one plough team, and the *brassiers,* literally those having only the strength of their own arms. But the distinction is not complete; there were intermediate groups and a *brassier* could be a small peasant proprietor rather than a proletarian. In fact each area tended to have its own distinctive social structure. See the discussion in B. H. Slichter Van Bath, *The Agrarian History of Western Europe* (London 1963), pp. 310 seq.
11. Was there a class division within the village community? Lefebvre speaks of *'les coqs du village'*, a rural bourgeoisie, employing wage labour. Soboul's article cited comes down against the existence of class divisions, on the grounds that there were no total and absolute rights of property. E. Julliard, whose *La vie rurale dans la plaine de Basse-Alsace* (Paris 1953) is a valuable addition to French agrarian history, contests this and reveals the different types of social structure—not based on differences in the fertility of the soil—to be found within a single region.
12. Lefebvre's article 'Répartition de la propriété et de l'exploitation foncière à la fin de l'ancien régime', first published in 1928, reprinted in *Etudes sur la Révolution française* is capital for this question. On Lefebvre's basis of ownership about one-third of the land belonged to the peasants; see *La Révolution française,* p. 58.
13. As much as one-fifth of the population was destitute.
14. There is no doubt that the peasant wanted his *own* piece of land, but his conception of property rights remained different from that of the bourgeois lawyers as the Revolutionary period was to show.
15. Especially, of course, in the works of E. Labrousse to whose *La crise de l'économie française à la fin de l'Ancien Régime et au début de la Révolution* (Paris 1943) the following paragraphs are mainly indebted.
16. Labrousse, *La crise . . . ,* Introduction, p. xxxi-xxxii. An English translation of part of this Introduction appears in R. W. Greenlaw, *The Economic Origins of the French Revolution* (Boston 1958).
17. See Labrousse, op cit. Part two.

CHAPTER II

Industry in the Eighteenth Century

THE INDUSTRIAL STRUCTURE OF THE OLD RÉGIME

In eighteenth-century France the society of the old pre-industrial type reached its apogee and at the same time became subject to new and intolerable strains from which the revolution of 1789 issued. However, this revolution was not made by industrial capitalists or businessmen and was not a consequence of rapid industrial growth. Rather can it be said that the failure of the old régime, despite its intervention in the economy, to provide the conditions for such growth prepared the way for its own downfall by aggravating social tensions and discontents.

The intellectual influence of France dominated the Europe of the eighteenth century, but it was a dominance based on the needs, tastes and outlook of the ruling class of the old régime.[1] The sway of French culture was exerted, in fact, over small minorities of the educated élite; the masses were not yet a force in history. The Revolution of 1789 and the industrial revolution germinating in Britain were to propel them onto the historical stage. This was not yet the age of mass production or of mass consumption. The industry which existed was mostly geared to the low purchasing power and customary needs of small peasants and artisans, to the luxury expenditures of the wealthy and to the strategic and administrative demands of the state. The social structure offered little incentive for breaking away from traditional methods of production and organization. What industrial expansion took place in the eighteenth century was thus, in large measure, along the old lines. It represented a response to growing wealth and to expanding population, but did not itself make a decisive contribution to the character and rate of growth of the economy as a whole. In short, the French economy remained an economy of 'the old type' throughout the eighteenth century and well into the nineteenth.

Factors in industrial development

The population of France throughout the eighteenth century remained overwhelmingly agrarian, although it grew considerably in size.[2] The agrarian population consisted predominantly of peasant households which had little to sell in the market and thus could only buy little. Most of what they needed to buy could be obtained from village craftsmen, from travelling salesmen or at periodical markets and fairs. In aggregate no doubt the market for cheap textiles and household articles was large. The reason why this market was not tapped earlier and more rapidly by large scale producers is to be found primarily in the fragmentation of the market. Although thousands of kilometres of roads were built for the state during the century the rural population was still poorly served and transport of bulky goods of low value on the roads was prohibitively expensive over long distances.[3] Markets for cheap commodities were mainly local, or at best regional in scope. Under these conditions there was little incentive for the transformation of production even had the technical possibilities for doing so existed. There was, however, no shortage of labour: in fact, growing population and the difficulties of many of the peasant families in maintaining the customary consumption levels, provided abundant labour in the rural areas which could be employed in domestic industry.

The towns of the eighteenth century were primarily centres for trade and administration, not for production. The industry which was carried on in them served the needs of the urban population itself, or found a market in the surrounding villages. Only a few towns, such as Lyons, had a wider national or international market. The organization and technique of production had, on the whole, undergone little change since the middle ages, especially in the complicated traditional crafts requiring trained skills. Some of these crafts served a broad market of townspeople and rural dwellers, others were of a luxury or semi-luxury kind, producing for the needs and sometimes to the order of the nobility and urban patricians. The disproportionate pull of the wealthy on the market under the old régime is revealed in the importance for the industrial structure of luxury production. Of greater intrinsic value, luxury articles could be distributed more widely and the prestige of French taste and artistry gave them entrance to a European market.[4]

The craft industries were deeply in the grip of custom and tradition. In most cases they were strongholds of the small masters, though they might be producing to the order of substantial capitalists, working alongside a few journeymen and apprentices. The routines of production changed little. They had behind them not only the ingrained conservatism of the craftsman, but also the regulations of the guilds and the state. The entry of fresh enterprise and capital into these fields was thus restricted, if not completely excluded. Any growth in demand could be taken care of without a major change in the scale of the unit of production or simply by an increase in the number of units of the old kind. But a revolution in demand imposing structural change in these industries was impossible under the circumstances of the old régime.

The pattern is not very different in many of the producer goods industries. The building up of industrial capital had scarcely begun. There was little demand for heavy and complicated machinery and what was required would be mainly built on the site. The peasantry was still using mainly wooden tools and implements. Iron was required chiefly by local smiths and artisans rather than by large processing units. The heavy metal industry continued to be geographically dispersed in small units near the forests upon which they depended for fuel.[5] Here, as in other sectors of industry, increasing demand could be met by a multiplication of units rather than by concentration.

What is characteristic of this pattern so far is the relative absence of spontaneous elements of change and expansion. It has a built-in tendency to reproduce itself rather than to accept growth or change. In this it accords with the nature of the surrounding social and economic environment. There were few impulsions towards more rapid change in industry; one of the major ones came from the State, with consequences which, in the circumstances, were bound to be ambivalent.

The regulation of trade and industry by the state was a matter of course in all countries before the rise of the doctrines of economic liberalism which only began to assume a coherent form in the course of the eighteenth century. It is important not to read into the policies of statesmen in this period a conscious desire to promote industrialization and economic development. Their motives were largely political and their object rather to stimulate particular sections of industry than to bring about a general transformation. They were concerned with the enhancement of the power and the security of the dynastic state, not with economic growth as conceived in the modern world. Thus Colbert and his eighteenth century successors thought largely in static terms. They shared the mercantilist idea that one nation could only increase its wealth at the expense of others. They manipulated the economy for fiscal and strategic reasons and the total result of their actions lacked coherence and is difficult to appraise. Certainly restriction and regulation were constant features of state intervention in the economy. The detailed industrial codes drawn up in Colbert's day, so far as they were observed, set strict limits to industrial change and innovation.[6] On the other hand, the officers of the state played a part in encouraging the implantation of new industries and used public funds to develop large scale production in some fields. It is scarcely helpful to conclude, however, simply that the rôle of the state was stimulating and inhibiting at the same time. No doubt more research is required on the nature of the relations between the state and the economy in eighteenth century France before a more significant judgement can be made.[7]

There are, however, some aspects of the problem which have to be brought into the picture. The state was not an independent organ standing above society; it expressed in a combined way a balance of interests between often discordant social forces. The pretensions of the dynasty towards greater independence and centralization of power, although they had made considerable headway, were opposed by the privileged classes. Events were to show that the Crown could not govern against the nobility and the nobility could not survive without the Crown. To balance its powers against the privileged hereditary caste of landed proprietors the Crown had found allies and support from those whose wealth consisted of liquid funds and resources rather than landed property. The sale of offices to ennobled bourgeois created new long-run problems for the monarchy. It raised up new centres of privilege, equally opposed to an extension of royal powers, and removed much of the growing pool of wealth from the grasp of the royal fisc. The whole social environment sucked the successive new layers of enriched merchants, men of law and industrial entrepreneurs into the orbit of a status society, where the goal was to live nobly from the proceeds of landed property or prudent investment, rather than to pursue accumulation for its own sake. Much wealth which might otherwise have found its way into industrial investment thus flowed into other, less productive channels. The state found itself financing, or assisting others to finance, industrial development which might have taken place through the operation of market forces—but only if the whole social and economic structure had been different. In the last analysis, then, it seems unlikely that the old régime could have made possible more extensive and rapid economic growth. The growth and change which did take place in the eighteenth century may have hastened its own end.

At the same time it has to be pointed out that the French merchant and industrialist of the eighteenth century took as a matter of course the presence of the state in the economy. When, after 1789, the bourgeoisie attained political dominance it did not make a clear break with the economic policies of the old régime. Indeed, it may be said that the state interventionism of Colbert established a strong and virtually indestructible tradition in French economic policy which the bourgeoisie was to use and interpret in its own interests, though one again with mixed results.

Varieties of industrial organization

Although the industrial sector of the French economy was relatively small, and its specific weight even smaller, it displayed considerable variety in size of the productive unit and type of organization. These characteristics have to be seen against the whole background of a mainly agrarian country with poor transport facilities and many artificial obstacles to the full operation of market forces—internal tariffs, gilds, state regulations and restrictions. At the same time other factors favourable to growth were present and becoming more potent. Population was growing and there was no general scarcity of labour, though there was of some forms of specialized and skilled labour. There was a general growth of 'wealth' to which many factors contributed, including improvements in agricultural productivity, the growth of foreign trade and an expansion of the internal market as witnessed by the growth of towns and the rise of the bourgeoisie. Despite the inhibiting effects of gild and state regulation an aptitude for technical change and innovation was being demonstrated in some fields. An examination of the industrial structure will help to explain why no major break through took place in the period before 1789.

In the accounts of French industry in the eighteenth century there is a tendency for those industries which have left most documentation, chiefly in the form of state regulations, to receive disproportionate attention. The widely scattered home industries carried on by the peasantry are apt to be overlooked although they made a much greater contribution to total production and were gaining ground at the expense of gild-dominated urban industry.[8] Some of these industries would be carried on by the peasants on their own account, others would be organized by commercial capitalists. The latter, who can be designated as merchant manufacturers, provided circulating rather than fixed capital: money for wages, raw material, work in progress, stocks of finished goods, rather than fixed plant and machinery. Although they might have central premises in which some of the processes were carried on, it was their ability to tap the cheap labour supplies of the rural areas which accounted for their success, a success based on organization and the dominance of capital over the direct producer rather than upon technical improvement. The splitting up of the process of production into component parts which could be reduced to a routine labour carried on by workers with little skill, not only undermined the position of the urban crafts, it also brought the rural workers completely under the control of the manufacturer. The producer could no longer deal directly with the market; he came to depend upon a middle man, necessarily one possessing capital, who could organize the passage of the material from one stage of production to the next. This applied to such comparatively skilled trades as cutlery, as well as to the production of woollen and linen cloth which was the most ubiquitous of the putting-out industries of the eighteenth century.

Small scale units of production employing mostly handicraftsmen prevailed in the urban industries which, in the larger towns, were still subject to gild regulation. Industrial towns, such as Lyons, were conglomerations of artisans working in their own homes or small workshops, not concentrations of large-scale enterprises. Thus, apart from a few islets to be noted later, France before 1789 had no proletariat of a modern factory type. The town working class, or that part engaged in industry, remained artisan in character. By their influence in the gilds the masters had succeeded in some trades in securing a hereditary position of privilege: high entry fees, impossibly complex *chefs d'oeuvre* demanded of the apprentice, excluded the majority of the artisans from hope of becoming masters because of the length of time involved in their making. In other cases, however, the social differences between masters and wage-workers do not appear to have been so great.

Artisan type organization covered a wide range of products, some of which entered widely into the consumption of the urban population, others of which catered for the wealthy, the urban patriciate and nobility. A hierarchy of grades of skill, earnings and status thus existed. Only the luxury products could be expected to find a market outside the limits of the town, except for certain specialities. The mass of the peasant population could hardly afford to buy the relatively costly products of urban artisan industry. Its own necessities would be more cheaply available from the village craftsmen or from the rural putting out industry.

The contribution of large-scale enterprises to French industrial production remained small, although there are signs that it grew in the latter half of the century.[9] But, before the Revolution, there were few genuine factories in France and the level of technique outside a few fields did not bring about concentration. A part of the large-scale industry was, it might be said, organically related to the needs of the economy. Thus, in the textile industry, finishing processes such as bleaching and especially printing required large premises and expensive equipment. In coal mining and in the iron industry the pull of the market and improvements in technique led to the investment of capital in large units, though even here the large-scale enterprise remained the exception. In the decades before 1780 some beginnings were also made in the development of factory production in the new cotton textile industry.

At the same time there existed the traditional policy of subsidizing and encouraging large scale manufacture by the state. These were strictly 'artificial' creations set up to serve the needs of the state, to reduce dependence on foreign imports or for reasons of a non-economic kind. They were examples of a general practice in the absolutist states of the time and were in no real sense precursors of modern capitalist industry. They were not intended to initiate a process of industrialization. In part they were, of course, filling gaps which private capital was unwilling or unable to fill, at least without special privileges and support. They indicated the still rudimentary basis of France's industrial economy rather than the beginnings of a real industrial transformation.

A number of *manufactures d'Etat*, including arsenals as well as the famous Gobelins tapestry establishment, were operated by the state. More numerous were the *manufactures royales* which were privately owned concerns encouraged and assisted by government grants, loans, contracts and privileges of various kinds. Similar aid might also be forthcoming from the provincial and municipal authorities. Frequently monopolistic in character, such rights might have to be won and retained by court intrigue and promises of a share in the proceeds, which could be very large. No doubt some of these establishments introduced new processes or techniques into the country. They impressed contemporaries by their size and organization and were among the first to introduce into France techniques and processes which were later to be at the heart of the 'Industrial Revolution'.[10] Even so, these enterprises were closely bound up with the old régime. They produced for the needs of the state and the wealthy, not for a mass market. They could not, for the most part, lead on to a breakthrough to more rapid growth in the economy as a whole. They may have diverted capital from other more productive uses, or blocked the flow of capital into some fields where monopolistic privileges were granted. In this particular sphere it may be that the state assisted a process of capital formation which would not otherwise have taken place, but, by its total action the state, and the social order to which it was bound, inhibited more rapid growth.

In fact, the development of the rural manufactures already alluded to were much more significant in preparing the ground for industrial capitalism than were the artificial creations of the state. In the last stages of the old régime its own officials were coming to realize the stifling effect of many of the old regulations and, responding to the increasingly pervasive influence of economic liberalism, brought about their modification. For example, in the 1750's, after much debate, the import and manufacture of printed fabrics was permitted. This opened the way for the development of the cotton industry and particularly for the investment of capital in the finishing of fabrics. Private capital was thus pushing its way into new fields in close association with rural industry, notably in areas where a landless or semi-landless peasantry existed. In any case, even the state-protected industries depended a good deal upon putting work out in the countryside, the central premises being concerned mainly with finishing processes.

Certainly new fields were being opened up for capital investment and the improvement of technique, including the adoption of the new textile machines which were coming into use in England.[11] State officials showed themselves aware of the new possibilities, as shown by the assistance proferred to Kay and Holker in the development of the textile industry. But the concern of the state with new fields does not appear to have been any differently motivated from its former policy; at best it is less restrictive, but its positive action is doing no more than keep up with changing requirements. The iron industry illustrates the way in which state intervention in industry was closely linked to power-political concerns. The backwardness of the French iron industry—itself closely related to the nature of its main markets—led the state to intervene to obtain anchors and cannon balls of adequate quantity and quality early in the century. The progress which was taking place in Britain caused further disquiet with the result that the government sent a technician across the channel to study modern methods of iron production, in 1764. In the following decade William Wilkinson was encouraged to settle in France to manage a state cannon factory. Later, in collaboration with the de Wendels of Lorraine, he worked on the preparations for the modernization of Le Creusot. This enterprise was commissioned by the government which provided part of its financial requirements. The de Wendels themselves were very much bound up with the old régime, and were ennobled by Leopold of Lorraine, rather than being entrepreneurs of a modern type, pushing their way forward from the ranks of unknown people. Le Creusot itself remained for some time an isolated phenomenon in an industry which fell increasingly behind its British counterpart.

The fact that the state was actively concerned with some of the most advanced units of French industry should not mislead one into misjudging its rôle in French industrialization. Although it could promote a few large scale enterprises it was not able to provide the conditions for a broadly-based economic advance because to do so would have involved a fundamental change in social relations, laws and institutions.

Technical conditions of industrial production

The technical conditions of French industry corresponded to the structure already outlined. Taken as a whole industrial production was still carried on in the old way and signs of a change only became visible in the second half of the century. 'Until about 1750-60', writes one recent authority, 'the industrial equipment of France remained practically what it had been in the past, and, with the exception of a few technical improvements made in the course of the sixteenth and seventeenth centuries, it remained faithful to medieval traditions'.[12] In most lines of production there had been little departure from traditional methods. Human muscle and energy, the skill of the human hand and eye were still of overwhelming importance. Tools and techniques changed slowly, if at all, over the centuries. Any gains in productivity took place rather from improvements in organization than from technology. Quality and uniformity in the product depended upon the level of skill obtained by the worker and only reached a high standard in expensive commodities. The substitution of the machine and mechanical power for human labour was still only at its beginnings. In short, industrial production had not yet undergone a revolution.

To say that there was little investment in industry is to make the same point from a different angle. No doubt there was no shortage of liquid capital in eighteenth-century France. Fortunes were built up both in trade and in financing the activities of the old régime. No doubt some of the newly accumulated wealth found its way into industry: but industry itself had not yet become a main source of accumulation. The outlets for industrial investment remained comparatively restricted. The newly rich put their money into the purchase of public offices, into land and buildings, lent it for the purpose of consumption by others. Some was no doubt simply hoarded. What was lacking was a powerful stimulus to invest in productive industry. The conditions of the old régime tended to militate against such a stimulus being offered. Even the investment it did require had to be encouraged and cajoled by special privileges or made directly from the public treasury. Neither the institutions for, nor the habits of, industrial investment yet existed in a developed form. On the other hand some members of the nobility, and even of the Court, did, at times, invest in industrial enterprise. Industrial entrepreneurs did emerge who built up their businesses by ploughing back profits. A process of capital accumulation and concentration in industry was already going on and was to gather strength in the second half of the eighteenth century. Industry began to emancipate itself from commerce and become itself the basis for important fortunes and even for new bourgeois dynasties which were to play a prominent part in the development of French industry and still exist to this day.[13] The rôle of mobile capital became steadily more important and sought profitable outlets in industry. But, although this process did quicken in the second half of the century, it was far from assuming the dimensions of a general movement able to alter the basis of the economy or set it on a decisive new course. Moreover, French industry, which, on the whole, had kept pace with that of Britain in the first three-quarters of the century was henceforth to be out-distanced by a more powerful rival.

Indeed, it is in this period that the origins of the problem of France's industrial lag may be said to be found. As this lag is relative, and as the standard of comparison for the next century or more is Britain, the question is why France did not begin an industrial revolution in this period? In fact there was no lack of technical knowledge or skill. There were French inventors and innovators and a constant flow of English entrepreneurs, workers and machines or know-how into France. The state actively assisted the process of introducing new techniques. Undoubtedly methods and equipment in industry did improve and the basis was laid for a modern large scale industry, notably in cotton textiles and metallurgy. But this development, significant as it was, remained limited in extent, while over the main field of production the forces of traditionalism prevailed. The new units and techniques were inserted into the old framework; as yet they did not lift it to a new level or instil a new dynamism into the economy as a whole. There was a slow and partial change, continuing that which can be discerned throughout the eighteenth century, but there were still powerful barriers to change and growth. These were to be found primarily in the social and economic structure which was conducive to the maintenance of privilege and acquired positions rather than to enterprise and innovation.

Even the moneyed and trading bourgeoisie, to a large extent, adapted itself to the possibilities offered by the old régime and adopted the outlook and goals of the reigning aristocracy. This can be seen in the avidity with which wealthy bourgeois purchased offices. It is shown, too, by the extent to which many of the richest financiers were closely concerned with the activities of the old régime. Tax farming drew off capital which might otherwise have found a more productive outlet and formed part of a regressive fiscal system which held back economic growth. The failure of the old régime to make any serious inroads into the traditional agrarian system, and hence the predominance of peasant agriculture, narrowed the market for industrial goods at the same time as it ensured that the surplus passed into the hands of those who had little idea of productive investment. In these circumstances, and reenforced by the burdensome internal tolls and tariffs, it is not surprising that France was made up of a series of local and regional markets, each of which was virtually self-contained. Some writers have stressed the importance of the lack of transport facilities in bringing this situation about, but the lack of an expressed need for improvement and the capital to effect them also has to be explained.[14]

In this environment the appearance of new techniques and inventions had less revolutionary effects than where, as in Britain, a whole series of precedent developments had, as it were, prepared the way for them. The purely industrial inventions of French origin remained, in this period, of limited application; the main new techniques were imported. Even when benefiting from government encouragement the technical inventions in the textile industry and in iron-making made only comparatively slight inroads into French industry before 1789. Indeed, the stimulus of the state gave them an essentially artificial character. They arose not from a spontaneous need for entrepreneurs investing capital to take advantage of market opportunities but from the intervention of a state which, at the same time as it ostensibly encouraged innovation in one direction, maintained a confused system of regulation and restraints on enterprise in others. It is not surprising, then, that the efforts of the state under the old régime were far from having the stimulating effects which, in different circumstances, state assistance to nascent industry has been able to achieve. In industry, as in other spheres, the efforts of the agents of the old régime were timid and piecemeal and perhaps helped to bring about its eventual downfall.

Growth and fluctuations

Despite the absence of an industrial revolution the French economy in the eighteenth century was undergoing growth and change which in some sectors were quite impressive. Taken as a whole the area in which the spontaneous operation of market forces held sway was steadily growing. Even large sections of the peasantry were being brought into a market economy as sellers of commodities, including labour power, and were buying in the market part of their requirements, including grain. As a result both peasants and townspeople were exposed to fluctuations geared, it is true, to the vagaries of crop returns but operating in a more complex way than in the past. A shortfall in the harvest of grain pushed up its price leaving all those who had to buy into the market at some time of the year, which included many of the peasants, short of income to buy other goods.[15] Industries thus faced a constricted market at the very time when urban consumers had to pay more for their food: real incomes in the towns thus fell, with industrial depression accompanying the harvest failure. On the other hand, periods of abundant harvests reacted favourably upon urban and rural industry by expanding the market. In fact, as has been seen earlier, the long term tendency was for the increase in total real income to be more than cancelled out by rising population and thus a fall in the average real income per head took place. Nevertheless, aggregate demand rose, wealth was being accumulated, a substantial urban middle class appeared. Hence the pull of urban markets increased both for imported and for domestic produce. This was a properous period for the merchants and particularly for the West coast ports, homes of a prosperous mercantile bourgeoisie. A bourgeoisie, be it said, whose businesses were susceptible to the fluctuations brought about by external disturbances as well as by the effect of harvests on internal demand.

Against this background it is clear why the development of industry takes on a spasmodic, even a cyclical character in the eighteenth century. Markets for industrial goods might also be affected by changes in fashion or by hesitancy in the policy of the state or its officials. The appearance of new techniques introduced the possibility of the displacement or decline of particular sections of industries as well as the rise of new ones. Although the industrial structure as a whole was still firmly marked by traditional routine and stability the breaking up of the old rigidities was beginning.

In a number of sections of industry substantial growth is indicated by such data as exists. For example, there was a rapid growth in coal production between 1700 and 1789; but output had been negligible at the earlier date and was still much below the British level at the end.[16] The growth in coal-mining, including the famous Anzin enterprise, was far from constituting an economic revolution. Even in terms of available techniques many mines lagged behind and markets were limited by the high cost of transport.[17] The growth in the metal trades was modest until the late eighteenth and early nineteenth century. Most furnaces and forges were on a small scale serving the needs of an agricultural community and belonging, often, to local landowners. The few larger and more efficient firms founded during the century did not change the general character of French iron production. As a new industry, cotton developed from an early stage using machines and concentrating some stages of production in central buildings, especially dyeing and printing, but its big expansion was to take place after 1789.[18] Silk manufacture was growing in Lyons and the surrounding area in line with the general prosperity, but certainly short of the rate necessary to warrant speaking of an industrial revolution. Apart from these fields, and a few new industries which had rapid rates of growth simply because they were new but whose net contribution to total production was small, the picture is one only of slow growth or even of stagnation.[19]

The spectacular growth rates achieved by a few sectors of industry cannot remove the impression that in the later decades of the eighteenth century the French economy was falling behind its British rival, although it continued to hold first place on the Continent. Indeed, industry failed to take full advantage of the opportunities offered to it. The rapid expansion of trade from the West coast ports, for example, had a less stimulating effect on French industry than the corresponding growth of Bristol and Liverpool.[20] Merchants had to purchase outside France some of the commodities needed for trade with West Africa. The possibilities of trade with the United States after the War of Independence could not be exploited despite a favourable commercial treaty and British industry rapidly resumed a dominant position in the American market.

All through this period, of course, the French market was protected by high or prohibitive tariffs; at this time, however, all countries were protectionist as far as home industry was concerned. It could not have been the tariff alone which encouraged routinism in French industry. In any case smuggling was itself an important economic activity in the eighteenth century and much foreign, especially English, produce, found its way into the French market through illicit channels. Only relatively high priced goods could support the high costs of contraband trade, though raw materials, notably wool, also found their way into France. That trade between two neighbouring countries, the most economically advanced, should have been so narrowed by protectionism was no doubt a fetter on the growth of both. The eventual decision to reduce the restrictions on trade in the 1780's, however, was political, rather than economic, in origin, the initiative coming from the French side. The opposition of industrial interests to the Treaty of 1786 which facilitated the entry of English manufactures into France, and found expression in the protests of Chambers of Commerce and in the *Cahiers* of 1789, reflected a fear of competition which was probably well grounded.[21] In those lines of production in which technical improvements had already taken place British manufacturers no doubt had a cost advantage over their French rivals. However, increased imports under the Treaty could not have become effective until the summer of 1787 and the responsibility of the treaty for the industrial depression is largely a myth.[22] It was easy to blame the treaty for a crisis which had deep impersonal causes the origin of which escaped the understanding of contemporaries. At the most it could only have impeded recovery.

As it was, the freer trade with England lasted for only a few years; too short a time, and too abnormal, for it to have lasting effects if not to confirm French industrialists in their attachment to protection. Some French industries had, of course, nothing to fear from more open competition in home or foreign markets either because they were technically superior or because they enjoyed a natural protection. Others would certainly have been pressed very hard as the industrial revolution gathered way in Britain. As it was, the Treaty perhaps revealed most of all the inability of French manufacturers, in some spheres, to keep up with changing tastes and needs, in part, at least, because of the rigid specifications as to sizes and qualities to which some products were subjected under the Colbertist industrial regulation. At the same time, apparently, some manufacturers had become masters at passing off inferior products as being in conformity with the legal requirements, thus opening the way for foreign competition by undermining the confidence of consumers.

In the French industrial economy of the eighteenth century elements of the traditional and the advancing were combined in proportions which still overwhelmingly favoured the former. Growth was still constricted by the prevailing social institutions and relations which were far from being attuned to the requirements of industrial capitalism. The tradition and momentum already established, despite the thoroughness of the work of the Revolution in some directions, were to continue to have their effects for a long period into the nineteenth century. The conclusion seems to be that the French industrial lag began under the old régime, began, perhaps unnecessarily, or became unnecessarily wide, as compared with England. It still has to be explained why it became wider still in the Revolutionary and post-Revolutionary periods.

Notes and further reading

1. On the importance of French cultural and intellectual influence see R. Mousnier and E. Labrousse, *Le XVIIIe. siècle* (Paris 1953); this contrasted with the lack of any major French contribution to the techniques of production or finance.
2. On the interplay of demography and the economic movement see the works of Professor Labrousse cited in previous chapter. Also C. Morazé, *La France bourgeoise* (Paris 1946) pp. 117 seq.
3. On transport in this period see H. Cavaillès, *La route française*, (Paris 1946) especially, Ch. XIV. Lack of local roads remained a besetting problem in the rural areas until the Law of 1836, and after.
4. For mainly descriptive accounts of industry see H. Sée, *Histoire économique de la France*, Vol. I (Paris 1957) and *La France économique et sociale au XVIIIe. siècle* (1st edn. 1925). For an excellent concise analysis of the situation, P. Léon, 'Tradition et machinisme dans la France du XVIIIme. siècle'. *Information historique*, jan. fev., 1955.
5. In addition many forges belonged to members of the nobility; the calling of '*maître de forge*' was considered to be compatible with the status of a lord of the manor. See P. Gille, *Origines de la grande industrie métallurgique en France* (Paris 1948). Gille sees the survival of feudal forms of property, bad administration of forests and lack of capital as being the main forces holding back

the iron industry. In 1789 the output of 60 furnaces was estimated at 60,000 tons.

6. C. W. Cole, *French Mercantilism, 1683-1700* (New York 1943).
7. The problem is not always solved in a felicitous way, even by specialists, perhaps because French authors, for reasons of national pride, seek to find something to be said for French policy in a period in which the economy, as they admit, was being outclassed. Thus Léon claims that the policy of the state was expansionist, that it had a 'growth policy', 'L'industrialisation en France en tant que facteur de croissance économique', *First Conference on Economic History, Contributions* (Stockholm 1960), pp. 172-3. His conclusion is that 'while the State acted from many points of view as a factor of impulsion, it often acted as a brake. *Dirigisme*, regulation, did not have only favourable effects, but led often to the impeding of fertile initiatives, the paralysis of the spirit of invention and to maintaining enterprises in the framework of the past', p. 180.
8. On this point see H. Kellenbenz, 'Industries rurales en Occident' and works cited, *Annales—Economies, Sociétés, Civilisations*, Vol. 18, No. 6, sept.-oct. 1963, pp. 838-882, especially pp. 845-7. He concludes his brief survey by saying that 'there existed in all parts of France rural industries of greater importance than has commonly been thought, though one does not find anywhere the concentration and intensity found in England, the Southern Netherlands and certain regions of Germany', p. 847.
9. J. Koulischer, 'La grande industrie aux XVIIIe. at XVIIIe. siècles', *Annales d'histoire économique et sociale*, Vol. 3, No. 1, 1931, pp. 11-46. According to Koulischer, 'even at the end of the XVIIIth century there existed in France very few establishments which really merited the name of centralized factories (*fabriques centralisées*)', p. 26. Even where a part of production was carried on centrally, and perhaps with machinery, a great deal of the preparatory and finishing work took place outside the establishment and was often performed by the peasants of the surrounding countryside working in their own homes.
10. W. O. Henderson, *Britain and Industrial Europe* (Liverpool 1954), Ch. II.
11. W. O. Henderson, op. cit., p. 37 seq.
12. P. Léon, 'Tradition et mechanisme . . .', p. 5.
13. This was especially so in the metal industry. Gille notes the following names already prominent in the XVIIIth century which were to remain so through the subsequent history of French capitalism: Le Creusot, Dietrich, Wendel, Guérigny, Ruelle, Indry, Gouvy, Ramboury. The Japy and the Peugoeut were already ironmasters. 'Of a hundred and eighty nine metallurgical companies existing in 1927, sixty-two, or about one-third, had as their basis establishments going back to the XVIIIth century or even earlier. Gille, *Les origines* . . ., p. 205.
14. Cavaillés, op. cit., L. Cahen, 'Quelques caractères de l'économie française à la veille de la Révolution', *Annales d'histoire sociale*, Vol. 1, No. 3, 1939, pp. 238-250, giving the poor state of communi-

cations as a major factor accounting for what he calls 'economic provincialism'—the existence of virtually isolated regions. A student of Mayenne in the XVIIIth century explains its backwardness, even compared with other parts of the country as being 'in great part' a result of the state of communications. J. Suret-Canale, 'L'état économique et sociale de la Mayenne au milieu du XVIIIe. siècle', *Revue d'histoire économique et sociale*, Vol. XXXVI, No. 3, 1958.

15. E. Labrousse, *La crise de l'économie française* . . .
16. According to Léon, 'L'industrialisation en France . . .', coal output rose from between 50-70,000 tons in 1709 to between 450,000 and 700,000 tons in 1789. Production in England and Wales was already 4½ million by 1750.
17. cf. the problems of the Littry mines studied by G. Lefebvre in the article reprinted in *Etudes sur la Révolution française* (Paris 1959).
18. The prohibition of printed fabrics in France had stimulated the industry in peripheral areas, notably Alsace and Switzerland, from whence the product was smuggled into the home market. The ending of the prohibition brought Swiss capital into the French industry which, still in its early stages, grew rapidly, especially in the Rouen area.
19. P. Léon's figures, using rates of growth, certainly set French industrial achievement in a more favourable light, but the volumes concerned remained small (at least compared with Britain) and, as he shows, the traditional industries were mostly stagnating.
20. G. Martin, *Histoire d'esclavage dans les colonies françaises* (Paris 1948), p. 44. This trade, with its demand for outgoing cargoes and the import of colonial staples, did, of course, encourage capital investment in industry: refineries, distilleries and textiles, including cotton in the later part of the century. See also Ch. III, note.
21. L. Cahen, 'Une nouvelle interprétation du Traité franco-anglais de 1786-7', *Revue historique, année* 64, 1939, pp. 257-285. 'The truth is that . . . the discussions of 1785-7 coincided with a very serious crisis, which, by confusion, the treaty has been made entirely responsible for', p. 275. There was already an import of keenly competitive English goods through illicit channels. See also W. O. Henderson, 'The Anglo-French Treaty of Commerce of 1786', *Economic History Review*, Vol. X, 1957, pp. 104-112.
22. Henderson op. cit.

CHAPTER III

Commerce and Finance under the Old Régime

THE structure of commerce and finance was shaped by the two basic features of the French economy in the eighteenth century: the overwhelming predominance of agriculture and the central rôle of the state and the social hierarchy bound up with it. Most productive activity was concerned with the extraction of a living from the land and gave rise to only a relatively limited volume of exchanges requiring the use of money and thus opportunities for the dealer in commodities or money itself. At the same time, the surplus scooped up from the direct producers in rents, taxes and tithes generally assumed at some stage a money form. They might be payable in money and thus require that the producers should have some dealings with the market. If received in kind, some part would find its way onto the market. The pull on the market of the receivers of the surplus was of great importance. It gave rise to a host of subsidiary activities which catered to their wants: commercial and financial intermediaries and professional services were supported, as well as the production of commodities. Closely interlocked with these activities were the direct and indirect repercussions of the needs of the state.[1] The state appears as a revenue raising, and even more, as a revenue spending agency; in particular, the fact that its income constantly fell short of needs made it a permanent debtor. Serving the financial needs of the state was an important source of profit, but it was a profit which derived eventually from the tax-payers, that is to say, in the main, the agricultural community.

In the circuits of exchange established in eighteenth century France the scope for the spontaneous development of industry and trade remained limited. In fact, the flow of capital and enterprise into the dynamic centres of the economy was inhibited by the all-pervasive influence of the state and of the hierarchical social structure which it maintained. The maintenance of the old régime required complex financial operations and opened up possibilities for the profitable investment of commercial capital. Merchants, traders, financiers and bankers—representative figures of developing capitalism—already played an indispensable rôle and waxed rich. But it was still only on the margin that productive investment in industry was taking place. This meant that French trade and finance, even though growing and enabling large fortunes to be made, were largely re-distributing a flow of income which they did little to generate or encourage. The accumulations made in these fields did, of course, tend to seek new outlets offering larger profits. This can be seen, for example, in the growth of the colonial trade, especially the slave trade, and in occasional waves of speculation. Generally, however, it was the new entrepreneurs pushing forward from below, rather than those already in position, who turned to the new expanding fields opened up by the technical improvements of the late eighteenth century.

Before the Revolution industrial capitalism was still in its infancy in France and, as has been seen, often in leading strings to the state. Until capitalism came to dominate production over large and significant sectors of the economy, turning the direct producers into wage labourers dependent upon the owners of the means of production for employment, the French economy could not be regarded as capitalist in the full sense. In the eighteenth century there were capitalists undertaking capitalist-type dealings and capitalist relations of production in some sectors of the economy but there had not as yet been a fundamental change in the way in which the economic surplus was produced and appropriated. However much the French economy may have changed since the Middle Ages and however the relations between lords and king and lords and peasants may have been modified, the term 'feudalism' remains the most adequate one to describe it. The capitalist elements in trade and finance were thus still subordinate parts of a feudal economy; many of them, indeed, were not at all antagonistic to the upholding of the traditional relations of production but depended closely upon them. However advanced the practices of eighteenth-century merchants, financiers and bankers they must be appraised within this context. The institutions and social structure of the old régime held back the development of capitalism. Successive attempts at reform from within failed and only after the Revolution had run its course did an environment conducive to the full flowering of capitalist relations come into being.

The relative weakening of France as a maritime and colonial power during the eighteenth century must be accounted as a further factor holding back capitalist development. The adverse consequences of the wars of the reign of Louis XIV were followed, under his successors, by the loss of possessions in India and North America and the establishment of English power in these areas. The governments of the old régime were unsuccessful at their own game. France's world position weakened. Outside the Antilles colonial policy achieved little but failure. The strength of the French navy was far from being matched by that of the mercantile marine which, in tonnage, was barely more than one-fifth of the English. The trade with the Antilles had serious limitations and could not replace the wide access to a growing world market which only England achieved. The failure of the old régime to establish for France a secure position in maritime trade must be accounted as a serious impediment to economic expansion. As compared with their English counterparts, French merchants had less scope for expanding trade, accumulating capital and finding their way into new markets. Likewise, French industry received less stimulus from the pull of markets and from the fertilizing stream of capital accumulated in trade, even had it been equipped to respond. Even before the further losses of colonies and the interruption of trade brought about by the Revolutionary wars, the French economy was in a much weaker relationship to the world market than its English rival. Perhaps, in any case, there was only room for one industrializing power in this market; France's chance of being that power was already small.[2]

Internal trade and communications

In France, as in other countries, internal trade in this

period is poorly documented compared with foreign trade. The activities of pedlars, small retailers and traders at local markets and fairs leave few traces and cannot be quantitatively measured. What can be said is that despite the improvements taking place in internal communications the sheer cost of moving commodities restricted the market for the cheapest and commonest to a limited geographical area.[3] France was thus made up of a series of local or regional markets. Long distance trade inside the country was virtually confined to river routes, with carriage overland of the goods where necessary. River ports thus played an important commercial rôle.[4] Great attention was paid by the administration to creating and maintaining a system of roads, a system which, like the later railways, radiated from Paris. Technically well conceived and constructed, many of the French highways carried little commercial traffic, having been built for political and strategic reasons and having only poor connections with the villages and small towns in which the majority of the population lived. Local roads remained poor and bridges were often falling in ruin; little was done to remedy the situation. As a result each area was bound to be highly self-sufficient: it could not sell its produce far afield and consequently it could exert little pull on distant producers. There could be no substantial growth of the internal market until communications had been improved; likewise, regional specialization was held back.

Internal trade was further impeded by tolls and charges imposed by lords, towns and market authorities and by the division of the country into separate tariff areas.[5] The abolition of internal tariffs was only to be accomplished after 1789; the failure of the old régime to take this step illustrates once again the incoherence and timidity of its policy.

Generally speaking the retail trader was not highly regarded in eighteenth-century France, though the wholesale merchant was winning esteem and an accepted place in urban society. Despite the limitations to which internal trade was subject by the high cost of transport and the internal tolls and tariffs there seems little doubt about its growth in the prosperous ports and market towns. It provided a basis for the growth of local fortunes which went into urban building and into land purchase. Some capital accumulated in local trade may have found its way into extending commercial control over the crafts or establishing industry of the putting out type.

Travelling salesmen and fairs provided an important means for supplying the needs of the peasants and townsfolk which could not be satisfied from local production, in the absence of a more permanent network of distribution. There were signs, towards the end of the century, that distribution was improving. There were a number of fairs which had more than a local significance and which continued to play an important part in national and international trade and finance. At such fairs samples would be displayed and orders taken for the coming year and international financial transactions could take place. The continued vitality of fairs having a regional or even a national and international significance testifies to the development of commerce, but also to the fact that it was still not backed up by an adequate system of transport, distribution and credit which, as it came, would make them superfluous.

External trade

French trade with foreign countries both by sea and by land expanded considerably and apparently flourished during the eighteenth century; but this expansion took place on what was later proved to be an excessively narrow basis. Owing to the general conditions of the French economy, therefore, this expansion did not have the same effects in preparing the way for industrialization which English commercial expansion in the eighteenth century had.

French overseas trade developed within a framework of state regulation along 'mercantilist' lines and in a climate of national rivalry and trade war. The expansion and prosperity of this trade cannot disguise the fact that French merchants and ship-owners were obtaining a relatively minor share of a rapidly growing world market. In the struggle for world supremacy, as one writer has put it, France lacked not so much the means to win battles as the resources to throw into the final struggle where economic strength was decisive.[6] The latter half of the century showed economically the growing superiority of England. Neither the policy of economic regulation, nor the timid steps towards economic liberalism were able to arrest this relative decline.

At first sight French performance in foreign trade shows up brilliantly; it was unquestionably the most dynamic sector of the economy. On it was reared the prosperity during the century of the West coast ports and of the commercial bourgeoisie which formed their leading citizens. These ports were engaged practically exclusively in trade with the West Indies sugar islands. Their merchants supplied the French colonies with slaves from West Africa and with the manufactured goods or primary products which they required; not least they supplied the colonists with credit. In return they provided the exclusive outlet for colonial products: sugar, coffee, rum, indigo and cotton.[7] This was an extremely lucrative traffic as long as the conditions for it were preserved, including slavery and the slave trade. But its basis was narrow and, apart from the dominating hold of Marseilles on the Levant trade, it provided by the 1780's the only important overseas trading sphere for French capital and enterprise.

One major weakness of this trade, though it showed itself as a geographical one, was linked with the level of development of the French economy at this time. That is to say, the ports which carried on the West Indian trade lacked a flourishing commercial and industrial hinterland and were unable to bring one into existence. Their activity thus tended to remain peripheral in an economic as well as in a geographical sense.[8] It did not bite deeply into the agrarian and state-regulated French economy. The ports did develop their own industries, mainly the processing of colonial imports and the manufacture of outward cargoes for exchange in the slave trade or for shipment to the colonies. However, this only heightened their dependence on the colonial trade and did not bring them into much closer relation with the economic life of the rest of France. Indeed, the relative backwardness of many French industries meant that some of the goods needed for the trade had to be purchased in other countries. The consequence of this was that when links with the West Indies were cut the West coast ports went into decline. The period of trade expansion had either not lasted long enough, or had not been adequately made use of, to develop a healthy economic life able to generate industrial development. Once again, the general conditions of the old régime have to be taken into account. The sugar islands were very much a part of the old régime, an economic appendage of a mercantilist economy.[9] The trade and industry to which they gave rise was never closely integrated into the economy of France and did not serve to set it on a definitely ascending curve of growth. The figures of trade, taken by themselves, can, therefore, be deceptive.[10] They signify less a breakthrough into something new than a kind of growth compatible with the existing social and economic framework and extending its life. Commercial capitalism, although it generated forces which sought new forms of expression, could in many ways accommodate itself to the conditions of the old régime. As far as the West coast ports were concerned, the Revolution was to bring disaster rather than liberation.

Banking and Finance

In the field of finance eighteenth-century France presents a picture of paradox and contrast.[11] Men whose speciality lay in handling money and credit and who emulated the most advanced techniques in the field of finance assumed an important place in the economy and in society. They undertook vast and profitable operations involving skill and judgement. They accumulated mobile funds for which they sought a profitable outlet. They personified, ostensibly, the abstract forces of the market and of rational calculation which were penetrating more widely into French society at this time. Yet, despite the attention which they drew to themselves then and have attracted since, they existed on the margin of an economy to whose alteration and growth they made relatively little contribution. While they undertook the large-scale handling of credit and capital, French banking institutions and financial techniques continued to fall far short of what was necessary for the promotion of a dynamic and expanding economy. It was to be well into the nineteenth century before these gaps were to be satisfactorily filled.

The contrast between the advanced large-scale money dealing at the summit and an economic base desperately short of credit media and investment capital can best be understood if we begin with an explanation of the former. The eighteenth century 'financier' was a man of a special stamp linked body and soul to the old régime whose function it was to supply with ready money the state and court. The old régime, whose financial needs constantly outran its revenues, came to depend upon private individuals to collect its taxes due and to provide it with credit to bridge the gap between expenditures and anticipated revenues. As a debt economy of a particular kind it had need of creditors and of men who could put it in touch with creditors. Always short of ready money, it had institutionalized its improvidence by the sale of offices and increased its own impotence by the creation in this way of a special form of propertied vested interest opposed to the extension of the powers of the state and the creation of a more rational political and financial system. The purchase of offices thus became a means for the bourgeoisie to rise socially and to become embedded in the old régime itself.

The significance of these opportunities for the enterprising commoner to enrich himself and rise socially, indeed into the privileged estate of the nobility, was considerable, both economically and socially. The financiers and office-holders of bourgeois origin remained linked to the feudal order by interest and outlook as well as through the source of their income. They used their own capital, and more particularly what they could raise from the public at large, itself partly 'bourgeois', to finance the military and other unproductive expenditures of the old régime. They used their advantageous position to extend their financial deals either into speculative fields or into the sheltered outlets provided by state-subsidized and protected industry. Undoubtedly energies and capital which might otherwise have gone into private industry and trade were drawn away into activities which, by their nature, could make little contribution to economic growth. Successful financiers founded families which acquired titles and merged with the nobility at the same time as they bought estates and built stately mansions. Yet they remained, at their most successful, the clients of the state and their financial activities were built upon the shaky foundations of monarchical absolutism. In a rational, strictly bourgeois society they could have no place, yet there is also a clear line of descent from the eighteenth century financier to the finance capitalists of nineteenth century bourgeois France.

In any case the financiers found it increasingly difficult to satisfy the growing financial demands of the state. They were obliged to put into circulation an increased volume of paper titles based on their own credit, and on progressively less favourable terms. The state was thus increasingly obliged to resort to other means and to other men.

The persistence of the problem of state finance in eighteenth-century France is well known. It contrasts strikingly with the relatively effortless manner in which, in England, the state financed its increasing expenditure. At the heart of this contrast lies the difference in political structure between the two countries, itself a product of different social relations. The impossibility in France of adopting new techniques of state finance was demonstrated most sensationally by the rapid rise to influence and equally rapid fall of John Law. This is not the place to anlayse his activities in detail, but it is relevant to note what he set out to do, why he failed and the effects which his failure had for the subsequent development of French finance. Law seized, like others in his age, upon the hallucinating possibilities of new financial techniques which had, apparently, proved their worth in England and Holland beginning with a 'fund of credit' against which paper titles, or even money, could be issued. At its height his project had two sides: a monopoly of whole spheres of foreign trade and of tax revenues and, simultaneously, the operation of a national bank whose notes, backed by the credit of the state itself, would take their place as the exclusive money supply. The launching of Law's Company as a joint stock concern set in train a fantastic speculation which involved the moneyed middle class and part of the nobility. Within a few months the increase in the value of the Company's shares was 3,600 per cent and vast fortunes were made by those who bought and sold at the right moments. The trade and investment activity figured by these shares had, however, no material existence. The Company was a paper project, no more. As some sense dawned on the frenzied speculators they hastened to sell their holdings and share prices collapsed. At the same time as this speculation had been proceeding, on the promise of taking over the state's debts and solving its financial problems, Law had, through his Royal Bank, put into circulation a large volume of paper money which he sought to impose as the only money acceptable in the kingdom. Despite Law's final efforts to avert a catastrophe the collapse in the values of the Company's shares was bound to ruin the Bank as well, lead to his own discredit and make necessary the liquidation of his 'System'.

If the state was bound to return to its old ways after the failure of Law's project to resolve its financial problems, the effect on the public at large was to produce a similar conservative relapse in which mistrust of credit institutions and instruments was prominent. The farming of the taxes remained and, from 1726, was based upon a consortium of financiers responsible for collecting all the indirect taxes. But other means had to be restored to raise money, as will be seen. Throughout the eighteenth century France remained without a central bank. The kind of banking techniques which were becoming commonplace in England and Holland were introduced only at a later stage into France or were much less widely used. The use of credit in business dealings, at least of the smaller scale, was less widespread. Even the large commercial centres and ports remained without formal banking institutions. Familiarity with credit instruments and procedures thus tended to remain confined to a small and wealthy inner circle and only spread slowly. It would be as mistaken to exaggerate the influence of Law's experiment on this situation as it would be to ignore it as a negative factor in the development of French banking and finance. The old régime, by its nature, by the confusion which ruled in its own financial affairs, could not induce that atmosphere of confidence which was essential for the growth of the investment and banking habit among the broad layers of the bourgeoisie. Moreover, despite the tolerance accorded the financiers and bankers when its own affairs were concerned, the state ostensibly upheld the ecclesiastical prohibition on usury which, although under discussion, remained in force during this period.

How far can it be said that the slow development of modern financial practices in France flowed from the fact that she remained a catholic country? The debate around the theme of protestantism and capitalism has been long-drawn out and there is no need here to summarize its course or to make a new judgement. Added importance is given to the question, however, by the fact that the Revocation of the Edict of Nantes, besides depriving protestants of religious as well as civil rights, forced many of them into exile, taking with them their commercial and industrial skills and experience. The latest study suggests, however, that the persecution of French protestants had less widespread effects than has sometimes been thought.[12] The fleeing Huguenots represented no more than 12 per cent of all French protestants or about 1 per cent of the total population and while some specialized industries may have been affected by their departure the net economic effect, even when the gain of the recipient countries is taken account of, cannot have been great. However, the international ties of family and religion created by the Huguenot diaspora had a marked effect precisely in the field of banking and finance in which protestants played a prominent part, and became indispensable to the state itself. That these men were Calvinist in religion was probably of less importance than their other attributes. While generally of French descent they had acquired a different nationality and, by virtue of their international family connections, re-enforced by business ties—the two inter-penetrated by conscious design—they brought to the business of handling money and credit advantages which the native catholic Frenchman did not possess. They were, for example, in intimate contact with the most advanced commercial centres—England, Holland, Geneva—from which derived the most sophisticated financial techniques and in which were to be found reserves of investible funds ready, and able, to move across state frontiers in search of the highest return.

As a counterpart to this must be seen the problem, as well as the opportunity, of the member of a suspected minority, subject to discrimination and standing outside the order established. Business, in its widest sense, especially its newest and most rapidly developing fields, would offer attractive outlets for his energies and talents. It would be an activity on the margin in which he began, not merely free and equal, but without the disadvantage of a constricting moral outlook or direct personal attachment to the traditional corporative order. The economic expansion of the reign of

Louis XV, and especially the fact that this saw the international commercial ascendancy of the Protestant countries, gave the French section of the Huguenot international magnificent opportunities for enrichment.

The protestant 'bankers' of the eighteenth century engaged, together with others who were not protestants at all, in international banking transactions—exchange dealings, commodity trade on a large scale including shipping and underwriting, the finance of governments. Some of them were pious, but most of them did not brandish their religious views; indeed it was not these views which accounted for their activities, but rather the social situation which the views of their forefathers had brought them into. Catholics did engage in activities which enabled them to become as rich as, or richer than, any protestant banker; but they were generally activities of a different sort which revolved around the financial needs of the state and the court. They clearly paid little attention to the strict letter of the Canon Law; but then catholic businessmen were generally not distinguished for their piety. In short, a pious Protestant could be a dedicated and successful businessman; a pious Catholic, who took seriously the teachings of the Church and obeyed its every injunction, could not and it is doubtful whether he would have had the time to engage in large-scale business enterprise in any case.

No doubt the fact that France remained a catholic country did mean that the social atmosphere, as well as the legal code, was impregnated with an anti-business virus which impeded industrial effort, productive investment, capitalist financial techniques and rational economic calculation. Nevertheless new men and methods were pushing their way forward; the inhibition was relative, not absolute and the Church itself, for over two centuries, had been adapting itself to the exigencies of a more complex economy. If the inhibition still retained some force, however, it was because it was in accord with the economic and social reality of the old régime: a corporate order based upon landownership and privilege in which the social surplus was derived predominantly from the peasantry and took the form of tribute of a 'feudal' kind. This reality was itself, of course, constantly becoming subject to more precise and critical analysis from a rationalist point of view which took its stand on the virtues of productive capital and enterprise. Without benefit of religion philosophers and economists were asserting the right of the active capitalist to a more honoured position in society, a position he already enjoyed in the protestant countries no longer subject to the kind of parasitism inseparable from the old régime.

In short it is perhaps true to say that had France not been a catholic country in the eighteenth century she would already have been much more advanced on the road to industrial capitalism; but for this to have been true it would also have been necessary for the old régime to have been overthrown. Only at a later stage was it possible for harmonious compromises between capitalism and the Catholic Church to be worked out.

This excursion, brief and inadequate, into a most controversial field was necessary in order to dispose of what might otherwise have been an obstacle to clear thinking in subsequent analysis. The rôle of the 'bankers', more properly merchant bankers, can now be discussed without excessive emphasis on the fact that many of them were protestants.

The bankers were the chief carriers of the financial techniques which, while not new to the more advanced commercial centres of Europe, had the character of innovations in eighteenth-century France. Without such techniques capitalist-type dealings could not develop and spread and the groundwork be laid for more rapid industrial development. It is noteworthy that such practices as the use of the bill of exchange, discounting and deposit banking were accepted late in France and that to the end of the century their adoption was slow. The maintenance of the prohibitions on usury no doubt played a part in this slow development. Thus the use of the bill of exchange, though becoming increasingly common, was still mainly confined to international trade and, until the establishment of the *Caisse d'Escompte* in 1776, bills were not legally discountable. Likewise, loan transactions were concealed behind the device of the '*rente*' whereby the lender became entitled to the annual rent from a given item of real or business property. Such inhibitions represented a reluctance to place financial dealings in an autonomous and impersonal sphere, to separate them from the relations between persons characteristic of the pre-capitalist order. In the course of the reign of Louis XV an important evolution in this direction was taking place of which the bankers were the main instrument.

Unlike the financiers the bankers were, by their origins as well as by their activities, outside the régime; at least on its margins. While the financiers channelled the spare funds of subjects of the king into the royal treasury either through the tax powers which they had acquired or through the raising of loans, the bankers engaged in the more alchemistic trade in bills, notes and foreign exchange. The financiers, if they infringed the law of Church and State, were a necessary part of the old régime. What was significant was that during the eighteenth century the bankers and their suspect dealings had to be accepted too, as they, without becoming fully part of the old régime, equally became indispensable to it. They were the agents through which, slowly and in a piece-meal way, the financial apparatus was brought closer to the advanced practices of neighbouring countries.

The strength and wealth of the bankers lay first and foremost in their international connections and in the international character of their business. Until the stabilization of the French monetary unit in 1726 playing the exchanges had been a lucrative source of profit. In the phase of currency stability which followed, with only small differences in exchange rates on the various foreign markets, such business became of relatively less importance. But the growth of European and overseas trade in the next half century gave rise to a growing demand for credit which the bankers were able to supply through the medium of the bill of exchange, to their great financial advantage. In this traffic the protestant bankers, especially from Geneva, or having connections with that city, played a central part. They seized upon the opportunities offered by the extension of overseas enterprise, the importation of new commodities, speculation, insurance, the fitting out of ships and the new outlets for investment in Europe itself which this activity gave rise to. Through the bankers, and the credit which their names and reputations inspired, the capital of the more enterprising bourgeois investors of Western Europe found its way into international trade and its adjuncts: that is, for France, the most dynamic sector of the economy in this period.

The connection was thus close between the prosperity of the reign of Louis XV—albeit a prosperity from which only a minority of the nation benefited—the wealth of the successful banking firms and dynasties and the growing sophistication of financial techniques practised in France and particularly in Paris. The centralization of a great deal of banking and finance in the capital flowed inevitably from its dominating rôle in the political and social structure of the age. Where the administration was highly centralized and had a finger in practically every great enterprise, whether in domestic business or overseas enterprise, the centre of its decision-making was bound to act as a magnet for the dealers in money of all sorts. By comparison the financial needs of provincial France remained sadly neglected.

At the same time, it was not surprising that the banking fraternity should be called into more intimate relationship with the old régime whose financial embarassments increased under the pressure of successive wars. This new turn was signalized with the appointment of the Swiss banker Necker to the post of Director of the Treasury in 1776 on the eve of French intervention on the side of the American insurgents.

Necker worked no miracles for the old régime in decline, but he did find new and ingenious ways of raising money to enable its financial day of reckoning to be postponed. In short he tapped the resources of the worthy protestant bourgeois of Europe and made the government of France financially dependent on the international bankers of whom he was an outstanding representative—a dependence which, paradoxically, was imposed by the reckless support for a revolutionary war the effect of which was to bring nearer the day of revolution in France.

The last decade of the old régime witnessed a considerable extension of banking and financial activity centred on Paris. Its basis, however, was not in a healthy growth of productive investment but the issue of government paper which brought prospects of speculative gains for every kind of financial intermediary. In this atmosphere a number of joint stock enterprises were launched—a new India Company, a Paris Water Company, projects for banks and insurance companies. The old inhibitions on unchecked dealings in money and credit seemed to have been swept away.

The combined effect of the Canon Law and John Law had apparently, at last, worn off and the Paris Bourse was ready to assume a new rôle in the finances of the country. Certainly leading figures took part in the new speculative ventures and sections of the nobility as well as of the upper bourgeoisie were drawn into the game. A vigorous public controversy was by this time being carried on. But all this feverish and modern-seeming financing, company floating and share-dealing remained confined within the limits imposed by the old régime, above all by the growing crisis in its own finances which, by the new loans to which it gave rise, was the main support of all this activity. In fact, its effects on the economy at large were slight. Existing wealth was re-distributed to the advantage of the insiders but little new wealth was created. For all the main industries were concerned the Paris Bourse and the world of high finance might as well not have existed. The main product of this whirl of money dealing associated with the ministry of Calonne was a further step towards state bankruptcy in a social situation moving towards crisis.

Notes and further reading

1. In the political field, of course, the centralizing policies of the monarchy had strengthened the dynastic state as against the nobility, reducing it to a privileged class of 'hangers on' with no economic function. In the course of this process that monarchy had allied itself, at certain periods, with bourgeois elements. As shown in the text, the existence of a powerful bourgeoisie within the old order was quite compatible with 'feudalism' and involved no change in the prevailing relations of production. On the other hand, in such a situation there could be no stable point of equilibrium and new layers of bourgeois pressed forward from below which could not be so painlessly accommodated.
2. On this see E. Hobsbawm, 'The General Crisis of the European Economy in the 17th Century', *Past and Present,* No. 6, 1954. 'It may be doubted whether before the 19th century the world market was large enough for the simultaneous industrialization of two or more countries on the modern scale', p. 56. The fact that France was not yet a 'nation of customers', i.e. lacked a large home market, was a vital handicap. See also below, note 3.
3. L. Cahen, 'Quelques caractères de l'économie française à la veille de la Révolution, *Annales d'histoire sociale,* Vol. I, No. 3, 1939, pp. 238-250.
4. H. Cavaillès, *La route française,* p. 62-4, stresses the crucial

importance of rivers for internal trade; roads tended to follow closely the course of the rivers—and the sites of bridges.

5. There were three main tariff zones. The first and largest was that of the Five Great Farms (the farming of the collection of customs duties still prevailed); secondly the provinces 'reputedly foreign' (such as Franche Comté) and thirdly, those 'effectively foreign' (including Alsace). Commodities paid duties, therefore, in crossing from one to another. In addition there were river tolls and local dues collected at town limits and at markets and fairs. There was no uniformity of weights and measures. In short, national economic unity had not been achieved by a long way.
6. Lüthy, in making the comparison between the French and English economies, in the work cited in note 11 below, vol. 2, p. 595.
7. A great deal of this colonial produce was re-exported to Western Europe.
8. C. R. Palmade, *Capitalisme et capitalistes français du XIXe. siècle* (Paris 1961), p. 19-20.
9. There were ample signs, moreover, that a serious crisis was brewing in the sugar islands by the 1770's. See G. Martin, *Histoire de l'esclavage dans les colonies françaises* (Paris 1948), *Nantes au XVIIIe. siècle. L'ère des negriers* (Paris 1931).
10. According to the figures given by Sée, *Histoire économique de la France,* Vol. 1, exports rose from 122 mn. livres in 1716 to 542 mn. in 1787, in the same period imports rose from 93 mn. livres to 611 mn. His conclusion is that 'However approximate these figures may be, it seems likely that foreign trade more than quadrupled from 1716 to 1789, and that despite three long wars . . . the considerable influence which the process of commerce exercised on the industrial development of the XVIIIth century can thus be understood', pp. 333-4. An interesting geographical breakdown of foreign trade is given in chart form by A. Rédmond in an article entitled 'Trois bilans de l'économie française aux temps des théories physiocratiques', *Revue d'histoire économique et sociale,* Vol. XXXV, No. 4, 1957, pp. 416-56. They show the key role of the Atlantic ports—Nantes, Bordeaux, La Rochelle—through which passed the great flow of imports from the American colonies. To be noted also is the close economic relationship between the North East and Eastern centres and contiguous countries. For Lyons the export trade to Germany was highly important.
11. In much of what follows the text is greatly indebted to H. Lüthy, *La banque protestante en France,* 2 Vols. (1959, 1961).
12. Warren C. Scoville, *The Persecution of the Huguenots and French Economic Development, 1680-1720* (Berkeley and Los Angeles 1960), p. 436 and passim.

CHAPTER IV

The Economy of the Old Régime: Conclusions

WHAT emerges from the foregoing chapters is the image of a country which remained predominantly agrarian and which can hardly be said to have begun to move forward onto the road of industrialization. Structurally the national economy had undergone no basic change in the course of the eighteenth century. Through the fluctuations of the century, however, the curve of income per head and total output moved unmistakably upward; at a rate, it has been claimed, comparable with that in England.[1] By comparison with other parts of the continent of Europe, moreover, France remained the leading state in terms of wealth, population and aggregate power. Certainly as long as the old techniques and forms of organization sufficed the French state could dominate the continent, as Napoleon was to show.

What seems significant is not the fact that growth took place or that the aggregate wealth and power of France continued to ensure her a leading position on the continent, but rather the lack of conditions for carrying through a structural transformation. To explain this it is necessary to look outside the sphere of production.[2] Partly this means taking account of the lack of favourable geographical and physical conditions. Whether these were decisive is questionable both for this period and later. It seems more likely that attention has to be directed rather at the character of the society. Stress has therefore been laid on the ways in which the general characteristics of the old régime limited the possibilities of economic transformation.[3]

I

Although the old personal ties of feudalism had largely disappeared social relations remained cast in a feudal mould. The great bulk of the economic surplus, over and above what was retained by the direct producers, was drained away by a privileged noble class using extra-economic means. The appropriation of this surplus took place through mechanisms by which the old régime itself has come to be defined. The state obtained its part through a highly regressive fiscal system; the Church was supported by its own estates and by tithes; most important of all, seigneurial dues in kind, cash and services drew a heavy toll from the dependent peasantry.

Changes were, of course, taking place. The sphere of market transactions was being extended. The fiscal and military needs of the state accelerated the appearance of merchants and financiers at the same time as they increased the burdens upon those at the bottom of the social ladder. The growing influence of physiocratic thought found expression in the 1770's in the freeing of the grain trade and the promotion of capitalist methods in agriculture. As has been seen, however, there was no agrarian revolution and these measures by intensifying social strains without the hoped for improvements in production, probably hastened the demise of the old régime. In some areas, it is true, lords began to run their estates on more commercial lines, large farmers producing for the market appeared and swelling numbers of the peasantry were forced into dependence upon wages. Other lords put their lands in the hands of middlemen or tried to increase their exactions from the peasants at a time when a growing rebelliousness made it more difficult for them to be accepted. In the rural areas the outbreaks of 1789 evidently had deep roots.

Attempts to modernize the old régime were made, but only in a partial or one-sided way. Increased fiscal and other burdens, growing inequality and dependence upon market as well as harvest fluctuations tended to make the whole balance of the economy more delicate. So far as there was undoubtedly an extension of capitalism in agriculture as well as in industry it only meant wider and more powerful sources of disturbance.

II

A basic characteristic of this type of society was the fact that relatively little of the comparatively large surplus produced found its way into productive investment. Of that part which passed through the budget of the state, military and administrative outlays took the lion's share. The subsidies and other financial assistance which it gave to industry, while significant in individual cases, could do little to promote a thorough structural transformation. The dynastic and mostly unsuccessful wars may have enriched a few merchants, industrialists and financiers and hastened the growth of a market economy but they contributed to the empoverishment of the many.[4] Moreover, they drove the state steadily towards bankruptcy.

Of the surplus going to the nobility the major part was devoted to conspicuous consumption, or, at least, to living nobly. Even empoverished estate owners strove to keep up appearances. In general, the income which the noble derived from his estate, for the most part from compulsory rather than contractual payments, gave rise to no comparable service on his part. The chateau was no longer a fortified place but a country residence[5] and its master had little or no contact with the lives of the community. His insistence on his rights, even those which had fallen into desuetude, raised antagonism; litigation between the villagers and the lords was frequent. If he was an improver he would make himself more obnoxious by his attack on communal practices. In other words, where the landowner did play the rôle of investor the temporary gains were dearly bought. The substitution of money rents for rents in kind and the extension of farming for the market in some regions acted remorselessly to drive many peasants into the ranks of the rural proletariat. The régime was not strong enough to confront successfully the resulting rancour.

Some lords did invest in mining or in industry, but they were conspicuous by their rarity, although the ties between landowning and entrepreneurship were necessarily close in the case of the former. The surplus appearing in industrial production must be accounted as a small part of the whole; on the other hand a large part of it would find it way automatically into new industrial investment. The growing commercial, financial and professional bourgeoisie also obtained a growing part of the surplus and a part of this, again, would go to build up their businesses. However, the bourgeois experienced the influence of the aristocratic style of life, also aspiring to live, or to enable his heirs to live, nobly. Saving was often directed to the end of purchasing land or real property and there were, in any case, few productive outlets available.

Needless to say the peasantry as a whole was left with little enough over bare subsistence needs once dues, rents and taxes had been met, to permit investment in the improvement of the land or agricultural methods. Outside the ranks of improving landlords and capitalist farmers, such investment was left to the better off *laboureurs* able to exploit the possibilities offered by the growth of markets. The differentiation taking place within the peasantry must therefore be accounted as favourable to investment, but the rate of agricultural improvement remained slow.

It is hardly possible to give any quantitative precision to these presumptions, but all the qualitative indications point towards a rather low level of net investment in the apparatus of production as a whole. Too much of the surplus went into war or into the consumption of the privileged orders, including building. At the same time mining and industry grew with reasonable speed, though still having only a low specific weight in the economy, through the re-investment of profits and the overflow of some of the surplus from other sectors.

III

A privileged and hierarchical society of this kind consumes in a special way. The extreme inequality of income distribution tended to concentrate consumption disproportionately on the luxury goods and elegant inessentials required by a hedonistic leisure class. It was pre-eminently a society of conspicuous consumption in which income was used to maintain a station and little went into developing the productive capacity of the economy. Only in the middle class and better-off peasantry were the habits of thrift likely to be much developed and even the middle class, at least the upper bourgeoisie, was much influenced by the trend-setters in the nobility.

Consequently industries and trades which catered for the needs of the wealthy flourished and reached high levels of artistry and aristocratically-determined taste. The predominance of French cultural standards and the high prestige of the material things connected with their maintenance had long given French quality products an entrance to the markets of the civilized world and sometimes a virtual monopoly. On the other hand, by their nature their market was confined to the wealthy and often to the wealthy who liked to consume in a certain way.

French industry's performance in these fields was long to remain a characteristic as well as a matter for national pride among writers on economic matters. From the point of view of national economic development, however, luxury and semi-luxury manufactures could have only a limited importance.

Such activities, by their nature, depend upon hand skills, not on machinery; what is sought by the customer is individual excellence in the product, not cheapness or utility. On the other hand, the limited income of the mass of the people tended to restrict the market for cheap mass-produced goods susceptible to mechanization and concentration. Until the last decade or so before the Revolution the chief examples of large scale enterprise in France were in luxury industries or those which served the needs of the state. These industries, while using the techniques and organization of modern industrialism to a growing extent, could not pioneer the way in the transformation of the economy.[6] On the other hand, although the needs of the peasants and little people of the towns, if satisfied through the market at all, could be supplied by local, small-scale industry, there was growing scope for a more organized production for the market. In addition, the rapid growth of overseas trade acted as another pull upon industry and attracted enterprise and capital into new fields.

Thus the French economy was by no means static in the eighteenth century. In particular sectors and areas it displayed a capacity for change and expansion which has enabled the claim to be made that the growth in production and in average income per head was about the same as that in England. However, this aggregate growth was not accompanied, to anything like the same extent, by the preparation of conditions for a structural transformation. By the 1780's therefore, the divergence becomes more sharply marked, with the strains and symptoms of crisis in the French economy contrasting with the strong industrial upsurge in England.

A more profound grip of the current of change in France was prevented by the interaction of a number of factors, some of which are common to all pre-industrial economies and need not, therefore, be dwelt upon in detail. By their nature such factors cannot be given a quantitative weight, they depend upon an analysis of social forces and particularly of the totality of social relations. Thus, France appears basically as a feudal society in the eighteenth century. Despite the growth and achievement already referred to and the evident extension of capitalism, not only into industrial production but also into agriculture, the forces of inertia bound up with the traditional society remained overwhelmingly strong. The absence of agrarian change on a scale sufficient to loosen the connection of the mass of the population with the land or to change fundamentally its way of life must be accounted of considerable importance in preventing a structural transformation. The peasantry was made up of highly self-sufficient, low-income households, separated from all but local markets by the lack of cross-country transport facilities. There were large numbers who were, to all intents and purposes, outside the exchange economy altogether. In any case, the fragmentation of the market into a series of regional or small local markets—the former institutionalized by internal tariffs—deterred investment in large-scale production of common articles of production, such as textiles and farm tools.

The slow growth of an internal market was not due exclusively to social factors. France was a country of large distances, by no means homogeneous in language, customs or tastes. Particular regions could, and did for decades, continue to exist with little economic intercourse with other parts of the country. The areas which moved ahead did not, therefore, necessarily have a stimulating effect on others, more backward. Regional diversity thus remained a marked characteristic of the country in economic as well as in other ways. Areas well favoured in soil and climate prospered. Others, stimulated by proximity to ports and markets, underwent significant change in agriculture or developed industries. Elsewhere the market economy made little headway and the medieval mould showed no signs of cracking.

The leaders of the dynastic state were interested principally in preserving its interests with the minimum of upheaval. Decisions affecting the economy were thus taken from an angle which, in terms of the exchange economy, were non-economic. The emphasis on administrative centralization, for example, was made in order to strengthen the royal government: but it had the effect of stimulating the growth of Paris as a great consuming, and thus producing, centre. The second half of the century witnessed a considerable effort by the state in the direction of road building. This was another part of the administrative centralization which characterized the last efforts of the old régime to meet its crisis. Good highways were built from the capital to the provinces and frontiers, using the *corvée* labour of the peasantry, but they had little economic significance for the people who furnished the labour or, indeed, for the country as a whole. Economically it was a case of mis-directed investment comparable to building magnificent motorways in a present-day underdeveloped country.

As long as the grip of the old social relations had not been broken or loosened and a juridical framework more conducive to enterprise created, capitalist development was bound to come up against definite barriers. The régime stimulated some activities, but essentially for non-economic reasons. In major fields of activity state support was essential for success. Corporate and state regulation, though not universal or always effective, was nevertheless a factor inhibiting enterprise. Even here, as time went on, moves were made to reduce the incidence of restrictions, including a temporary abolition of the gilds. *Intendants* tended to become more concerned with encouraging entrepreneurs than with enforcing regulations.[7] From the 1750's there were growing signs of a change and increased emphasis on the desirability of a liberal economic climate.

A complex criss-crossing of the new with the traditional thus resulted, making generalization hazardous and quantification misleading. There were points of brilliant growth, especially the ports, as well as vast 'deserts' of medieval backwardness and poverty. Evident signs of material prosperity were to be found amongst much misery and distress. New sources of strain and crisis accompanied the penetration of new ways into the old structures.

IV

Who prospered where prosperity there was? In the rural areas a few progressive landlords, the 'strong' peasants, the grain dealers, cattle drovers and the like. In the towns and ports openings in trades and the professions multiplied. Prosperity and growth, even of a relative kind, meant more merchants, shopkeepers, money-lenders and master-craftsmen: the nucleus of a business class of the new, rather than the old medieval type. Such men were geared to an expanding market economy; their incomes and property grew and while no doubt many aspired to buy an estate and live nobly, the relative weight of mobile wealth had significantly increased. The urban patriciate and lesser bourgeoisie created a demand for professional services from men of their own social stamp but with a specialized education or training. Thus the educated middle class of lawyers, doctors, journalists, teachers and other professional men gained a large and influential place in society. Under the special conditions of the old régime, however, the dynastic state also offered possibilities of security and advancement to members of the middle class through its sale of offices, though on a lesser scale than in the previous century. Within the old régime the men of law, for example, could become a powerful and privileged corporation having as their property stake the royal office which they had purchased or inherited. By means of offices they could acquire titles of nobility; with their money they could buy estates and become ensconsed in the traditional social structure. The same road was also open to the successful businessman who, in any case, might well have required backing from the state in order to become successful.

In fact, the whole nature and atmosphere of the old régime tended to bring the upper layers of the bourgeoisie into association with it. The state had definite material awards to bestow upon men of wealth. Compared with the prestige of public office and the acquisition of a landed estate, and perhaps a title, the rewards of business might appear of lesser worth. There was a tendency, therefore, for the business élite to be drawn into the meshes of the traditional society rather than to form a self-contained and self-confident alternative with its own scale of values.[8] In turn this tended to dull the edge of business enterprise itself: to give it a 'feudal' rather than an uncompromisingly acquisitive character. Instead of accumulation of capital being an end, the successful businessman was likely to seek an honorific course for himself and his family through the purchase of offices and direct his sons into the professions or into state service. With exceptions, therefore, the French businessmen seem to have made their peace with the régime and to have adapted themselves to its conditions. The prevailing 'feudal' environment was extremely difficult to break free from and, while it did not prevent a steady growth in agricultural or industrial production, it inhibited enterprise of the kind which innovated on a scale sufficient to effect a real structural transformation. The pursuit of profit, the accumulation of capital, therefore took place within the definite limits imposed by the traditional social framework.

It was, therefore, the inhibiting nature of the relations maintained by the old régime itself which account, above all, for the relative lack of enterprise in French industry and trade and for the weakness of the effort brought to bear against the other growth deterrents. It must be emphasized, of course, that there was a development of some advanced financial dealings, a rapid growth of foreign trade, some expansion of internal demand and the establishment of new industries or technical and organizational change in existing fields: capitalist methods and capitalist relations were making a sustained attempt to find fuller expression. At the same time these forces, or rather the men who personified them, were not able to break out of the limits imposed by the estate society of the old régime.

In appearance French capitalism made some important steps forward in the eighteenth century. Great fortunes were made in financial operations involving the manipulation of large volumes of liquid capital and the employment of capitalist techniques. But these transactions arose out of the needs of the dynastic state and the feudal nobility and had nothing to do with the extension of capitalist relations in production. Despite the expansion of foreign trade and the commercial prosperity which distinguished the reign of Louis XV, fortunes were made rather from the redistribution of existing wealth than from a great increase in production or a growing control over it by big capital. Those in the sphere of banking and finance who appeared to be representatives of advanced finance capitalism were really closely tied in with the traditional order and shared in its downfall. The operative sphere of 'modern' capitalism—controlling production, looking to further accumulation and disruptive of existing institutions—was still circumscribed and could hardly be extended until major juridical, political and social changes had taken place. Even when the Revolution had affected a good deal of this re-modelling the legacy of the eighteenth century remained potent.

The fact that growth took place, in some spheres at an impressive rate, does not, therefore, seem to be the significant thing about French economic development in this period. Rather the emphasis must be upon the comparatively narrow scope for entrepreneurship of a modern kind in a society which remained overwhelmingly agricultural and traditional. In order to maintain its place in a competitive world, influenced by the 'demonstration effect' emanating from across the channel, the monarchy did embark upon a policy of encouraging industry. In some of the new industries it literally created entrepreneurs who were provided with every facility except freedom from the favours and protection of the administration. So little did these hot-house conditions produce the desired result that the turn was increasingly towards encouraging businessmen to develop greater independence.[9] In the searchings for a new way, which occupied some of the keenest minds at the time, the influence of economic liberalism became increasingly potent. But no consensus did emerge as the political and financial recklessness of the old régime carried it closer to the abyss. In the balance, the aid which it gave to innovators, the capital it supplied for industrial development, were far out-weighed by the lack of overall policy objectives and the incoherence and confusion in which its policy was carried on. The upholding of fiscal immunities for the privileged orders, the maintenance of traditional barriers to enterprise and the draining away of resources into calamitous wars and inexcusable extravagance had an incalculable net negative effect on the potentialities of the economy. In terms of population, resources, inventive capacity and reserves of wealth and human talent France was second to none among the states of Europe in the eighteenth century. It was an indictment of the old régime that it was unable to realize on them, or only in a very partial and one-sided fashion. Meanwhile the changes occurring of which it was by no means master, flowing from the development of market relations and the increasingly critical importance of prices and their movements, revealed its own inadequacy and created the conditions for its revolutionary overthrow.[10]

V

The relationship between the economic developments of the eighteenth century and the origins of the French Revolution has long been a matter for debate and there is no intention here to deal with it fully. At least that the economic background and changes in the social structure have to be closely examined to explain the growing weakness of the monarchy and the chaos and confusion of its institutions, to understand the rise and nature of the bourgeoisie and to account for the timing of the events themselves would today be scarcely questioned. Already at the time, Barnave, who came from Dauphiné in which significant industrial development had been taking place, sketched out an economic theory of the Revolution to which Jaurès drew attention as a brilliant anticipation of later interpretations.[11] The leading academic representatives of French historiography of the Revolution have insisted at length upon the importance of economic forces in preparing the ground for the downfall of the old régime. Such historians as Lefebvre, Labrousse and Soboul have, moreover, not hesitated to speak of a 'bourgeois revolution' and to find its source, like Jaurès in his pioneer history, in the flowering of commercial and industrial activity which brought onto the stage a growing bourgeoisie increasingly conscious of its strength.

This interpretation, with its Marxist overtones, has not gone unchallenged and, indeed, in recent years the debate has been re-opened at a new level. The very features of the economic life referred to in previous chapters—the association of much 'capitalist' activity with the administration and the court, the small scale of most industrial undertakings, the greater emphasis placed upon status than upon business success—have been adduced to show that the Revolution could not have been the work of a rising capitalist class.[12] Certainly, the largest accumulations of liquid wealth under the old régime were in the hands of men bound to it by many ties of interest and outlook such as the tax farmers, financiers and office holders. Their revenues were not drawn from ownership of the means of production but were more in the nature of a rent; they had a right to an income created by others. Consequently they did not undertake the kind of risks inseparable from production or dealings in the market place. They did not seek to increase their incomes or add to their accumulations by the methods of the business entrepreneur; in fact their rôle was entirely different from his. Since they did not control the factors of production, but merely what has been called 'proprietary wealth', any increase in their income was more likely to come from a drain on production than from its increase through innovation. Such men can scarcely be regarded as 'capitalists'; their fortunes and fate were closely bound up with the old order.

The merchants, on the other hand, were definitely both capitalists and bourgeois: they ventured their wealth as capital in the buying and selling of commodities, they took risks and entered into complex market relations. It is true that as their wealth grew they tended to withdraw it from trade, buying land and building houses, purchasing offices and aspiring to live nobly; in other words they shifted it into a proprietary form. This may have been because this was safer or because they sought status. However, although individuals and families took this step, the general growth in trade extended the numbers and wealth of the merchants as a whole. As well as those engaged in large scale foreign and wholesale transactions there were the many lesser tradesmen and merchants in the market towns, and those whose interests extended into the rural putting-out industries. This broad base of the commercial and industrial bourgeoisie, which widened with economic growth, cannot be overlooked. From its ranks came many who, through the purchase of *biens nationaux* and speculation, were later to consolidate their fortunes.

Nobles were also attracted into trade and industry. Indeed in some of the fields in which large capitals were required, such as mining and metallurgy, they were especially prominent, as witness the Anzin mining company. Others engaged in speculation or took an interest in trading companies. In short, some nobles assumed the rôle of entrepreneur and deployed and accumulated wealth in liquid forms: they could hardly be described as 'bourgeois' though in an economic sense it can not be doubted that they were capitalists.

This brief excursion into a controversial field at least reveals some of the complexities of the problem. It does not mean, however, that the economic interpretation of the Revolution as essentially a bourgeois revolution has been invalidated. Certainly there was no conscious and determined onslaught on the old régime by a homogeneous class of capitalists intent on reshaping society in their image. In particular, the industrial capitalists, owners of fixed capital in the means of production, operated on too modest a scale and had too little influence to play any determining rôle. But this does not mean that the Revolution must be seen as a primarily political event issuing from the inability of the monarchy to overcome an acute financial crisis and that it is now old-fashioned or doctrinaire to see it as a bourgeois revolution.

In the first place, the financial dilemma of the monarchy raised the question of the tax exemptions of the privileged orders and aroused their antagonism in what has been called 'the aristocratic revolt'. However, the monarchy was not able to ally itself with the Third Estate against the nobility because its own institutional basis presumed the social predominance of the latter. At the same time, by undermining the monarchy the nobility weakened its own position as a privileged section of society. The significance of this lay in the fact that as the fissures appeared from 1787 onwards the régime as a whole was brought into question. In particular it exposed it to the criticism of the growing bourgeoisie, not necessarily persons of great fortune, which the expansion of the economy in the previous decades had brought forward. It is true that they did not prepare a Revolution, but they had begun to formulate some social claims of their own. This bourgeoisie was itself highly stratified. Much of its wealth was still in landed rather than mobile forms. Its industrial component was small; it was a class of modest individual fortunes on the whole, weighted towards trade and the professions. Its members were ambitious and resentful of privilege; the financial crisis of the régime gave them an unbelievable opportunity. But it was not until their representatives actually met in 1789 with the summoning of the States-General that they could constitute themselves as the leadership of a revolutionary class. Even then it was because their elementary demands could not be met within the framework of the old order that they were obliged to take up a revolutionary position. Their aims, as embodied, for instance, in the Declaration of the Rights of Man, were profoundly 'bourgeois'—directed against the abuses of the old régime but otherwise moderate, individualist, respectful of property rights and insistent on the 'bourgeois' freedoms.

The opportunity which the crisis of the old régime offered for the statement of bourgeois claims for change coincided with a growing crisis in the agrarian sector. For many decades there had been little sign of open revolt by the peasantry but there appears to have been a growing rebelliousness and resentment at seigneurial dues and obligations. The extent and violence of the explosion in the summer of 1789 was, however, a complete surprise; in fact, the peasants carried out a revolution of their own which became interwoven with, but was really distinct from, that of the urban middle class. It was a revolution which put an end to the seigneurial régime in the countryside, the decomposing 'feudalism' which drained away so much of the peasant's income without return; it did this on the peasants' terms in ways which the Revolutionary Assemblies would not have chosen but were obliged to endorse. Finally, the conjunctural factors associated with harvest fluctuations and price trends had plunged the country into a simultaneous food shortage and industrial depression. Both the rural population and the urban artisans, traders, shopkeepers and wage workers were thus highly susceptible to revolutionary measures as a way out of their hardships. These factors seem to explain the timing and the violence of the events of 1789 which brought the old régime to an end.

Notes and further reading

1. P. Léon, op. cit. and especially François Crouzet, 'Angleterre et France au XVIIIe. siècle: essai d'analyse comparée de deux croissances économiques', *Annales—Economies-sociétés-civilisations*, Vol. 21, No. 2, mars-avril, 1966. English translation by J. Sond-

heimer in R. M. Hartwell, ed., *The Causes of the Industrial Revolution in England,* (London 1967). The point had already been made by John U. Nef, The Industrial Revolution Reconsidered', *Journal of Economic History,* Vol. III, No. 1, 1943.

2. See Louis Cahen, 'Quelques caractères de l'économie française à la vielle de la Révolution', *Annales d'histoire sociale,* Vol. I, No. 3, 1939, especially for emphasis on lack of transport facilities and of communication between the ports and the interior.
3. The question of the character of the French economy at this time is obviously of importance to students of the history of economic thought. In particular, why should the Physiocrats, with their emphasis on the exclusive productivity of agriculture and their call for the single tax on land, arise at this time? Luthy, op. cit. p. 771 suggests that they were 'the last and highest manifestation of traditional catholic thought on economic matters'. For Ronald Meek, on the other hand, they reflected more closely the economic interests of 'the new class of agricultural entrepreneurs'. They were advocating 'a capitalist society in which the landowning classes, by accommodating themselves to new conditions, would be able to retain their old position of predominance', see *The Economics of Physiocracy* (London 1962), Ch. V. passim. Their policies were thus aimed at clearing away the obstacles to a form of agricultural capitalism, one that is, which would retain the predominance of agriculture and of the landlord. They looked forward to a reformed and modernized version of the society in which they lived, a kind of harmonious extension of the sphere of the market within an economy whose social relations remained basically antithetical to it. Meek perhaps overlooks the extent to which industrial capitalism was making headway.
4. This point has been emphasized by Paul W. Bamford. He points out that foreign policy was determined by dynastic aims to which economic interests were sacrificed. 'In summary', he writes, 'it can be maintained that the subordination of economic interest to the achievement of political aims in foreign affairs, and the frequency and peculiarly burdensome character of French participation in the wars of the period, exercised a generally depressive effect on French economic life and business enterprise'. 'Entrepreneurship in Eighteenth Century France', *Explorations in Entrepreneurial History,* Vol. IX, No. 4, April, 1957, p. 205.
5. 'Le château devient la plus belle maison bourgeoise du lieu', P. de Saint Jacob. *Les paysans de la Bourgogne du Nord* (Paris 1960), p. 416.
6. Care has to be taken not to see production for low income consumers as necessarily leading to mass production. In France such goods as the peasants bought in the market would be crudely and cheaply made under the putting-out system. British industry mechanized to an important extent by producing high quality goods for a middle class market, Crouzet, op. cit., p. 281.
7. See P. Léon, *La naissance de la grande industrie en Dauphiné,* 2 Vols (Paris 1954), Vol. I, p. 138 for this point.
8. As note 5 in the following chapter.

9. Léon, loc. cit.
10. The historiography of the Revolution, in its economic and social aspects, is a subject in itself which can only be touched on here although, of course, in the preceding chapters a number of references have been made to it. A useful introduction for the student is the selection made by R. W. Greenlaw, *The Economic Origins of the French Revolution* (Boston 1958). See also G. Lefebvre's *Études sur la révolution française* (Paris 1959).
11. See J. Jaurès, *Histoire socialiste de la Révolution Française, la constituante* (reprint, Paris 1922), p. 119 seq. In his treatment of economic life Jaurès lays particular stress, of course, on the rise of the bourgeoisie, the expansion of the economy and the complex nature of its institutional arrangements which restricted the continued development of capitalism. These ideas were also discernable in Barnave.
12. See George V. Taylor, 'Noncapitalist Wealth and the Origins of the French Revolution', *American Historical Review*, Vol. LXXII, No. 2 (January, 1967) and 'Types of Capitalism in Eighteenth-Century France', *English Historical Review*, Vol. LXXIX, No. 3 (July, 1964).

CHAPTER V

The Economics of Revolution and War, 1789-1815

PERIODS of revolutionary upheaval are inevitably unfavourable to economic growth whatever effects they may have in preparing the ground for it. The French Revolution was no exception. It broke out in a period of agrarian crisis, industrial depression and imminent state bankruptcy from which it offered no immediate way of escape. Indeed, the deep social conflicts and the administrative difficulties of the early years of the Revolution, followed by the effects of the civil and foreign wars into which France was plunged, could hardly fail to have an adverse influence on many sectors of the economy. A hectic inflation, followed after a number of years by a drastic deflation, brought new problems. The loss of overseas markets and contact with the colonies meant a great setback to the most flourishing field for investment and enterprise in the eighteenth century. Industry was adversely affected in many ways by these events and, except for those parts which were stimulated by war demand, suffered a decline. Business conditions were disturbed, confidence impaired, long-term investment discouraged; some businessmen and industrialists emigrated or perished on the scaffold. As for agrarian France, which contained the great bulk of the population, it underwent its own social revolution but otherwise remained the main stabilizing force in the whole economy, with methods of husbandry unaffected by the great changes of the time. Whatever interest the revolutionary period has from an economic point of view stems not from an examination of growth, or even change, but rather from the dislocations and distortions which political events promoted in the economy.

The Revolution was the work of the bourgeoisie, but not of a bourgeoisie of industrial entrepreneurs and merchants, many of whom, like the financiers, were economic dependents of the old régime. The leading protagonists of change, while including some members of the business fraternity, were, in the main, lawyers, professional men, even office-holders. They fought for social and legal reform at the expense of the privileged orders. They did so as, and on behalf of, men of substance, men of property. But the very nature of the economy in which the Revolution took place meant that there were few concentrations of great wealth outside the field of landed property. Great fortunes were made in subserving the financial needs of the state, or with the assistance of state privileges, but not yet in a freely developing industry and only in a few areas, and to a limited extent, in merchant business and banking. The legislation of the Revolution was tender of property rights and established the conditions for the full and free flowering of capitalist enterprise—[1] but only as the other conditions for it came into existence, and, as has been seen, the years after 1789 did not, and could not, create those conditions. In fact it was in the agrarian field that the most far-reaching social changes of economic consequence took place; but these changes were not part of the programme of the revolutionary bourgeoisie. They took place because there was inextricably inter-woven with the bourgeois revolution a peasant revolution which had objects, and a momentum, of its own.[2] By challenging the privileged orders, who derived their social position from the rights they exercised over the land and the peasantry, the bourgeoisie opened the way for the entry onto the scene of the latter with claims of its own to make.

The agrarian changes of the revolution

In 1789 and 1790 in many parts of the French countryside the peasants rose against their lords, both lay and clerical, burned the documents on which their obligations to the lords were inscribed and pillaged or burned the manor houses in which they were kept. This spontaneous outburst of violent anger by an oppressed class followed many decades of relative calm in the rural areas. Behind this calm, as has already been seen, was a mounting agrarian crisis. There were numerous indications that some kind of change in agrarian relations was due: all that remained to be seen was whether it would benefit the landlords or the peasants and under what conditions it would take place. By the efforts which they made to re-impose obligations on the peasants which had fallen into desuetude and by the half-hearted efforts to carry out enclosures the lords had accelerated the grievances of their nominal vassals. Yet neither the lords, nor the state, were able to carry through an agrarian reform which had long become overdue.

The harvest failures and price trends of the 1780's provided the immediate background for a sharpening of rural antagonisms.[3] The conflict between the nobility and the Crown, and then between the Third Estate and the privileged orders, gave the peasantry its chance. Already, in the *Cahiers de doléances* of 1789, peasant grievances find a public and coherent expression. With the calling of the States General and the aggravation of rural distress in the spring and summer of 1789 peasant hatred of the aristocracy and of the clergy reaches burning point. Independently of the bourgeois Assembly, which itself sought to give legal expression to the need to end feudal anachronisms, and always outstripping it, the peasants made their own revolution. From the point of view of the bourgeois jurists, as much as from that of the landed aristocrat, the violent intrusion of the peasantry onto the scene was most unwelcome. It detracted from the main business, the drawing up of a new constitution, and threatened all property rights with attack. Unable to suppress the peasant uprisings, the National Assembly sought to remove their cause by abolishing the most obnoxious of the feudal obligations. Indeed, in the famous session of the 4th August some noblemen took the initiative, whether from sincere concern for reform or to save what could be saved—perhaps thinking that any concessions made would be purely provisional—it is difficult to say.

By the decrees of 5th-11th August, 1789, the lords, in fact, relinquished in principle only those rights which appeared to issue from compulsion and for which no counterpart was received by the peasantry. The abolition of personal services was the only part of the decrees to come into immediate operation. The rest were to be subject to further legislation. Those dues and payments taken to have a contractual origin in the nature of a rent were to be subject to re-purchase by the peasantry. The Assembly announced the destruction of the feudal order, but it intended to uphold the sanctity of private property by assimilating the old forms of land ownership to a general law of property based on the model of the Roman Law.

If the peasants ever heard of or understood the fine distinctions of the jurists they had scant respect for them. As far as they were concerned feudal property was abolished and the obligations which the Assembly held that they should re-purchase were no less objectionable than those which were to be abolished outright. They neither waited for the passage of the necessary legislation nor took account of the differences between one form of obligation and another. Peasant disorders spread and created a situation which either had to be endorsed by the revolutionary Assemblies or changed by the use of force against the peasantry. But, as the bourgeoisie required the support of the peasants against the royalists, concessions had steadily to be made to the peasant revolution. At all times, however, these concessions were made reluctantly and, as far as possible, the provisions of the law sought to strengthen the rights of individual ownership in a way which ran contrary to the desires of the peasantry. Even the burden of proving that particular obligations should be abolished without indemnity fell on the peasant. The landowner, not the *métayer* or tenant, benefited from the abolition of tithes. By the laws of May, 1790 provision was made for the purchase of those obligations held to be legitimate through a contract between the peasant and his lord at a price of 20 to 25 times their annual value. In some areas, where the burden of these obligations was not too heavy, feudal obligations might have been gradually extinguished by purchase, but over a large part of the country the peasants had not said their last word. By their opposition to the continued payment of obligations of any kind, and thus to the distinctions built into the laws of the Constituent Assembly, the peasants forced its successors to accept the abolition of all the feudal obligations which weighed on their land.

The more radical turn of the Revolution after the 10th August, 1792 made peasant support more indispensable to the new leaders. From that month the burden of proof of the legitimate nature of payments for land fell upon the landlord. Then, in July of the following year, the Convention abolished all dues and obligations derived from the seigneurial régime without indemnity. Peasants who held land subject to payments of some kind to the lord, except where they resulted from a contractual agreement—tenancy or *métayage*—were now confirmed as full owners. But most peasant land was still subject to the inherited complex of rights and obligations upheld by the village community. On this score the conceptions of the peasantry still differed widely from those of a bourgeoisie committed to the absolute rights of private property.

In the meantime the course of revolutionary change made its impact on the agrarian system at a number of points. Punitive measures were taken against the Church and the *émigré* nobility, notably through the confiscation of their landed property. Food shortages in the towns and a sustained price rise offered opportunities for speculative gains to some and brought hardship and famine to many. Through the sale of confiscated land—*les biens nationaux*—an important change was effected in land ownership. This, and the new possibilities for enrichment offered these peasants, the better-off minority, who had a surplus for sale in the market, brought to the fore the already existing, but generally concealed, conflicts of interest within the peasantry. United in its detestation of feudal burdens it became more divided as it was caught up in the mechanism of an exchange economy.

The lands of the Church were confiscated in November, 1789, and put up for sale in an effort to cope with the acute financial problem inherited from the old régime. The distribution of Church land was very unequal so that in some areas considerable transfers of property took place while in others little land came onto the market. In all 4-5 million hectares were affected. From 1792 the property of *émigrés* and then of 'suspects' was also liable to confiscation and sale. Once again the land involved was unequally distributed over the country and was composed of woodlands and common as well as arable and pasture land, cultivated, for the most part, by small peasants. These lands were sold off over a period of years by methods which varied over time, or from place to place. There were, therefore, widely different regional results of the operation which must be taken into consideration when an attempt is made to describe the general outcome.

The French countryside suffered from chronic land hunger. The peasants were anxious to acquire land; they do not seem to have been much deterred either by attachment to the Church or by fear of a restoration of the land-owners. In most areas, therefore, the *biens nationaux* sold well. These who acquired them did so for personal gain, not from attachment to the Revolution; on the other hand, no owner or purchaser of former noble or clerical land could wish to see a restoration of the old régime. However willing the peasants were to acquire the confiscated lands many of them lacked the wherewithal to purchase. From the beginning, therefore, members of the bourgeoisie appeared on the scene as purchasers. With the advance of the inflation land became a worthwhile investment for money acquired elsewhere as well as a source of speculative gains. Such gains were at least made possible by the land hunger of the peasantry which, if it could not buy land, was ever ready to rent it for money or take it on a *métayage* tenure.

The confiscated lands were put on the market at a relatively low price, though, in some cases, prices were bid upwards during the auction. The method of selling varied from place to place: in some cases large tracts were disposed of as single lots, in others small pieces were sold off. A law was passed to prevent combinations of purchasers, as in some villages the peasants banded together to buy an estate up for sale to keep down the price and prevent its acquisition by strangers. The laws of the Convention, on the other hand, favoured the splitting up of the estates and their disposal in smaller parcels. In some areas, therefore, depending on the timing and conditions of sale, most of the *biens nationaux* were acquired by the peasants. In others, especially around the towns, bourgeois purchasers took the lion's share. All in all the peasantry was able to acquire a good deal of fresh land, though, of course, most of it went to the better off peasants; land purchased by bourgeois might later be sold off in smaller lots to the peasants. Some land was bought back by the nobility or people acting on their behalf. In any case, voluntary sales by the landowners, already taking place before 1789, continued during the revolutionary period and added to the volume of land transfers.[4]

The general effect of revolutionary legislation was to assimilate the old feudal forms of property into the general category of what can be called bourgeois private property. It also enabled many bourgeois to accede to the ownership of landed property through the purchase of *biens nationaux*. Some retained this land and rented it to small tenants on a contractual basis, just as nobles not dispossessed henceforth derived their income from contractual rents and not from feudal dues and obligations. For many bourgeois acquirers of *biens nationaux*, however, the operation was seen as a speculative one in which they bought on a rising market in a depreciating currency and sold off the land later at a handsome profit. There were great opportunities for rapid enrichment by those who began with small capitals; the origin of some of the great fortunes, and industrial capitals, is to be found in this process of speculation.[5]

The Revolution brought no general re-distribution of land and advocates of an 'agrarian law' were despatched to the guillotine. It did not, therefore, enable those without land to acquire it; rather did it permit those with some land, or some means, to acquire more. The numbers of the landless or semi-landless continued to be large in many rural areas. Where it was customary for the family lands to be divided up between the heirs on the death of the head of the family land holding tended to be dispersed. The inheritance laws of the Revolution and the Empire confirmed and extended this tendency. If this meant *morcellement*, which was harmful from the point of view of agricultural efficiency, it also opened up wide opportunities for the acquisition of land. This must be seen in relation to the fact that the peasantry had now been confirmed in its ownership and, as a class, had come into possession of more of the total available land. Those who held land as tenants or *métayers* before the Revolution were not, as such, directly benefitted. Likewise, large estates, whether belonging to noble families who survived the storms of the period or constituted by bourgeois proprietors, continued to form a feature of the agrarian landscape in many areas. In short, the Revolution, while bringing about substantial changes left untouched many of the established features of the rural scene.

This is also to be seen with respect to the customary practices of agriculture with which the village community was entwined. The bourgeois revolutionaries were no more successful than the functionaries of the old régime in bringing about enclosure. The most they could do was to make it legally possible for the individual peasant to choose his method of cultivation and to withdraw his land from the collective servitudes and for the division of the commons to take place. Despite the growing differentiation within the peasantry the force of custom and the antagonism of the peasantry to change prevented much use being made of these facilities. The abolition of the open fields was a long drawn out and uneven process which was to take place in the course of the nineteenth century as the members of the village community were persuaded of its advantages.

In the field of technique and the mutual operation of husbandry, therefore, the Revolution brought no change. Agriculture remained in the hands of the peasantry to be conducted on traditional lines. The bringing of the peasantry more fully into an exchange economy was bound to be a slow process once it was confirmed in its rights without having to re-purchase its obligations and more of its members acquired land. Rather than being forced off the land the peasants were more firmly attached to it. Even those who had little or no land had perhaps some hope of acquiring it through inheritance or purchase. The peasant revolution, whatever else it might have done, undoubtedly held back the economic development of France. By operating against unchecked individualism and capitalist agriculture it thus prevented the full possibilities of the successful bourgeois revolution from being realized. The full programme of agrarian individualism could not be carried through because almost every part was opposed by some section of the peasantry. On the other hand, the peasantry was now more divided against itself than in the past and the slow disintegration of the old agrarian system had begun.

The economic legislation of the Revolution

From an early stage, responding to the desires of the middle class as reflected in the *Cahiers de doléances*, the Revolutionary Assemblies destroyed many of the restrictions on economic freedom which had existed under the old régime. New laws were passed which embodied the bourgeois conception of property and provided the legal conditions for the maximum freedom in its use. These measures, taken from the standpoint of the jurist rather than the businessman, thus established conditions necessary for the full functioning of a market economy. Distinction between different types of property was abolished together with the division of society into orders or estates. Privileges based upon heredity, favouritism or membership of closed corporations were swept away. The rights of property, on the other hand, were clarified and extended as an essential part of the new, bourgeois order. These rights were a central part of the comprehensive re-modelling of the law which was begun by the Constituent Assembly and completed under Napoleon. A legal structure was thus created which was wholly in keeping with the needs of capitalist enterprise.[6] However, its creation could not in itself bring about an accelerated economic growth which was inhibited by the structures inherited from the pre-1789 period and by the disturbing and distorting effects of revolution and war. In fact, for some time into the nineteenth century France was to display a marked disparity between an advanced legal code and an industry which still displayed many symptoms of weakness.

Already, in 1791, a number of measures were taken which opened the way for the widest application of technical improvement and capital investment. By the D'Allarde decrees of March, 1791 the gilds and corporations were swept away and all trades and professions were declared open to those wishing to practise them, subject to the payment of a new tax on trade and industry (*la patente*). Unlike Turgot's edict of 1776, the new law did not expressly forbid the formation of associations or combinations by those exercising the same trade or profession. Such associations did, however, exist or were formed by workers in a number of trades and in Paris a certain amount of agitation for wage increases took place, notably among the carpenters, who sought to establish a minimum wage. There was nothing essentially new about such demands, but the Paris municipality and the Assembly were concerned and opposed to these embryonic combinations the classical middle class arguments about freedom of labour. Re-enforced by petitions from complaining employers, the Assembly passed, in June, 1791 the law presented by Le Chapelier which made associations of wage-earners or employers for professional purposes illegal. 'There are no longer corporate bodies in the state,' declared Le Chapelier, 'There is only the private interest of each individual and the general interest.'

By these two laws a free market for labour was upheld against the old forms of restriction practised by the gilds and the new menace of combined action by the wage-earners. Capital and enterprise could flow freely into what seemed likely to be the most remunerative fields. The employer was free to make his own bargains with individual workers without the intervention either of the state or of collective action by the workpeople. As for the latter, they were obliged to sell their labour power where they could without the protection of the state and without being able to bargain collectively. Economic inferiors through their lack of reserves, they were deprived of protection from the law and prevented from organizing collectively in their own defence.

These legal changes gave an indication of the intention of the revolutionary legislators to create a 'liberal' society based upon free contracts between individuals pursuing their own self-interest within the context of the law. No doubt it is possible to exaggerate the practical effect of the laws relating to labour. There was, as yet, no more than an embryonic industrial proletariat and large-scale enterprises of a capitalist type were very much the exception. Even in Paris there were few workers in large enterprises compared with the great mass of small masters, artisans and workers in productive units of the traditional type. Conflicts between employers and workers were as yet of little importance. Social disturbances were sparked off by food shortages and high prices and were aimed against hoarders and speculators: wage-earners and small masters could thus be found together, side-by-side, even, with members of the middle class of property owners and small capitalists.

The period of the Constituent Assembly showed, almost without alloy, the desire of the bourgeoisie to uphold and strengthen the individual rights of the property owners. Through all the vicissitudes of war and revolution this remained a permanent theme, to find its crowning expression in the Civil Code of 1804. The jurists who drew up the new laws took their inspiration from the Roman law whose conception of property and property rights coincided so exactly with the needs of bourgeois property owners desiring both to free property from traditional, or 'feudal', encumbrances and to protect it from the encroachments of the state or of the non-owners. Property was thus divested of duties towards subordinates or neighbours. It was given a purely individual connotation, and this was carried into the laws of succession which provided for equal division on inheritance. Still designed for a society in which land was the main form of property, the law of partible inheritance—which, however, only confirmed a long-standing custom in many provinces—was to have its most far-reaching effects in agriculture. The splitting up of landed property contributed to the *morcellement* which was to be the besetting problem of French agrarian society. But, to counteract the consequences of the law, peasants and other property owners tended to limit the size of their families and thus to bring about a demographic trend of small families and slow population growth which, again, was to have far-reaching and long-enduring effects.

From the point of view of its effects on economic growth, therefore, the legislative achievement of the Revolution is, to say the least, ambiguous. Positively it stood unequivocally for the rights of property and it was in the light of these rights that equality and liberty were legally interpreted. By relieving the peasantry of feudal burdens and other sections of the population of indirect taxes—which were to be restored in a different form—by opening up new opportunities for social mobility, it prepared the way for the unhampered operation of economic motives.[7] In the nature of things this left the poor and disadvantaged unprotected. Fields like social welfare and popular education were spoken about with enthusiasm during the revolution but the practical steps were negligible. Nothing was done to deal with the grievances of tenants and *métayers* and the ruling bourgeoisie, as a whole, expressed no concern for the landless or semi-landless peasantry. In dealing with the traditional agriculture it passed laws which facilitated its dissolution by enabling the village communities to allocate and enclose the arable lands and divide out the commons. In practice, however, it was no less timourous in dealing with this question than its predecessors had been. Dependent at every stage of the revolution on peasant support, it could do nothing to speed up the course of agrarian change by directly intervening.

Tenderness for property rights, with a marked reluctance to disturb the established situation more than was necessary, was a distinguishing mark of the new bourgeois régimes after

1789. However, the exigencies of revolution, coupled with the threat of invasion, led, within a few years, to the adoption of measures of economic regulation and control which cut across the set course to competitive individualism. Despite themselves, the representatives of the bourgeoisie were obliged to curtail the rights of property and intervene in the market to requisition what was required for the war effort and deal with soaring prices on the home market.

The abandonment of economic liberalism during the period of revolutionary dictatorship, 1792-4, took place empirically and reluctantly, under the pressure of events. The apparatus of control thus established had the characteristics of an improvised, siege economy; it was by no means the result of a conscious design or conviction of the superiority of a controlled economy. In any case, the apparatus of controls was bound to work loosely. The government lacked information, factual and statistical; it lacked trained and experienced personnel. It operated under conditions of severe stress and bitter in-fighting between the revolutionary factions. Even under the best conditions, the size of the country and the lack of communications would have impeded anything like a national and uniform system of economic regulation. With a large part of the country out of its control or occupied or threatened by the enemy such uniformity became an impossibility. In these conditions the government was bound to depend upon nationalist and pro-revolutionary fervour which operated unevenly and arbitrarily rather than upon a coherent and workable system of regulation. It was not surprising, therefore, that the results were very uneven and that there was ample scope for evasion and for the piling up of illicit fortunes in hoarding and speculating in scarce commodities.

These, then, were the conditions for the ventures into economic regulation and control which reached their peak during the period of Jacobin dominance, 1793-4. The state became the main factor of economic impulsion, controlling and regulating private enterprises in order to ensure a supply of arms and other essential supplies. It did so by regulation of raw material supplies which were either directly requisitioned from the home producer or purchased abroad. In some cases, notably in the manufacture of weapons and munitions, new enterprises had to be established under state control. The overriding pressure of military need thus, for a time, pushed aside the bourgeois concern with private enterprise and profit. It yielded considerable results in increasing the output of war supplies without which, no doubt, the Revolution would have been crushed. To some extent this must have been done by bringing new resources into use, stimulating technical improvement and increasing the productivity of the labour force by providing a new incentive. However, the costs of the experiment were high and it was, throughout, in the grip of the conflict between intention and possibility.

This conflict was shown most clearly on the issue of price control. Control of prices was the logical accompaniment of the other measures of control and requisition which the revolutionary government was taking and the counterpart to the sacrifices which were being demanded of the people as a whole. Need for popular support in the critical months of 1793-4 had probably more to do with the adoption of the famous Law of the Maximum than any chain of economic reasoning. The immediate need was to check the rise in prices and speculation and ensure a supply of basic foods and other essentials for the civilian population. But the establishment, and even more the enforcement, of maximum prices over a wide field and including wages as well, raised insoluble problems for the authorities. The administration of the national law had to be left to the municipalities and other local authorities. Local conditions varied enormously and so did the extent to which price and wage control was enforced. The main beneficiary was the government itself, which was able to hold to the Maximum for the commodities it requisitioned. As for traders, artisans and peasants, they were by no means satisfied to sell at the fixed price however much they might have liked to buy at it. From one angle the Law of the Maximum embodied the hankering after a regulated, pre-capitalist order which was widespread among the masses of the urban population upon which the rule of the Jacobins depended. Yet, in its operation, it did little for those it was supposed to benefit. Because it was not enforced, prices continued to rise and the speculators were enabled to operate with impunity. The price rise, which was kept in check during the period of the Jacobin dictatorship, became a hectic inflation as the Directory allowed the conditions of a free market to be restored. In fact this was the only way in which the circulation of commodities could be ensured without more far-reaching and effective measures of economic control.

It should be remembered that the Revolutionary régimes inherited all the financial and fiscal problems of their predecessor and were unable to solve them. They lacked a stable system of public credit and an efficient tax system and events rapidly moved against any possibility of establishing the conditions necessary for the emergence of such a system. Hence the expedients, such as the issue of paper money, the *assignats*, ostensibly backed by the *biens nationaux*. Whether or not this expedient could have worked under different conditions, it proved to be the means for a vast inflation whose social and economic effects were intertwined with those of the Revolution itself. Rising prices and scarcities, coupled with generally unenforceable regulations, offered great opportunities for speculative deals. The virtual end of the Maximum in December, 1794 and the dismantling of economic controls by the Directory left a free field for the rapid amassing of new fortunes. Speculation in land, speculation in commodities, a depreciation of the currency—these were the classic conditions for the rise of a crop of new rich. Some of the men who accumulated fortunes at this time no doubt took their origin from the bourgeoisie of the old régime, others were new, or relatively new, men. At the same time, part of the old bourgeoisie was ruined or emigrated at this period, aided by the collapse of foreign sea-bound trade and the shrinkage of the home market for certain (e.g. luxury and semi-luxury) commodities.

After an initial stimulus, the Revolution had a baneful effect on some important sectors of industry owing to lack of raw materials, loss of markets and labour difficulties.[8] The emphasis on military needs no doubt stimulated some sectors of industry but it held back others. In any case, outside a few fields, the conditions prevailing in the decade after 1789 were hardly propitious for healthy industrial growth. For all the favourable legal conditions for enterprise now proclaimed, the structure of French industry was not such that it could immediately take advantage of them, even in the absence of the largely unfavourable environment created by revolution and war. Moreover, the latter, by the opportunities they offered for rapid, speculative gains, tended to draw enterprise and capital into speculation in land, commodities and currency. Over most of the industrial field, however, the old traditional methods and forms of organization persisted. For many industrialists the Revolution failed to realize its early promise; some, indeed, like Claude Perier, became involved in these lucrative operations.

The bourgeois families which consolidated their fortunes or rode to wealth in this period were not, for the most part, therefore, based on industry. Landed property remained a main outlet for their investment and a source of income, at least once their fortunes had been acquired. Economic freedom could not mean for them quite what it meant for an industrial capitalist. They were men of affairs, not men concerned with the organization of production or with long-term industrial investment. They looked to the state for protection and for the means of enhancing their families' fortunes or reputation. They were the beneficiaries of the downfall of the old régime, but they had not entirely broken with its outlook and they operated within the framework of an economy which remained distinctly of the old type. That it was 'old' showed up more clearly as industrialization moved ahead in Britain. Partly cut off from the stimulus of technical and other contacts with Britain by the wars, the general response to this challenge was to be a protectionist one.

Markets and the economic blockade

The most serious loss to the French economy brought about by the wars which followed on the heels of the Revolution was that of overseas markets. The initial measures of the Revolution promised well. Internal tariffs were abolished and measures were taken to facilitate the free movement of goods within the country. By 1791 a moderately protective tariff system had been instituted and the following year the tendency towards freer trade signalized by the Eden Treaty of 1786 was definitely reversed. Evidently the bourgeoisie was alarmed by the threat of English competition and sought to close not only the home but also the colonial market against foreign competitors. In the first stage of the revolution, therefore, there was no sign of a desire to break with what might be called the Colbertist tradition.

The establishment of a war economy had inevitable repercussions in the field of foreign trade. Above all the war exposed French overseas trade to the decisive blows of British naval power with devastating effects, especially for the Atlantic coast ports. The most dynamic and brilliant sector of the economy of the old régime rapidly wilted, with adverse effects on those sections of industry closely connected with it. Prolonged trade war, followed by economic blockade, brought the trade of the main and once prosperous French ports to a virtual standstill. Their industries declined, they lost population and ceased to be leading centres of enterprise and capital accumulation. The Revolution thus brought about a sharp discontinuity in the development of areas which might have been expected to lead the way in subsequent French industrialization.

Economic warfare was systematically pursued by both Britain and France in the conflict which divided them almost without interruption from 1793-1815.[9] The former's command of the seas made it possible to seize the French colonies and greatly reduce France's seaborne trade whether carried in her own or neutral ships. The French aim was to exclude British goods from the continental market and to harry British trade on the seas. The methods used varied over time and became more stringent and effective although, being based on balance of trade theories, they stopped short at complete trade embargo. Moreover, they were limited at all times by the difficulties of enforcement and the reluctance of traders and consumers in both camps to comply with the regulations.

The French attempt to exclude British goods began in October, 1793 and, at the same time, a navigation law sought to confine the carrying trade to French ships or ships carrying the products of their own countries. It was hoped by these means, not only to stimulate French manufacturing and shipping, but also to strike a mortal blow at British trade by depriving it of markets. The idea that in this way the 'nation of shopkeepers' could be brought to its knees remained a cardinal point of all subsequent French economic strategy during the wars. On the British side French ports were declared to be in a state of blockade and neutral ships seeking to enter them were stopped, searched and seized if found to be carrying contraband. In the period up to the Treaty of Amiens the commercial war left Britain in possession of an increasing trade with the United States and the colonies as well as with the other neutrals. British goods continued to find their way all over the continent mainly through the Scandinavian and north German ports. All French efforts to heighten the trade war had thus failed, although severe losses had been inflicted on British shipping. French overseas trade, notably that through the Atlantic ports, had declined catastrophically. On the other hand, the victories of the French armies on land permitted some extension of French markets across the land frontiers. The importance of these markets fluctuated with the fortunes of war. In any case, the stimulus which they gave to those industries in which French entrepreneurs had a technical advantage, once British competition was excluded, did not compensate for the losses elsewhere. All this time the dislocation and disarray of French industry contrasted with the rapid growth taking place in Britain.

With the resumption of the war Napoleon and his advisors re-imposed the blockade, seeking to build up French economic strength and undermine English commerce. However, for the first few years its application was distinctly cautious. Neutral trade was not interfered with and efforts were made to encourage export industries. This ensured manufacturers a certain protection against English competition, apart from smuggled goods, while enabling them to obtain raw materials from overseas. Policy was based on the mercantilist canon of ensuring a favourable balance of trade and wearing down the British economy by depriving it of markets. This, in turn, would prevent England from paying subsidies to Napoleon's continental enemies and enable him to bring the wars in Europe to a successful conclusion. As under the Republic, this thinking ran in harness with the object of protecting French industry from British competition and thus enabling it, with state encouragement, to grow more rapidly and promote national prosperity.

In practice, then, Napoleon's policy would depend upon whether Britain could be denied markets for her growing industrial output and whether this could be done without harming France and her allies. The final phase of the trade war came with the Orders in Council and the Berlin and Milan Decrees which established a severe sea blockade of continental ports and brought into being the so-called Continental System.

The extension of the Napoleonic Empire thus entailed the extension of the Continental System, but the means were lacking to maintain an effective wall around this territory. It proved impossible to exclude British goods from the Continent, but it was even more impossible to cripple British trade as a whole since it was able to find growing markets across the Atlantic and in other parts of the world which more than compensated for the losses inflicted by the Continental System. On the other hand, the combination of the British sea blockade and the Continental System paralysed the trade of most European ports. Trade was driven into illicit channels and new fortunes were erected on the basis of smuggling.

Neither side was concerned specifically with depriving its enemy of all supplies from outside on the lines of the economic warfare of the twentieth century. Consequently trading with the enemy was not regarded as reprehensible by British merchants nor repressed by the government. As for Napoleon, bending to necessity, he issued licences permitting the export of French agricultural or industrial products to Britain in return for specified commodities or currency. From 1810, by the Trianon decree high customs duties were levied on the 'prohibited' articles imported under licence. The needs of the Treasury took precedence over the logic of trade war, which, above all, should have prevented the export of grain to England during the grain shortage of 1810. Even from the stand-point of his own theory Napoleon's application of the Continental System was inconsistent. It involved him in campaigns which proved disastrous without striking a real blow at British trade primarily because command of the seas ensured its maintenance and extension. Attempts to enforce the blockade more rigorously on occupied and allied countries, while permitting breaches in the interests of France, undermined Napoleon's own political reconstruction of Europe and involved him in further campaigns which brought about his downfall.

Economic development in Napoleonic France

The desire of the bourgeoisie for internal security and stable government in order that the gains of the Revolution could be digested lay behind the acceptance of Napoleon's dictatorship. For most of those who rallied to the Consulate and Empire support was always conditional and it was progressively alienated as the Empire had nothing more to offer than interminable wars accomplished by economic disruption and tax burdens. Throughout this period economic development was much more directly affected by the special conditions brought about by social upheaval and war than by the positive measures of government. There could not be a coherent policy of encouragement for industry and Napoleon's measures are more impressive on paper than they were in practice. They can be regarded, in any case, as still in the tradition of the old régime, just as Napoleon's own attitude towards businessmen, however much he needed them, remained deeply suspicious. He combined respect for property and wealth, and a recognition that military and political notables had to be endowed with property if they did not already possess it, with a deep prejudice against the practices of advanced commerce and finance (although he was not averse, himself, to a little speculation on the side). For him industry and trade had to serve the state, and that meant, in the circumstances inseparable from his régime, serve its military needs. Under these conditions there was no room for rounded economic development.

State intervention thus became a further arbitrary factor in a complex situation dominated by the effects of revolution, war and economic blockade. Taken as a whole, the French economy, while not prospering or undergoing any notable transformation, did show itself capable of bearing the burdens of the war and supporting the disadvantages of the blockade, though not without heavy losses to particular regions, industries and sections of the bourgeoisie itself. This ability to bear the war was, however, very much attributable to the relative backwardness of the national economy. The worst hit sectors included shipping and external trade centred on the ports, the luxury trades (though they had periods of revival as well as of depression) and internal transport and trade. These were among the most dynamic sectors before the Revolution but they did not penetrate profoundly into the lives of a population composed predominantly of peasant households still only loosely tied to the exchange economy. Much of the population could thus retrench and accommodate itself to the storms which blew around it. More real to many were the actual gains which the situation brought which enabled the peasantry to enjoy a larger proportion of its product. Many, too, had made gains at the expense of the

Church or the former landowners and were laying the basis, through land speculation and the buying and selling of commodities in scarce supply, for solid bourgeois fortunes. Some no doubt suffered from high prices and scarcities, or from the effects of the wars. The effects were less than they would have been in a more advanced economy. The deterioration of the roads, for example, did not disrupt the internal market for commodities in common consumption because national markets for them did not yet exist. Local and regional self-sufficiency was thus a shield against economic disaster. Such surplus as could be mobilized in each area went to support the war effort, but this was in the nature of a stimulus to activity rather than a burden for the area concerned.

The cutting off of trade with England offered some industries a kind of protection which they would not otherwise have enjoyed. Other industries were stimulated by military needs. Substitutes had to be found for products formerly imported, such as cane sugar and some dye-stuffs. On this basis the Empire could take credit for a quite rapid growth of some 'new' industries. The cotton industry was one which went through a phase of rapid growth, able to adopt new techniques but shielded from English competition. The artificial protection thus offered had, as its counterpart, a shortage of raw cotton which became chronic in the later years of the Empire. The restoration of peace thus completed the discomfiture of an industry which, across the Channel, had been going through a major transformation which gave it an unchallenged competitive power on the world market.

The patchy performance of French industry, with contrasting sectors of slow and rapid growth, was characteristic of the eighteenth century. What the Revolution and the Empire did was to introduce external factors which had their own distorting effects. Where they accelerated growth it could not be sustained once peacetime conditions had been restored; where they held it back, the restoration of peace did not automatically prepare the conditions for new expansion. Under conditions of arbitrary fluctuations in demand, high labour costs and the influence of military needs entrepreneurs, and businessmen generally, could hardly plan their investment far ahead. The emphasis tended to be upon quick and speculative returns, upon improvisation and quick adaptation to temporary market requirements. Fortunes could be built in this way, but it was not a satisfactory basis for an industrial transformation of the type which was taking place in England, especially as it was accompanied by the decline of a number of the main commercial areas which could have been expected to make an important contribution to such a change. The expansion which did take place, therefore, tended to be largely upon the old lines, without bringing about any major changes in structure. There were some factories and large enterprises, but over industry as a whole the old techniques and the traditional productive units held their own, and multiplied. We are justified, therefore, in speaking of the economy, throughout this period, as being still of an eighteenth-century type: predominantly agrarian with industrial production still mainly subordinated to commercial capital. More advanced techniques and business personalities were appearing but they had not yet altered substantially the inherited structures.

And yet, the Revolution and the Empire brought into existence and consolidated a social and legal order thoroughly attuned to bourgeois property owners, clearing the ground of all pre-existing barriers to individual enterprise. In this, perhaps, lays the essential paradox of nineteenth-century France. The very events which brought the bourgeoisie to power at the same time retarded the development of industrial capitalism. As has been pointed out, the base of the revolutionary bourgeoisie was not in industry, but rather in trade, the professions and the land. The new men who thrust themselves forward as a result of the opportunities created by social upheaval were also mainly interested in the same forms of wealth and enrichment. Opposed to all the obstacles to enterprise upheld by the old monarchical order, demanding commercial and industrial freedom, they did not see in industrial investment and production the main avenue for taking advantage of the new-won freedoms. Fortunes could be built up far more quickly in speculation in land and commodities. They might later find their way into industry, but only as and when opportunities presented themselves. The wealthy capitalists of the Empire were still mainly financiers and bankers whose operations were closely linked with the financial needs of the state. In personnel and in function there was considerable continuity with the old régime, but there was also something decisively new: the legal conditions for the full flowering of capitalism in all its forms had been established.

In this sense, then, the Empire completed and consolidated the accomplishments of the Revolution. Within a short time the legal codes and institutions of French society were re-shaped in the image of the bourgeoisie. Thus, at the centre of the Civil Code of 1804 was the absolute principle of private property, derived, it is true, from the Roman law, but now given a connotation which could not fail to be of tremendous importance for the development of capitalism which required, at this stage, that restraints on the individual's right to use his property as he thought fit should be reduced to a minimum. The rights of property were basic to the freedom and individualism which the bourgeois felt as a pressing everyday matter as he went about his affairs and not as an abstract thing. Proclaimed by jurists and idealists, these principles became the passwords of those who wanted no restriction placed on the manner in which they utilized their property and accumulated more. As written into the Civil Code they thus became the charter for the new, emerging sections of the bourgeoisie as industrialization took place.

The legacy of the revolutionary period was complex and ambiguous. The old barriers to enterprise and the free exercise of individualism were, formally, destroyed. Capitalism in France had, in this respect, the most favourable conditions possible for development. On the other hand, the economy was disrupted and distorted by all the accompaniments of revolution and war and its vital links with the world market were almost wholly cut off. So far as the war and the blockade proved a forcing house for economic change the resumption of peace destroyed practically all the gains. One sector, and that the largest of all, agriculture, had proved inflexible to major change in organization or technique once feudal relations had been overthrown. The peculiarities of the revolution, the inter-twining of a peasant with a bourgeois revolution, left agriculture largely in the hands of a backward peasantry. By its very individualism the Revolution confirmed the peasant custom of division on inheritance and thus prevented the emergence of a really individualist agriculture over the country as a whole. The inheritance clauses of the Civil Code contributed to *morcellement* of the peasants' lands where they did not encourage the limitation of family size. No doubt they helped to conserve the peasantry, albeit at a low standard of living, but at the price of impeding the expansion of the internal market and the creation of an urban, industrial proletariat. Even in its strictly legal effects, therefore, the Revolution took away from developing industrial capitalism some of the pre-requisites with which it had, in other ways, so freely endowed it.

In the nature of the society which emerged after 1789 some of the brakes on subsequent development can thus be discerned. They concern, not only the direct impact of war, but also the peculiarities of the triumphant bourgeoisie and its relationship with the peasantry without whose assistance it would have been unable to overthrow the old régime. French society thus combined the most advanced features of a wholly bourgeois society with strongly built-in carry-overs from the old, pre-industrial, pre-capitalist society in such a way that the whole subsequent development of capitalism was to be affected. The break with the past was thus not clear-cut. Only as industry became strong enough to push against the limits opposed to it could a disintegration of the old forms take place.

Notes and further reading

1. As a leading French jurist has put it: 'Je crois que l'on peut dater l'avènement du régime capitaliste en France de la Révolution de 1789. En détruisant l'ordre ancien qui aurait pu s'opposer au développement du capitalisme, elle a permis la création d'un régime nouveau qui devait en assurer le triomphe. Il importe peu qu'elle ne l'ait pas voulu. C'est souvent longtemps apres les événements qu'apparaissent les effets d'une révolution.' G. Ripert, *Aspects juridiques du capitalisme moderne* (Paris 1951), p. 11.
2. For the 'peasant revolution' consult the works of G. Lefebvre, whose principal articles are collected in *Études sur la révolution française* (Paris 1954). The social and economic aspects of this period are given their due weight in the two volumes of the Peuples et Civilizations series for which he was responsible, *La révolution française* (3rd ed. Paris 1963) and *Napoléon* (5th ed. Paris 1965). The best available treatment of the social changes of the Revolution by an English scholar is N. Hampson, *A Social History of the French Revolution* (London 1963).
3. E. Labrousse, op. cit. Hampson, op. cit.
4. On the revolutionary land settlement see Lefebvre, *Études* . . . .
5: A point strongly emphasized by E. Beau de Loménie, *Les responsabilités des dynasties bourgeoises*, Vol. I (Paris 1943).
6. Ripert, op. cit. Pernoud, op. cit.

7. It was characteristic of the new tax structure that the taxes were levied on things, not on people or their incomes.
8. e.g. in the industrial areas of Dauphiné studied by P. Léon, op. cit.
9. A valuable summary of the economic effects of the war for Europe in F. Crouzet, 'Wars, Blockade and Economic Change in Europe, 1792-1815', *The Journal of Economic History,* XXIV, No. 4, December, 1964.

CHAPTER VI

Continuity and Change in the French Economy, 1815-1848

THE period in French economic history which begins with the Restoration of the Bourbons and ends with the Revolution of 1848 has been variously seen as an extension of the eighteenth century and a period of transition in which, if there was no Industrial Revolution of the English type, the first steps were taken towards the establishment of a modern industrial society.[1] The literature reflects the fact that this period witnessed a complex interplay between the forces of continuity and the pressures of change. Striking contrasts were thus to be found between the archaic and the novel. In the harvesting of grain the sickle still held its own against the scythe.[2] In the iron industry Le Creusot reared itself against a background of small-scale, charcoal-burning forges. From what sources did the old forms and structures derive their strength and to what extent had their hold been broken by 1848? It is to these questions that this chapter principally addresses itself.

I

The main economic significance of the Restoration of the Bourbons was that it brought to an end a long period of warfare extending back to the seventeenth century and almost uninterrupted in the preceding quarter of a century. Louis XVIII returned to a country whose economic structure still essentially retained its pre-revolutionary shape. Forms of property and economic relations in the agrarian sector had, of course, changed fundamentally, but only to leave the actual operations of husbandry in the hands of the peasantry.[3] Freed from seigneurial obligations the peasants, as a whole, were brought into more intimate contact with the market because they had more to sell. Nevertheless, the self-sufficiency of the peasant household remained high and the restraints of the village community on individual enterprise were only slowly undermined. The land transfers and legal changes affecting property which had characterized the Revolutionary period, and which the restored monarchy was obliged to accept, benefitted mainly the bourgeoisie, giving this class an unusually strong basis in the ownership of real property and re-enforcing its non-industrial character.[4] The effects of the Revolution on the social structure helped to determine the character of the French economy in the nineteenth century.

The Revolution had not been made by a bourgeoisie based on industry, nor did it do much to elevate the industrial and commercial capitalist to a higher social standing than he had under the old régime.[5] Conditions after 1789 had not been conducive to large-scale investment in new lines of production; industry had advanced slowly and unevenly in wartime conditions. Overseas trade had suffered severe blows from which it only slowly recovered after 1815.[6] The economic infrastructure, especially commercial highways and ports, had scarcely been added to and in some cases had deteriorated. Industry generated little capital for its own expansion and had as yet little access to outside sources of supply. Some sectors had been stimulated by wartime demand, but loss of markets or shortage of raw material supplies had handicapped the progress of others: notably those upon which, at this time, industrialization was most likely to be based. In short, the economy remained predominantly agrarian, with a peasantry which had been confirmed in its property rights and a bourgeoisie composed of owners of real property, practitioners of the professions and holders of state office in which the businessmen remained a detached segment having little standing.[7] Technical change, growth in wealth and incomes, remained confined within this inherited framework with its strongly marked 'eighteenth century' character.

II

What had greatly changed was the international environment. The rapid growth and economic transformations which had continued in Britain during the war period placed the French economy at a much greater relative disadvantage than before. Bordeaux was no longer comparable with Liverpool; France, as yet, had no Manchester. British industry, through its technical superiority, and with the assistance of naval power, had established a hold over the world market for manufactured goods which was to become even more secure in the decades after 1815. It was this industrial giant which French manufacturers confronted with the coming of peace; in almost every sector their inferiority in technique, financial means and business experience was clear.[8] On the other hand there was an industrial tradition and in certain lines of production French goods had an international reputation. The hold on the home market given by distance and government support, together with a long-time borrowing and improving of technique made French industry, in aggregate size and modernity, the leader on the Continent of Europe.[9]

In a sense France was the first 'late-comer', whose entrepreneurs were able, in principle, to take over and assimilate innovations which had been tried out and developed in Britain, the industrial pioneer. However, in the decade or so after 1815 these techniques were still evolving and had not been completely applied even in Britain.[10] The direct and adverse effects of British competition and the pre-emption of a world market which grew more slowly when French exporters again had access to it than when the British had been establishing their hold over it weighed much more heavily in the balance. The inferiority of French industry, even apart from the lack of the stimulus which abundant supplies of cheap coal may have offered, grew out of deep differences in social development between France and Britain. The contrast between the bourgeoisie in the two countries offers a significant index of this.

In France the bourgeoisie was distinguished by its ownership of property but property which existed mainly in the form of land and buildings. The legal changes of the Revolution had assimilated the feudal property of the nobility to that of private property in general and they ceased to be a privileged class. Under the old régime the bourgeoisie had already had the form of a class of office and property holders; the Revolution opened up more opportunities for the acquisition of land, mainly through the purchase of *biens nationaux*, though some military and civil officials were also endowed with land under the Empire.[11] The fortunes of the nineteenth century bourgeois families can be traced to a large extent to the old régime and particularly to the acquisition of, and speculation in, land during the revolutionary period.[12] After 1815, therefore, it is safe to assume that the French bourgeoisie derived its income largely from rents paid by tenants of houses and apartments, farm land or commercial property.[13] Those who passed into the professions generally came from families which had some real property: already established bourgeois or peasant families on their way into the ranks of the bourgeoisie. Both these men, and 'little people' who built up even modest fortunes in trade or in production, tended to buy land and buildings as the safest and perhaps most lucrative investment available as well as to consecrate their status as men of wealth and position.[14] For this there had to be a free and active market in land, with those of the peasants who could economizing to add to their holdings. In a period of monetary stability and falling prices a steady appreciation in land values took place; the bourgoisie consolidated its position and became richer and itself displayed great social stability.[15] Its monetary income derived to a large extent from rents paid by householders, by commercial tenants and by peasants and farmers who were commercializing agricultural produce. The growth of markets and improvement in agriculture, as well as industrial development, tended to increase automatically the incomes of the bourgeoisie, thus making further wealth available for accumulation. The emphasis fell upon conservation rather than upon the rapid expansion of fortunes through investment comporting a high degree of risk. Apart from the land, therefore, the wealthy bourgeois tended to prefer government stock to investment in business unless he was himself an active participant. There was little in the way of a capital market and few institutions concerned with banking and finance until the 1830's or 1840's.

The French bourgeoisie, for all it had carried through a revolution and re-shaped the legal system to its needs, was still profoundly marked by the conditions which had prevailed under the old régime. Twenty-five years of revolution and war had made it conservative to the point of timidity and had provided little opportunity for the growth of large numbers of dynamic entrepreneurs of the type which had emerged in Britain.[16] Across the Channel the old families retained their grip on landed property and the peasantry had disappeared. There was little basis for the rise of a land-owning middle class and even in the towns the land was often owned by large landowners. In a sense, then, the English middle class was more 'bourgeois' than its French counterpart; it was more exclusively urban and held relatively little of its property in the form of land. It had built itself on strictly capitalist activities in trade, finance and industry at a time when politics and administration remained the virtual monopoly of the landed nobility and gentry. It saw the state as an outside force from which little good could be expected, the offices in which were filled by patronage and purchase.

Compare the relationship to the state of the French bourgeoisie, even under the Restoration. State offices which had once been bought and sold (mainly, of course, by members of the bourgeoisie) were open to the talents: which meant to the educated minority drawn mainly from the bourgeoisie. Its members looked to the state to extend and consolidate their fortunes. The new rich, as well as the older families, had built their wealth under the protection of the state, which offered their sons steady employment, influence and social prestige. A quite different relationship existed between the state and business from that in Britain. The state was seen not as an alien force whose powers had to be reduced but rather as a necessary agency for the protection of *positions acquises*.[17]

The French economy offers the paradox in the early nineteenth century of growing wealth and a substantial and prosperous bourgeoisie without industrial development on a scale comparable with that in Britain. Property remained mainly in the old forms; mobile capital, as distinct from real property, had not yet become a decisive force. The surplus accruing to the bourgeoisie itself came largely from land rents. Bourgeois property was protected by the maximum of legal guarantees and the juridical basis for the full development of capitalist relations had been laid.[18] In this respect the Restoration accepted the very foundation of bourgeois social supremacy as it had emerged from the Revolution. Even the attempt to strengthen the old hereditary élite could have little effect;

in the administration itself there was a great deal of continuity with the Empire. Other attempts to alter the law by permitting corporations and establishing primogeniture in the 1820's came to nothing. With the Revolution of 1830 surviving vestiges of the *ancien régime* were swept away, and with them all hope of a revival of noble privileges. The July monarchy gave the bourgeoisie all the legal guarantees it required and enabled its wealthiest sections at that time, the financiers and bankers, to exercise a predominating influence over policy. Apart from that, and despite the hopes of the July days, as Adeline Daumard puts it: 'It was above all for the upper classes that the revolution of 1830 marked a break while for the bourgeoisie taken as a whole the chronological division 1815-48 conserves all its value.'[19] Relatively little wealth was transmuted into forms which enabled these opportunities to be put to use through the promotion of industry. The industrial sections of the bourgeoisie remained somewhat to one side, whether rich, enterprising and exclusive, or small fry beset by inadequate capital and limited horizons. Business success in such an environment might lead to early retirement, to running the enterprise much as a family estate, to purchase of land and to education of the oncoming generation for the professions or a career in administration or politics.[20]

The bourgeois nature of French society, the close relationship between the middle class and the state apparatus established before industrialization had been carried out, favoured the steady growth of wealth rather than a rapid surge forward in the economy. Although there was little industrialization under the Restoration and only the first steps in the direction of modern capitalism were taken during the Orleans monarchy a momentum of change had been established. Both by accretion and by a quickening of the rate of growth the process was carried further in the 1850's; the years from 1815 to 1848 were years of preparation rather than of achievement. New techniques, new forms of business organization and finance were being implanted but they had not yet proved strong enough to effect a structural transformation, except on a local or partial scale. The forces which tended to conserve the old structures and forms of economy remained deeply entrenched.

III

If the French economy remained through most of this period of 'an eighteenth-century type' it was principally because of the predominance of peasant agriculture. The peasantry not merely survived; its rights to the land, of which it owned almost half, were guaranteed by the same laws which protected the property of the bourgeoisie. This was the price which the peasants had been able to exact for their participation in the Revolution. As a result strong barriers were erected around the forms of agriculture and land use inherited from the past, protecting them from the corroding forces of individualism. These barriers were not, of course, impenetrable. The peasants' need for cash tended to undermine the subsistence basis of agriculture and the growth of markets favoured the division of commons and the slow abandonment of the old practices of husbandry. Nevertheless a large proportion of the peasant households produced largely for subsistence and only appeared in the market to a small extent, whether as sellers or as consumers. And the peasantry tilled a larger proportion of land than they owned, since many of the former noble or bourgeois landowners saw their estates merely as a source of income, to be derived from small tenants or *métayers*.

Peasants holdings were generally small and the legal provisions concerning the division of property on inheritance tended to make them smaller still. For lack of knowledge and capital the peasants continued to make use of primitive techniques; labour was not scarce, so that even new tools were substituted but slowly for the old. Apart from the long-standing specialization of some areas, the principal function of peasant agriculture was to provide for the needs of the household. Uneconomic use of the land was added to *morcellement* to hold down yields to low levels and thus to limit the surplus available for sale.[21] Possession of land or the possibility of acquiring it through inheritance, the readiness of landowners to lease land in small parcels or on *métayage* tenure, tended to fix the population on the land. Except in a few areas of high population growth and particularly poor soil there was little permanent migration from the villages.

The social position of the French peasantry was extremely secure and its weight in French society remained considerable, though as a passive, rather than an active force. Economically its preservation under such favourable conditions could not but act to retard development. The peasant households which made up such a large part of the French market had but a low average purchasing power. The commodities they required in the largest amounts—cheap textiles, farm tools and domestic utensils—would generally be obtained from local sources and be produced in small units or under the putting out system.[22] The persistence of local differences in customs and dress re-enforced the lack of standardization. Until the coming of the railway, an uneven process since it did not penetrate into some rural areas until the 1880's, the village population lived in a state of isolation from the outside world which is now difficult to imagine. The difficulties in the way of the movement of men and goods remained considerable.[23] France thus consisted of a series of local and regional markets grouped around one or two country towns; such markets had only loose connections with each other and a national market scarcely existed.[24] In such an economy there would not be a powerful need for improved means of communication and those which had the most effect were not necessarily the most spectacular. The improvement of local roads from 1836 no doubt had more effect on the peasantry than the main line railways. The impulse for improvement came, as might have been expected, mainly from the centre: from the state and from technicians, economists and financiers. Before the coming of the railway the lack of transport facilities reflected the structure of society rather than explained it. The bulk of the population already lived in an exchange economy, it is true, but one which remained localized and insufficiently developed, not primarily because of the lack of transport, but because it only slowly generated an effective demand for these facilities.

In a mainly agrarian economy of this type, made up of regionally almost self-contained markets and with low per capita purchasing power, industry will also be organized in small units and on the old lines. Entrepreneurs will adapt themselves to the market situation with which they are confronted. It would be risky and foolish for them to make large capital outlays on new techniques which could only be operated economically if their costs could be spread over a larger volume of output than the market warranted. In this period textiles remained the main field subject to such expansion. Most other industrial activities, outside a few towns associated with *la grande industrie*, were concerned with the transformation of local materials and agricultural products by traditional village craftsmen and small-town artisans for a mainly local market. Even the iron industry was largely oriented towards the production of tools and implements for local use; the small forge using local ores and charcoal thus sufficed.

It is well known that in a peasant economy the production of textiles, beginning with the yarn, is the first activity to be carried outside the home as a specialized industry on a scale which makes possible the growth of capitalist industry. Even so, this does not necessarily mean that actual production leaves the home; generally it requires organization of the rural labour supply on putting-out lines, particular processes going into the factory only as power-driven machinery is developed. The rate at which this change takes place will depend on many factors: it can be said, however, that an abundant supply of cheap labour in the rural areas will tend to prolong the life of the putting-out form of organization, especially if it is combined with a shortage of labour for work in the factories. The reluctance of the French peasant to leave his village where he or his family had land, combined with low rural incomes, tended to prolong the life of the putting-out system in the textile industry. Mines, ironworks and even factories often drew upon the peasants for their labour supply without the need to separate them from their rural roots.[25] The more rapidly growing factory industries had to call upon low grade labour from the fringes of rural society and from the impoverished semi-nomadic elements, one time beggars and paupers. In the larger towns, and especially Paris, skilled as well as unskilled workers came from the villages as temporary and seasonal labour.[26] There were signs, therefore, that French capitalism, mainly through the size and stability of the peasantry, was only able to assemble an industrial proletariat in a slow and difficult manner. This is not to say that there was a general or acute labour scarcity. There was plenty of surplus labour in the villages, unwilling as it was to move on a permanent basis. The fact that industrial firms grew slowly, for reasons that can be traced elsewhere, prevented labour scarcity from becoming a crucial problem though, as always, the larger firms and more centralized industries encountered difficulties in recruiting and retaining skilled and supervisory workers (a problem which, to some extent, could be overcome by hiring English workers).

IV

The predominance of 'textile capitalism' remained an outstanding feature of the French industrial structure throughout this period. It was in textiles that the most significant strides were taken in establishing a factory industry and creating a modern type of industrial environment.[27] Of the main textile areas Alsace displayed the most advanced features, adding to the adoption of English machinery technical innovations of its own, particularly in the field of printing. The main problem of the Alsatian industry in this period seems to have been one of markets: the home market did not grow rapidly enough and the established position of Lancashire in the foreign market impeded the growth of exports. The Alsatian entrepreneurs were among the most dynamic in France at this time but their businesses were of a family type, closely attached to their trade secrets and having little need to resort to outside supplies of capital.[28] Mechanization of the Northern textile industry came somewhat later than that of Alsace but the whole growth of the region was rapid from the 1830's, when cheap textiles, particularly cottons, manufactured by machinery were brought within the reach of the mass of the population. In particular, the Northern manufacturers had the advantage of a thickly populated area from which workers could be drawn and markets found. This area was clearly affected by its proximity to England and Belgium and was becoming part of the industrial complex of North West Europe. The third main area of cotton production, Normandy, conserved more of the traits of a semi-rural putting-out industry. Its entrepreneurs made the most of their favourable location, abundance of water power and cheap labour and concentrated on the coarser lines for the home market. They may be taken as an example of an adaptation to French peculiarities which inhibited growth. Landes suggests that there was less profit in the production of the cheaper textiles than in the quality lines.[29] In the absence of a large foreign market for the former there was little incentive to mechanize and in the production of coarser varieties the machines might not yet have a decisive advantage.

While these were the main areas of the cotton industry, at this time undergoing expansion and technical change, regional specialization was less pronounced than in England. These areas produced other textiles than cottons and there was textile production in other parts of the country, apart from the Lyons silk industry. Small, high cost producers could survive with the help of protection and the lack of transport facilities by selling in a local market or turning out specialities. The silk industry owed its importance to intricate organization and skilled hand labour employed in small units of production. Despite some technical improvements it continued to represent an old-style capitalism; it was geared to changes in high fashion not to mass markets. Although silk manufacturers were as apprehensive of foreign competition as those in other fields the French industry had an international reputation and a large export trade. But it cannot be considered as a pole of growth or change.

From the 1830's the growing industrial capitalist sector associated primarily with textiles became of greater relative weight in a still predominantly agricultural economy. As has been seen, textile capitalism tended to adapt itself to the existing environment in the absence of an expanding foreign market. Businesses in textiles had in some cases a continuity going back into the eighteenth century,[30] more recent creations had begun in a small way and had grown, as in England, by the ploughing back of profits into family firms and small partnerships. In some areas the industry was controlled by a relatively small number of families, sometimes assuming the form of wealthy, interlocking dynasties which had established themselves over a period of decades. These firms had, as it were, grown almost imperceptibly into the prevailing structures without 'revolutionary' consequences. Machine had been added to machine, workshop to workshop following a search for profit no less rational than that pursued in England. But the opportunities offered by the environment were different from those in England and the industrial entrepreneurs, as part of a wider bourgeois class, adapted to them. They were concerned with the preservation and accumulation of capital in an historical background of state support of industry, political uncertainty, availability of landed property, access to public office and international competitive inferiority. There was no rapid expansion of demand. Technical change had been absorbed slowly and made use of selectively over a protracted period. Markets and sources of supply had been subjected to the vagaries of war during a period in which the basis for industrial expansion might otherwise have been laid. There was a strong protective reaction and an acquired preference for security and stability among those with large investments in fixed capital. Established entrepreneurs sought to hang on to acquired positions and eschewed the unknown and thus insisted on having a protected home market.

Although, as will be seen, a new, more modern type of capitalism began in the 1820's and 1830's to make its first forward steps, its connection with the main established industries was at first small. The new capitalism was concerned with the mobilization and disposal of large amounts of capital required for extending the economic infrastructure and building up heavy industries. While the balance remained with the textile industries the industrial entrepreneurs had little need for outside sources of capital and avoided it as far as possible. Even bank capital was not much sought after and the banking facilities remained primitive. There was no demand from industry for changes in company law or for improved financial institutions.

In the industrial field, it has been suggested, textiles tended to lead the way in economic development. As they grow, however, complementary changes take place elsewhere. A demand is created for machinery and fuel. New markets are offered for the metal industries. The areas of France in which the changes associated with an Industrial Revolution were apparent combined textile industries with the availability of coal and ores upon which an iron and machine-making industry could be based. These areas, in turn, generated a need for, and the means to construct, railway lines. New dissolvents were introduced into the peasant economy. Labour was drawn into the growing industrial centres. New forms of accumulation appeared and purveyors of credit responded to, or induced, the growth in demand for capital.

Fear of English competition and addiction to protection on the part of many French manufacturers did not prevent a rational adaptation to the opportunities for profit in the foreign as well as the home market. The advantages of the Northern England textile producers lay mainly in the lines where machinery and large-scale production at low unit costs were decisive. In the finishing processes and in the higher quality cloths, or where it was important to be able to follow frequent changes in fashion, French firms were able to do more than hold their own. Economic growth in other countries expanded the international market for such commodities and the export of quality products expanded steadily. There was a tendency, therefore, for mechanization and advanced processes to appear first in the later stages of production and then, as the industry grew, to extend back into the primary stages. As a market developed for machine-makers something similar happened in the metal industries. By the time that railway building had begun a basis had been laid for the production of locomotives and rolling stock and the process of transforming the furnaces and forges to the use of coke and the concentration of iron-making on the coalfields was in full swing.

In some areas of France, notably in the North, the development of a textile industry created a demand for machinery and fuel and offered a new and growing market for the metal industries. A need for improved means of transport was generated and capital became available to finance the railway lines which industry was now equipped to undertake. This was more in the English style of industrialization, but it was a pattern which not many areas in France were endowed with the means to follow. Elsewhere, however, industrialization followed a different and necessarily slower course in which investment and enterprise were attracted into those branches of production nearest to the consumer. By their nature these industries produced commodities which were made on a smaller scale and sold at a higher price than did the cotton yarns and cloth of Lancashire. The emphasis on quality was not, however, irrational in the circumstances in which many French entrepreneurs found themselves, all other considerations apart. They were, in fact, able to take advantage of rising incomes produced by industrialization elsewhere in Western Europe and North America at a time when they were ill-equipped to challenge the hold on the markets for cheaper and semi-finished goods possessed by their English rivals. In this way, it may be argued, they made an intelligent adaptation to the international division of labour.

Taken as a whole the economy was moving forward rather than stagnating in these decades. Textile production and exports were growing. French inferiority compared to neighbouring and competing areas was most evident in heavy industry. Some writers have therefore seen the relative lack of good coking coal as a major reason for the lag in French industrialization in the nineteenth century.[31] Certainly industrialists generally had to pay more for coal than their rivals and although this may have encouraged them to economize in fuel it might also have deterred investment in coal-using processes and steam engines. The pattern of industrialization was perhaps more clearly affected by this than was its rate. Of course, had coal resources equivalent to those of the Ruhr been opened up during this period in France the economic development of the country would have been quite different. This does not mean that all the discernable weaknesses in metallurgy or elsewhere can be ascribed to the scarcity and high price of coal. Even in the iron industry the prevalance of small-scale, scattered forges using charcoal seems to be related to the nature of the market, particularly the localized demand for agricultural tools and implements, as much as to the shortage of good coking coal. Only the railway could change this, as it was already beginning to do by the 1840's, both by its own demand for iron and by overcoming the local and regional fragmentation of the market.

V

Two departures in the 1830's, more than anything happening in the field of manufacturing or mining, announced the appearance of the new-style capitalism—the spread of new methods and forms of organization in business and banking and the coming of the railway. Both acted upon, yet were held back by, the same resistances in the environment which shaped the course of industrial change. There was bound to be a close relationship between the nature of the society and its business structure; transport facilities, in turn, were adapted to the needs of such a society. Exceptionally powerful forces were required to push them beyond the existing limits and bring about a real re-shaping of the inherited structures.[32] Certainly in neither sphere did this happen before 1848. By and large the banking and financial structure reflected closely the physiognomy of the economy as a whole and the railways, of which more will be said later, did less than might have been expected to stimulate change. Yet the adoption of new business methods, the introduction of more advanced forms of credit and changes in the capital market, as well as the building of the first railway lines, foreshadowed the rise of a capitalism of a more complex and advanced type.

Bankers and businessmen in France were able to take over and develop the most advanced methods and forms of organization found elsewhere, in some ways at a rate and with a facility greater than was the case with industrial techniques. As in the eighteenth century, the needs of the state and overseas trade and financial transactions offered scope for the merchant banker. The coming of peace thus saw the revival of *la haute banque*, essentially a collection of wealthy banking families resident in Paris but with international connections which were vital for the type of business in which they engaged.[33] Hence the predominance of Jewish and Protestant names. An economy which remained of the eighteenth century type nonetheless provided opportunities for enrichment by handling public loans, dealing in exchange transactions and financing international trade. The success of this business depended upon the ability to provide relatively large amounts of money capital or credit for operations in which there was little risk and which had a self-liquidating character. It was business of a kind which had been practised since the Middle Ages and which could grow in line with the expansion of the economy without fundamental change. The firms involved in it were able to adapt themselves to the changing demands for financial services which arose out of the developments of the nineteenth-century economy.[34] In fact they assumed a central rôle in the long-term capital market: issuing and dealing in state bonds and, increasingly, promoting the joint stock companies without which the capital for the advancing projects of large-scale capitalism could not be raised. For this it was no longer enough to rely on the resources of the family and its immediate circles of associates. *La haute banque* had to learn how to overcome the timidity of the small savers, so numerous in France, and bring together from many sources the large capitals increasingly required.

The sources of saving, and the habits and preferences of the savers, reflected the nature of the society and the character of its peasantry and bourgeoisie. It is evident that while the old-style capitalism, typified by the family firms in the textile industry, drew its capital for expansion from its own resources, every big new investment, whether in industry or in commerce or transport, had to obtain its capital to start with from already existing accumulations, accumulations which had arisen in the course of the circuit of exchange of a still predominantly land-oriented economy.[35] Yet the bourgeois owners of real estate and the better-off peasants, saving to buy more land, to educate a son or provide a dowry for a daughter, had as yet no experience with the modern practices of deposit banking. In the 1820's the provinces were largely a desert as far as banks were concerned and there was no opportunity for middle class Frenchmen to acquire the banking habit.[36] Alternatively, their unwillingness to trust bankers or hold their spare funds in paper money acted as an obstacle to the spread of banking. Had France possessed a more developed banking system it is not difficult to assume that its economic development would have been more rapid than it was; had its banking system been more adequate, however, that would have been because the economy, by its development, had made the opportunity for bankers. As it was the financial practices and institutions were created in the image of the society. Credit there was, and therefore financial intermediaries and recognized financial instruments: but they were of a sort consistent with a pre-industrial society. The transactions of the provincial notaries who found outlets for the funds of their clients in mortgages or usurious loans could just as well have taken place in the seventeenth century. The ubiquitous usurer who financed the needs and emergencies of a peasantry lacking financial reserves or other sources of credit was not inherently different from his predecessor of two or three centuries before. On the other hand, the spread of a market economy in the countryside and the growth of towns, going on now at an accelerated pace, was accompanied by a pressing shortage of money and credit in the absence of an adequate mechanism for bringing lenders and borrowers together. The downward price trend after 1815 expressed and intensified the difficulties of a society which had not as yet learned how to make full productive use of its surplus or to speed up the creation of wealth by a ready multiplication of 'fictitious' values.

In the provinces there were few banks and those which existed carried on a business which resembled, on a smaller scale, that of the merchant bankers of Paris. Often originating in a commodity trade, these firms performed a limited range of financial services for a narrow and localized clientèle: transmission of funds, discounting of bills, acting as intermediaries for wholesale transactions in internal trade. As time went on they were able to branch out and begin to meet the needs of local industrialists and add deposits attracted from the moneyed middle class to their own resources. These institutions no doubt made an important contribution to such regional economic growth as took place, but they hardly did so as active promoters of change. Their services expanded in accordance with needs; tending, if anything, to lag a little behind.

At the apex of the banking structure stood the Bank of France, founded under the Consulate and remaining a link between the topmost circles of the Parisian business community and the Government.[37] The state furnished the major part of its capital and its fund of credit was constituted essentially by the account of the Treasury in which tax receipts were held. In addition the bank had a monopoly of note issue and carried out a high class discounting and lending business. After 1815 the Bank of France may be seen as an embryonic central bank, a state supported extension of *la haute banque.* It remained primarily a Bank of Paris and reflected and reenforced the centralization of high finance in the capital. Its autonomy increased during the Restoration and, after closing its two provincial branches in 1816, it remained without representation outside Paris for another twenty years. Like the Bank of England, it contributed to financial stability without promoting economic development in any active sense.

While the bankers concentrated in their hands the most important reserves of liquid capital needed by developing capitalism, they made it available sparingly and only to narrow and privileged groups: hence the appearance of a new 'feudalism'. Developing industry was able to make use of the short-term credit facilities provided by the bankers through the discounting of bills of exchange, but apart from this the banks offered no impersonal mechanism which industry could use to satisfy its needs for capital and credit. There were, of course, some close personal connections between financiers and industrialists, and banks might lend on personal security or mortgage to entrepreneurs. However, until they would tap the idle or under-used funds in the hands of the saving public the ability of the banks to engage in industrial financing was bound to be limited.[38] The note circulation of the Bank of France rose in line with growing prosperity—the modest prosperity of a 'bourgeois' society—but its notes remained of large denomination and did little to oil the wheels of provincial trade and industry which remained, all through this period, close to a cash basis. The prudent peasant or bourgeois held a large part of his savings in hard cash and only slowly became accustomed to the idea that pieces of paper—banknotes or shares—might be as good, or better. A great change was required before a significant inroad could be made into this habit.

The predominance of the bankers in the reign of Louis Philippe, while marking an advance compared with the Restoration period, was still a symbol of French economic backwardness. The banking oligarchy, although it took a prominent part in the financing of railways and became more involved with industrial development, still followed rather than led the course of change. It adapted itself to the new opportunities, it did not go out and look for them or much alter its traditional practices. Its relative power grew because of the increasing need for capital and because, where its own resources were insufficient, its reputation enabled it to raise more from the public. To have to go to the public was a new departure, as was, for some, participation in industrial financing through the *société en commandite*.[39] But the French bankers were not yet capable of leading the way in change. The financial oligarchy exercised its influence on the government and found new openings for enrichment in railway finance. It was, in a sense, a substitute for a more broadly based business bourgeoisie, exercising power because there was no serious contestant and not because France had become an advanced capitalist country.

Change, of course, did become more marked in the 1840's and banking and finance began to reflect the growth of wealth and the increasing and more diversified demand for capital and credit. The major influence in promoting change was the railway, both because of its demand for capital and because it contributed to the breaking down of regional isolation and the changing of traditional habits concerning finance within the bourgeoisie and peasantry. This process was still in its early stages when the Revolution of 1848 broke out.

It would be tempting to explain the relatively slow pace of industrial change by reference to the defects of the financial structure and particularly the difficulty in obtaining long-term loans. Of the latter there can be no doubt and entrepreneurs could only partly and unsatisfactorily overcome it by mortgaging their real property or by having a large floating debt. It might be argued that if only investment banks had come earlier then French economic development would have been different. The attempt was made in 1837 with the creation by Jacques Lafitte of the *Caisse générale du commerce et de l'industrie,* precursor of the great investment banks of the 1850's.[40] Lafitte's idea was to assemble a large capital through the issue of shares which, because the *Caisse* assumed the form of a *société en commandite,* enjoyed limited liability. In addition, the *Caisse* was to accept deposits in return for interest-bearing notes of 5, 15 or 30 days duration. These notes enjoyed some success until the crisis of 1847 when the *Caisse* foundered on the rock which more prudent institutions avoid: lending at long-term and borrowing short. A number of similar institutions were set up, in the provinces as well as in Paris, only to suffer a like fate in the financial troubles which marked the period 1846-8 and without making any significant impression on the credit problem.

Meanwhile, the inadequacies of self-financing were making themselves apparent in established industries and the old financial practices were unable to cope with the requirements of new large-scale enterprises in industry and transport. Working capital remained chronically scarce in all fields of business. The provinces, in particular, were starved of capital and credit, with middle class savings hoarded or drained off to investment in Paris. Parisian finance, concentrated in the hands of the big merchant bankers, even when it found new outlets, did so in line with established habits and preferences. The bankers preferred large-scale transactions which promised handsome returns within a short period. The increasing number of stocks and shares, including government bonds, which were, to begin with, the staple commodity of the Bourse, offered just this kind of outlet. Business grew rapidly in the thirties, with a rapid increase in the volume of railways shares, and kept the interest of the bankers turned mainly to this speculative type of gain rather than to catering directly for the needs of industry. This was a built-in characteristic: not so much a failure to see opportunities as it was an anxiety to grasp those which offered the greatest earning potential in the shortest possible time. Consequently, in the period before the 1848 Revolution, the bankers, for all their political and social predominance, played little creative rôle in the development of French industrial capitalism. The bankers reflected not only the image of the Citizen-King but that of the solid bourgeois society of the type already described upon which the throne was based.[41]

French society grew and offered possibilities for enrichment but it was only slowly losing its eighteenth century, pre-industrial characteristics. So far the bankers were not acting as a motive force in such a transformation, though they were willing to profit from the opportunities offered by railways, and even by industry, as they became apparent. Even so the focal point was the issuing and dealing in shares, not providing means for accelerating the rate of new capital formation.

VI

Nothing demonstrates more vividly the financial and industrial shortcomings of French capitalism in the reign of Louis Philippe than the slowness with which it established a railway network, or rather the beginnings of one.[42] On the face of it the lack of a transport system was one of the main besetting weaknesses of the French economy. Until improvements had been made France would remain a country of virtually self-contained regional and local markets. Industrial capitalism required a unified national market which, for a country with long distances to traverse, an inadequate river system and insufficient natural harbours, could only be provided by large-scale projects involving considerable investment. A major system of canals might have gone some way to fill this gap, but the advance made by steam locomotion in England meant that from 1830 a faster, more reliable and proven form of transport was available.

The first French railways were built principally to carry coal, were partly financed from local sources and raised no issues of general public policy. Their powers were obtained from the royal government without parliamentary discussion and their construction was supervised by a government department, the Corps des Ponts et Chaussées. From 1833 railways became a matter of public debate as their potential financial success and economic value stirred the interest of bankers, engineers and publicists.[43] The outstanding difficulty was how to raise capital to build the projected lines. While in Britain this was no problem in France the habit of blind investment had not yet become established and institutions for mobilizing the savings of the middle class and peasantry for projects of this kind were still rudimentary. Moreover, although railways were discussed in intellectual and business circles they do not seem to have gripped the public imagination to the same extent as in England. This was not purely a psychological phenomenon. While on the face of it France needed railways more urgently than Britain, which had carried through the first phase of the Industrial Revolution without their help, this did not show itself so potently as a felt need. An economy split into local and regional markets did not generate a powerful demand for the new means of transport, or only for lines of local interest. The initiative in railway promotion thus largely came, as it were, from 'outside': from the bankers of the big towns, especially Paris, from the government and, in the North, from British financiers. The bankers had, or could raise, the necessary capital provided that the government offered them some guarantees against loss. That the government should concern itself actively with what was seen as a new form of public works was accepted as natural enough. Ostensibly it had the duty to safeguard the public against abuse by private firms and to ensure that national security requirements were taken into account in the routing of railways. In practice the interests of the government, the parliament and the financial fraternity criss-crossed and collided. Until 1842, therefore, no coherent railway policy emerged and new investment in any case fell off as a result of the financial crises of the late 1830's. Some lines were built during this phase, but with only 600 kilometres of track in use by 1842, and those in a few localities, it is clear that the railway had, as yet, made little impact on the economy.

From 1842 to 1848 the length of track in operation had tripled: the total was still modest compared with Britain, but at last the railway was beginning to influence development by its demand for capital and the effect of its expenditure on construction. In 1842, after much groping, a compromise between the government and the financiers was worked out. The Act of 1842 (Dufaure law) provided for a number of main lines for which the government was to supply the land and build the infrastructure. The permanent structures were then to be leased to private companies furnishing the rolling stock and operating equipment. An important part of the initial cost of the railways was thus laid squarely upon the general revenue. In addition the companies were to receive further assistance from the same source in the coming years.

The law of 1842 preceded several years of economic expansion in which new railway construction played a prominent part. Under the generally favourable conditions provided by the law all the main financial interests in France, as well as financiers from England, Germany and Switzerland, were induced to participate in the promotion of French railways. A notable rôle was played by the Rothschilds who, by 1848, controlled eight major lines. Railway shares came on the market in increasing numbers in a mounting frenzy of speculation and began to tempt the conservative savers who up till then had not thought of holding shares in joint stock companies. Nevertheless, the flow of funds from the home investor fell far short of the actual expenditure on the new lines; as much as two-thirds of the share capital raised in the 1840's is said to have come from abroad, mainly from England.

The speculation of the mid-1840's ran into inevitable difficulties. Share prices fell, shareholders failed to meet additional calls, foreign funds were withdrawn from the market and capital to continue construction could not easily be raised. When the February revolution broke out France still had only about 1,800 kilometres of track and a number of lines were unfinished and in difficulties. On the financial side the experience of the railways had begun to bring about a change in the habits of the French investor and had added greatly to the business of the Bourse. Construction itself opened up a new market for the metallurgical and machine-making industries which had previously lagged behind.[44] In particular the demand for railway iron and other materials, which could not be made in the old type charcoal-burning furnaces, stimulated the change over to coke and thus to large-scale production. By cheapening iron made by these processes a further market was created and the high-cost local producers were steadily driven out of business, though this process still had far to go in 1848. As a salient example of a large-scale, concentrated enterprise the railway stimulated business change in the same direction especially as the main railways were closely controlled by the *haute banque*. The British contractors operating in Northern France demonstrated a new model of labour organization from which French enterprise may have learned something.

It cannot be said of this period that the railway awakened France from her slumbers, as would be true of Germany. Neither the rate nor the consequences of the railway building were revolutionary. While the railway stimulated the iron and machine-making industries, increased or strengthened those elements in the economy making for change as against those which stood for continuity with the past, its development was still shaped and constricted by the inherited structures and established habits of French bourgeois society. The railway did, by 1848, connect up some of the main centres with a cheaper, faster and more reliable form of transport, but it left untouched the life of most of rural and small town France. The activities of the bankers, the bickering of the deputies and the ups and downs of the Bourse were still largely froth on the surface as far as the deeper currents of French life were concerned. But forces had now been released which could begin to change their direction. The French economy and French society were being disturbed by strains and conflicts which testified to the passage from one sort of structure to another; in part the Revolution of 1848 testified to the strength of the tensions thereby produced.

VII

Throughout this period French industrialists, as well as agricultural producers, remained masters of their own home market. Despite the growth of the ideology of economic individualism and its enshrinement in the codes of the Empire, French businessmen had little time for the doctrines of free trade. In the sphere of foreign trade they looked to the state to protect them from foreign competition as of a right while at home, despite the persisting tradition of Colbertism, business was carried on in the first half of the nineteenth century in an environment of greater freedom from interference and restraint than had been known under any previous régime. That is not to say that the state abandoned all concern with the economy or that the French industrialists and merchants were not on occasion prepared to call upon it for support or succour. As has been pointed out, the relationship between the bourgeoisie and the state in France was more intimate than in England. Moreover, the state had important privileges to dispense which could assist individual and corporate accumulation. The formation of joint stock companies with limited liability (*sociétés anonymes*), which enabled the funds of the investing public to be tapped, was subject to ministerial approval. Railway concessions, opening the way to the greatest new investment field of the time, were likewise an administrative matter. In the field of banking relations between the ministers and officials of the state and the leading financiers remained close and became closer under Louis Philippe. It was accepted that the power of the state could assist in private enrichment and might be indispensable for it. Businessmen looked to the state to diminish their risks and safeguard their *positions acquises.*

In the circumstances of French industrial inferiority after 1815 a policy of high protection was demanded by most manufacturers. Agrarian interests likewise, and more irrationally, feared the effects of an influx of cheap imported raw materials and foodstuffs. Consequently the pressures on the Restoration government for high tariffs, amounting often to prohibitions, were irresistible, accepted by ministers even against their better judgement.[45] However, this policy was part of a continuing protectionist tradition which had been endorsed by the Revolutionary Assemblies and by Napoleon. The only important deviation from it had been the Treaty of Commerce with England of 1786 which had opened the French market to cheap English manufactured goods,. Not only had the Treaty been bitterly opposed at the time by manufacturers but it had been blamed, probably inaccurately, for the industrial depression of the late 1780's. The triumphant bourgeoisie showed how it viewed the matter by returning to high protective tariffs in 1791. It was assumed that an opening of the market to low-cost English goods would threaten many French firms with extinction and undermine national economic strength. Napoleon's economic policies were strongly protectionist, even apart from his wartime attempt to undermine the English economy by blocking the access of its exports to the European market.

The Continental system and the opening of European markets in the wake of the conquering armies did little to compensate for the loss of overseas markets for French goods and the rapid growth of the English industrial apparatus. Consequently, after 1815 the disparity between costs and efficiency in England and France, at least in the industries to which the new techniques were applicable, yawned even wider than it had done in 1786. The sense of inferiority among French industrialists was extreme and found expression in a defensive reaction.[46] The advantages enjoyed by their English competitors were greatly exaggerated and the general refrain could be summed up as protection or ruin. The Restoration Government had little choice but to withdraw into a 'customs fortress' under the pressure of its most influential subjects.

In the circumstances, then, free trade arguments had little chance of success; though they might be persuasively expressed by economists and publicists their public was a restricted one. Few economic groups saw any advantage in the adoption of free trade.[47] Protectionism, on the other hand, with its nationalist appeal, could unite otherwise discordant sections. For the state the tariff was a convenient way of collecting revenue and, for the businessman, it served the double purpose of defence against foreign competitors and against a possible tax on his earnings.

After some initial steps taken after 1815 to moderate or remove tariffs, the Restoration went on to make the French market one of the most heavily protected in Europe. Tariff schedules were not only uniformly high, even prohibitive, they were designed without any regard for the effects they might have on the economy at large. For example, not only was the duty on coal maintained at a high level, but it was based on differential scales which rose highest on imports through the West coast ports, that is from England. In view of France's deficiency in coal resources restriction on importation was illogical from the point of view of economic development. The same could be said of the heavy duties on iron, which deprived users of cheap supplies, thus acting adversely on the machine-making industry. The outcome was that the old-style industries and techniques were able to retain command of the home market without the incentive to change. Other industries, which might have expanded upon more modern lines had they had access to cheap imported raw materials, fuel and semi-finished goods, had a limited market and therefore higher unit costs.

Since industry did grow in this period at a rate which would look quite respectable were it not for the more rapid rates achieved across the Channel it may be said that French entrepreneurs did get the most out of the protectionist system.[48] It may not be fair to accuse them of slumbering behind the tariff barriers.[49] They adapted themselves to them and it should be remembered that poor internal transport also gave them virtual monopolies of the local or regional markets. Within the limits of the protected home market, which was itself growing as per capita income rose, the pursuit of profit did bring about accumulation, investment and growth. But it also brought rigidities and reluctance to change which loomed larger the longer protection endured. The differential advantages of the English manufacturer did not diminish and they possessed, in addition, the inestimable advantage of a large and expanding export market. For French industry command of the home market was distinctly second best; grow as it did it could not grow fast enough to support the rapid expansion of the technologically most advanced industries of the kind necessary to support an industrial revolution.

Obviously a voluntary reversal of protectionist policy on the part of French manufacturers was out of the question. They were no doubt correct in believing that any sharp lowering of duties would be catastrophic, at least for them. What was chiefly wrong with the free trade argument in France was that it was not practical politics. Manufacturers and agrarian producers knew that from their own short-run position the easiest way to maintain profits was to exclude foreign competition. If cheaper foreign (i.e. English) commodities penetrated the home market this would require, at the least, a painful and costly re-adjustment and might end in bankruptcy. This was a case, therefore, where the pursuit of individual self-interest had consequences for national economic growth which the consensus of historical opinion regards as unequivocally adverse. On balance protection strengthened the conservative tendencies among French entrepreneurs and the traditional agrarian structures. Old processes and forms of organization survived longer than they should have done and some activities, such as beet-sugar refining, were artificially stimulated. The environment of enterprise was thus profoundly modified.

Although eloquent voices were raised on behalf of free trade, or at least a reduction of tariffs, the French bourgeoisie, in the main, remained deaf to them. Small firms as well as larger felt threatened by any change in tariffs in a downward direction. The newly enfranchised voters after the 1830 Revolution were just as protectionist as the rest and the government, despite instituting enquiries, was too timid to venture on serious reductions. Every sectional and local interest, with but few exceptions, contributed its quota to the protectionist pressure. Nothing less than the 'industrial *coup d'état*' of Napoleon III was necessary before a change could be brought about. As it was, nationalism and Anglophobia, prevalent in all classes, prevented French economic influence in other European countries from being extended by a policy of tariff concessions. Hence the defeat of the proposed customs union with Belgium and the failure to prevent the South German states from being drawn into the Zollverein. Instead, high French tariffs encouraged other countries to keep high their own protective walls over which the low-cost British commodities could generally leap more easily than the French.

VIII

Some of the specific and distinctive characteristics of the French economy in the period 1815-48 should by now have emerged, and some conclusions should be possible regarding its slow and incomplete transition to industrial capitalism despite the social predominance of a prosperous bourgeoisie. The attempt has been made to set this problem in a broad framework, making use of the work and conclusions of social historians as well as of economic historians and economists, in the belief that only a total view can arrive at interesting and valid explanations.

The impression that the French economy was undergoing growth during this period at a steady rate has been confirmed by the detailed quantitative studies of Jean Marczewski,[50] and by the work of Pierre Léon.[51] However, contrary to Rostow, Marczewski holds, and with that there seems no reason to disagree, that France did not experience a 'take-off' in this period. The picture he presents of French industrial growth is one of acceleration from the mid-eighteenth century, that is about the same time as in England. 'But for a number of historical reasons', he concludes, 'the most important of which no doubt resides in the two countries' different agricultural structures, industrialization proceeded much more slowly in France and within narrower limits than was the case in England'.[52] The present writer would concur with this and has, indeed, sought to grapple more closely with these 'historical reasons'.

The French economy during this period was, indeed, relatively prosperous; in particular it saw a steady growth in the social surplus accruing to the bourgeois property owners. This enabled them to live more comfortably, build more houses and begin to engage more extensively in 'blind' investment, a growing part of which was of a productive character which increased its surplus still further. Throughout, however, a significant part of the revenues of the bourgeoisie continued to come from the agrarian sector. This was still, until the 1840's, an economy of 'the old type'. But it was moving steadily towards a more complex, more modern, capitalist structure in which the surplus was increasingly being generated in industry. In this respect, the first, often painful steps on the new path, with the spread of new techniques, products and forms of business organization, which were being taken in this period were of decisive importance for French economic development. To explain why it did not proceed faster then and later a variety of interacting, structural factors have to be taken into consideration. Basic to these was the nature both of the bourgeoisie and the peasantry, and the relationship between them, established in the Revolutionary decade. The economic environment and the conditions for enterprise could be said to have been built in the image of these two classes which together made up the bulk of French society.

A number of specific features making for structural inflexibility and resistance to faster growth may now be enumerated.

Firstly, government policy was narrow and parsimonious and granted whatever the dominant bourgeoisie wanted, especially in the field of tariff protection. Government did not promote economic growth, but through sound finance and protection kept it within narrowly defined limits. Secondly, French industry lacked the stimulus of a large and expanding foreign market and compensated itself with a protected home market. By its nature, however, this market could grow only slowly and tended to confirm the conservative traits of the business middle class. Thirdly, the monetary and banking structure also reflected the nature of the bourgeoisie. Its policies were generally 'sound', which is to say that they restricted the supply of credit which might otherwise have been available, thus making new projects essentially dependent upon what could be obtained from existing accumulations. This leads on to the fourth and final point: that while there was no lack of capital in the system as a whole there was a gap between savings and investment with the former generally outrunning the latter.

In this period, therefore, France lacked state policies for the promotion of development, since the tariff was a restrictive rather than a promotional instrument. She lacked the growing foreign market which has frequently been a stimulus to rapid economic development and saw only the first beginnings of investment banks which could overcome the timidity of savers and break through the credit barriers of the 'eighteenth century' society. The fact that there was steady growth and accumulation of wealth suggests that the full growth potential was far from having been realized in this period. However, some preliminaries to the full emergence of industrial capitalism were being put in hand to be carried further, with more obvious and impressive results, under the Second Empire.

Notes and further reading

1. The most accessible factual account of industrial development in this period is to be found in Arthur Dunham, *The Industrial Revolution in France* (New York 1955). Unfortunately the analysis of the material is unsatisfying. Dunham is inclined to explain the characteristics of French society and economic life as reflecting the French people's love of the land, aesthetic taste, awe in

the presence of bureaucracy and so on. The most recent detailed French study is by Maurice Lévy-Leboyer, *Les banques européenes et l'industrialisation internationale dans la première moitié du XIXe. siècle* (Paris 1964) which reaches some original conclusions about French industry and entrepreneurship by examining them very thoroughly in an international context. The economic position of France in 1815 is usefully summarized in Shepberd B. Clough, *France: A History of National Economics* (New York 1939, reprint 1964); the general emphasis is on economic policy and institutions. See also Henri Sée, *Histoire économique de la France* (Paris 1951) and the useful article by Louis Cahen, 'L'Enrichissement de la France sous la Restauration', *Revue d'histoire moderne*, 5, 1930. The best account in a general history of the period is perhaps that by Berthier de Sauvigny, *La Restauration* (Paris 1955) who uses the concept of the 'eighteenth century' nature of the economy and suggests that 'From the point of view of the economists the great Revolution was almost a negligible episode and the France of Restoration was nearer to that of Louis XV than to that of Napoleon III', p. 284. To this it may be added, however, that the changes of the intervening period were by no means devoid of significance for long term economic development, though it is true that the basic framework had not been transformed. Moreover, as stressed in the previous chapter, the catastrophic effects of the Revolution and the wars must be taken into account. The idea that the economy remained of a pre-industrial or 'eighteenth-century' type until some time in the 1840's seems to derive from Ernest Labrousse's work on French cycles. It is put forward in his mimeographed Cours, *Aspects de l'évolution économique et sociale de la France et du Royaume-Uni de 1815 à 1880* (in three parts, Paris, n.d.), Introduction, Chapter II and Livre II. Finally, for a valuable discussion of sources and methods with a bibliography by a leading French historian, see Paul Leuillot, 'Notes et remarques sur l'histoire économique et sociale de la France sous la Restauration', *Revue de synthèse historique*, 1953.

2. According to André Chatelain the substitution of the scythe for the sickle was a slow and uneven process not completed until the mid-nineteenth century. The scythe economized labour but meant higher losses in grain when used to harvest wheat. *Annales—Economies, Sociétés, Civilisations,* Vol. XI, No. 3, 1956.
3. For a summary of the changes see Frederic O. Sargent 'From Feudalism to Family Farms in France', *Agricultural History*, Vol. XXXV, No. 4, 1961.
4. It does not seem to be necessary here to enter into the question of the definition of the 'bourgeoisie' upon which a great deal of intellectual effort has been expended. Even such a detailed study as that of Adeline Daumard, note 12, has been reproached for lacking a real definition of this class: see the review by Pierre Léon, 'Une grande thèse sur la bourgeoisie parisienne', *Revue historique*, Vol. CCXXXIII, January-March, 1965. It is evident that it is intended to include a much wider segment of property

owners than those who own the industrial means of production. In this period France was still in the early stages of industrial capitalism; the majority of the bourgeoisie was still of the old type and a large proportion of its revenues came ultimately from rents. There were, however, particular areas in which a bourgeoisie owning the main means of production was becoming the dominant social force even in the eighteenth century. Such a town was the Norman woollen centre of Elbeuf which has been studied in great detail by Jeffry Kaplow, *Elbeuf During the Revolutionary Period: History and Social Structure* (Baltimore 1964), especially pp. 57 seq. There were many other towns in which a property owning class, properly designated as a bourgeoisie, dominated social life but did not derive its income from the ownership of industrial property; in these towns, then, the typical features of a pre-industrial economy were much more strongly pronounced. Moreover, as is indicated in Kaplow's study, the bourgeoisie is itself a stratified class; it is also one subject to considerable mobility—largely upward in this period—and to recruitment from below, cf. Daumards' study.

5. On the nature of the bourgeoisie in 1789 see Paul Leuillot, 'Reflexions sur l'histoire économique et sociale: à propos de la bourgeoisie en 1789', *Revue d'histoirc moderne et contemporaine*, I, 1954, with very full references to the literature, and Marcel Reinhard, 'Élite et noblesse dans la seconde moitié du XVIIIe. siècle', *Revue d'histoire moderne et contemporaine*, III, 1956. Reinhard's conclusion that until the reign of Napoleon II the industrialists were not integrated into the 'official élite' and enjoyed little prestige seems to be acceptable. For him the Revolution brought about the embourgeoisement of a functional élite. Leuillot brings out the great regional diversity in class structures and in the nature of the bourgeoisie itself, part of which was ready to collaborate with the counter-revolution.
6. France was, of course, an exporter of finished goods, principally textiles, of which by far the most important in the 1820's were silk and silk goods, followed by wines and spirits, leather, pottery and paper goods.
7. A considerable literature exists on the nature of the French entrepreneur and his alleged responsibility for the slow growth of the French economy in the nineteenth century. See in particular, David S. Landes, 'The French entrepreneur and industrial growth in the nineteenth century', *The Journal of Economic History*, IX, 1949, and 'French Business and the Businessman' in *Modern France: Problems of the Third and Fourth Republics,* ed. E. M. Earle (Princeton 1951); John E. Sawyer, 'Social Structure and Economic Progress: General Propositions and Some French Examples', *American Economic Review*, XLI, No. 2, 1951, and 'The Entrepreneur and the Social Order in France and the United States', in *Men of Business: Studies in the History of Entrepreneurship;* William Miller (Ed.) (Cambridge, Mass., 1951). Rondo C. Cameron, 'Economic Growth and Stagnation in France', *Journal of Modern History*, XXX, No. 1, 1958. See also Ben. T.

Hoselitz, 'Entrepreneurship and Capital Formation in France and Britain since 1700', in *Capital Formation and Economic Growth*, edited by Moses Abramovitz (Princeton 1955); Gerschenkron's comment in the same volume, p. 373 seq. and 'Social Attitudes, Entrepreneurship and Economic Development', Ch. III of *Economic Backwardness in Historical Perspective* (Cambridge, Mass., 1962).

8. The French businessman was constantly looking over his shoulder at his English rival as Peter Stearns has shown, see 'British Industry Through the Eyes of French Industrialists (1820-1848)' in *The Journal of Modern History*, Vol. 37, No. 1, 1965.
9. The general characteristics and course of development of French industry can be studied in John H. Clapham, *The Economic Development of France and Germany* (Cambridge 1921) and William O. Henderson, *The Industrial Revolution in Europe, 1815-1914* (Chicago 1961).
10. For French borrowings from Britain see William O. Henderson, *Britain and Industrial Europe* (Liverpool 1954).
11. On the history of the bourgeoisie in France, see Régine Pernoud, *Historie de la bourgeoisie française*, Vol. II (Paris 1962). For the importance which Napoleon attached to making his generals and officials bourgeois men of property and founders of families see Ch. IX.
12. This is the thesis of the opinionated but not to be neglected diatribe against the bourgeoisie of the royalist Beau de Loménie, *Les responsabilités des dynasties bourgeoises* (Paris, Vol. I, 1943; Vol. II, 1947; Vol. III, 1954). See especially the Introduction to Vol. III. For him the upper bourgeoisie, definitely constituted under the Directory, grew in power and self-consciousness after 1815 and achieved full power in 1830. While theoretically economic prizes were open to all, in practice they were bestowed by those who held political power on the members of their own circle.
13. Adeline Daumard's impressive study of the Parisian bourgeoisie, *La bourgeoisie parisienne de 1815 à 1848* (Paris 1963) illustrates this very well. The proportion of the family fortune held in real property varied with individuals, of course, but it was higher in the case of the richer bourgeois. Under the Restoration about two-thirds was held in real property, p. 496. To a growing extent, however, this property was located outside Paris and the growth of the economy permitted greated diversification of investment, especially by holding shares in *sociétés en commandite*. Also there were large holdings by wealthy Parisians in the farm lands of the Paris basin and in forest lands, p. 501.
14. But in Paris the smaller property owners held a large proportion in the *rentes*. There were some large holders of *rentes*, but the typical *rentier* had only a modest fortune. Daumard, op. cit., p. 501.
15. This picture of steadily growing prosperity, assumed by the bourgeois to continue indefinitely despite periods of crisis and pause, comes through very strongly in Daumard's study. So does the emphasis on stability and solidity.

16. See David S. Landes, 'French Entrepreneurship and Industrial Growth in the Nineteenth Century', *The Journal of Economic History*, IX, i, 1949.
17. Charles Morazé, *Les bourgeois conquérants* (Paris 1957) especially pp. 151-2. See also *La France bourgeoise* (Paris 1946).
18. See Georges Ripert, *Aspects juridiques du capitalisme moderne* (Paris 1951) and Pernoud, op. cit.
19. A. Daumard, op. cit., p. 245.
20. Landes op. cit. In characterizing the French entrepreneur Landes detaches him from the French bourgeoisie as a whole, whose traits he tended to follow—at least as far as Landes' version of his behaviour is valid.
21. In so far as the peasant produced all or most of his own food land was retained in uses in which it was less productive than it would have been under a more complex division of labour.
22. On this see also T. Kemp, 'Structural Factors in the Retardation of French Economic Growth', *Kyklos,* XV, Fasc. 2, 1962.
23. On migratory patterns see Louis Chevalier's article, 'L'émigration française au XIXe. siècle', *Études d'histoire moderne et contemporaine,* Vol. I (Paris 1947).
24. There have been a number of local studies which show this very clearly. It comes out particularly well in periods of economic crisis as shown, for example, in E. Labrousse (ed.), *Aspects de la crise et de la dépression de l'économie française au milieu du XIXe. siècle* (Paris 1958).
25. Even to-day it is characteristic that many urban workers conserve some connection with their native village, perhaps returning to retire there on a piece of inherited land. The low retirement age in public services in the nineteenth and twentieth century is said to be attributable to the same cause.
26. Louis Chevalier, *La formation de la population parisienne dans la première moitié du XIXe. siècle* (Paris 1950). Many of these workers, attracted to Paris by a high nominal wage, and ready to put up with overcrowding and a low standard of living, were saving to buy land at home. What counted was how much money they could earn in a given period, see p. 102.
27 There is an excellent description of the French textile industry in this period in Landes' contribution to Vol. II, part I of the *Cambridge Economic History of Europe* (Cambridge 1965), p. 387 seq.
28. On the economy of Alsace in this period see Paul Leuilliot, *L'Alsace au début du XIXe. siècle* (Paris 1959), Vol. II, *Les transformations économiques.*
29. Landes, op. cit.
30. The stability and solidity of the French industrial dynasties paralleled that of the bourgeoisie as a whole. Thus Bernard Gille notes that 'of a hundred and eighty-nine metallurgical companies existing in 1927, sixty-two, or about one-third, had as their basis establishments going back to the eighteenth century or even earlier'. *Les origines de la grande industrie métallurgique en France* (Paris 1948). Not only firms, but families, have preserved

their position. Peugeot and Japy were already established in the eighteenth century. So were Le Creusot, Dietrich, Wendel, Guérigny, Gouvy, etc.

31. Thus J. H. Clapham's *The Economic Development of France and Germany,* still the most used English language text on French economic history, makes this a main point in explaining the relative slowness of industrial development in this period. For a critique and further references, Kemp, op. cit., pp. 345-6.
32. For a study of the reciprocal relationship between changes in the economy and those in banking and finance see Jean Bouvier, 'Le système de crédit et l'évolution des affaires de 1815 à 1848. Les premiers pas du grand capitalisme français', in *La Pensée, revue de rationalisme moderne,* 1957, Nos. 71 and 72.
33. For a detailed study of the activities of *la haute banque* before the Revolution see Herbert Lüthy, *La banque protestante en France* (two Vols., Paris 1959, 1961).
34. David S. Landes, 'Vielle banque et banque nouvelle', *Revue d'histoire moderne et contemporaine,* Vol. III, 1956, for the activities of the merchant bankers and their adaptability to changing conditions and especially the need for long-term capital. This valuable article is now available in English translation in F. Crouzet, W. H. Chaloner and W. M. Stern, *Essays in European Economic History 1784-1914* (1969); translation by M. A. Lehmann.
35. For an interesting description of the financial scene at this time, with some illustrations from the novels of Balzac, see Guy Palmade, *Capitalisme et capitalistes françaises au XIXe. siècle* (Paris 1961), Ch. II passim.
36. On banking in this period the principal work is by Bernard Gille, *La banque et le crédit en France, 1815-1848* (Paris 1959).
37. A-J. Tudesq has studied the administrators, staff and shareholders of the Bank of France in 1840. He confirms the great social stability of the groups concerned and points out that political agitation and economic vicissitudes strengthened the need for stability and confidence. The bourgeoisie, with its basis in the ownership of real property, was more concerned with maintaining its revenues from existing sources than with seeking for others through industrial development. 'La Banque de France au milieu du XIXe. siècle. Étude des structures sociales', *Revue historique,* Vol. CCXXVI, Oct. 1961.
38. Thus the reply given by the banker André de Cottier to one of his clients: 'il est tout à fait contraire à nos usages de faire des avances sur des garanties hypothécaires qui sont toujours d'une réalisation plus ou moins difficile . . . tandis que comme banquier, il nous importe de pouvoir disposer de nos fonds d'un instant à l'autre', Daumard, op. cit., pp. 474-5, who adds that loans depended much more upon a personal relationship than a client relationship between the borrower and the banker. The reply of de Cottier is the very epitome of sound banking policy.
39. Under the Commercial Code the formation of *sociétés anonymes* was subject to administrative control but *sociétés en commandites* could be formed freely. This form was thus used both by old

established firms and by many of the new enterprises established in the 1830's and 1840's in mining, iron works, glass, canals, insurance and so on. See, for example, Bouvier, op. cit., pp. 64-6.

40. Gille says of Lafitte that 'he should have the honour of having initiated the first formulas for the great credit establishments which burst forth with a singular power under the Second Empire', op. cit., p. 106.
41. Bouvier, op. cit., p. 37-8, explains the retardation of French banking as a case of the relative immobility of the 'superstructure' compared with the base. It was only after the construction of a railway network that it was possible to establish a banking and credit network. Until then: 'The modifications in the banking apparatus could only *follow* the impulses and needs, which appeared first of all elsewhere, that is in the system of production'.
42. The following table illustrates the relatively small impact which railways could have had in this period.

FRENCH RAILWAY DEVELOPMENT IN THE PERIOD 1840–1848

Year	*Kilometres in operation*	*Gross receipts: in million francs*	*Receipts per Km in* 000 *francs*	*Passengers in millions*	*Metric Tons millions*
1841	573	12.9	9.3	6.3	1.0
1842	600	14.2	8.8	6.2	1.5
1843	829	21.0	13.4	7.3	1.5
1844	831	28.3	17.3	8.1	1.9
1845	880	31.9	18.8	8.8	2.3
1846	1,322	41.1	20.6	10.4	2.5
1847	1,832	65.2	22.4	12.8	3.6

Source: Andre Liesse, *Evolution of Credit and Banks in France.* National Monetary Commission, Washington, 1909, p. 69.

43. On the railways in this period Dunham's account is the most accessible, op. cit., Ch. IV. See also, Georges Lefranc, 'The French Railroads, 1823-1842', in the *Journal of Economic and Business History*, Vol. 2, 1830. Dunham stresses mutual distrust between the government and the Parisian bankers 'increased by the whims of the legislature and public opinion and by the uncertainties of business', p. 70. But these, in turn, have to be explained. There were plenty of problems and frictions in England: but the railways were built.
44. Bernard Gille, *Recherches sur la grande entreprise capitaliste* (Paris 1959), pp. 29-30.
45. Ernest Levasseur, *Histoire du Commerce de la France,* Vol. I (Paris 1912). Book three, Ch. II, 'La formation du système douanier ultra-protecteur' for details.
46. Stearns, op cit.
47. For a perceptive analysis of the attitude of the bourgeoisie, see Claude Fohlen, 'Bourgeoisie française: liberté économique et intervention de l'état', *Revue économique*, 1956.
48. In the last of a series of articles on 'La politique du Libre Echange' Cochut, writing after the Treaty of 1860 made an in-

teresting comparison between the development of the English and French economies in the previous fifty years. Dealing with the undoubted expansion of the French economy despite the vices of protectionism which he deplored, he suggested that France 'a fait sortir d'un système faux tout ce qu'il était possible d'en tirer'. *Revue des deux mondes,* 1st February, 1862.

49. Compare the conclusion of Rondo E. Cameron in *France and the Economic Development of Europe* (Princeton 1961). According to him 'It is difficult to exaggerate the effect of this commercial policy in retarding the development of French industry and France's relations with other countries. . . The protective system slowed the development of the economy in several directions', pp. 36-7. In other words, he adopts a clear free trade position and attributes too much weight to the tariff as a causal factor in what he regards as France's economic retardation. But the historian also has to ask why the policy of high protection was adopted and maintained. The basis of the tariff was the desire of the economically influential to maintain their profits; compare Fohlen's article.

50. See Jean Marczewski, 'The Take-Off Hypothesis and French Experience', in Walt W. Rostow, Ed., *The Economics of Take-off into sustained Growth* (London 1963), Ch. 7 passim and Discussion of the Paper, pp. 354-466, and 'Some Aspects of the Economic Growth of France', in *Economic Development and Cultural Change*, April, 1961. Many problems raised by Marczewski fall, of course, outside the scope of this study. He seems to have created some surprise by his findings that there was steady growth in the economy during the period 1815-1848 and by his statement that railways 'did not begin to exert any sizeable influence on the economy as a whole until the 1850's'. Both of these positions seem to be sound enough, for instance, although railways had begun to stimulate some industries they certainly had not had a major influence on the economy 'as a whole' before 1848; see Landes' different view expressed in the Discussion.

51. Pierre Léon expressed similar views on French economic growth at the *First International Conference on Economic History* (Stockholm 1960). See his paper, 'L'industrialisation en France en tant que facteur de croissance économique du début du XVIIIe. siècle à nos jours'.

52. Marczewski, op. cit., p. 138.

CHAPTER VII

Crisis, Revolution and Stabilization

YEARS OF CRISIS: 1846–1851

INTO the years 1846-51 was compressed a succession of crises ranging from the age-old threat of famine to the seizing up of the credit mechanism and accompanied by a prolonged political uncertainty only ended with the taking of power by Louis Bonaparte. Accompanying the economic disasters, and closely involved with them, came social struggles of a new type and intensity.

For all the changes which marked the early progress of the industrial revolution in France the country still retained the deep imprint of the past on its economic life. The crisis years centred on that overwhelming disaster of an agrarian society: harvest failure and the consequent threat of famine. Much of the country still lived on the periphery of the exchange economy; each region had its own pattern of economic development and was affected by the events of these years in contrasting ways. Economic, as well as political, centralization gave, of course, special importance to events in Paris; it was in the capital that the great decisions were taken. It was here that contending social forces fought to a finish, but without necessarily making any deep impression on the life of the provinces,

One characteristic of the time was the heightened social content of political conflicts. As is well known, the preceding period had seen a luxuriant growth of socialist theories in France. Broadly these theories can be defined as utopian in nature; they hoped to find a speedy path to the new society but they hardly yet discerned the motive forces of change in society as it was. In so far as industrialism was understood it was disliked and opposed. The workers who followed these theories, or who devised their own, based their vision of the future upon the old-style workshop and the homely virtues of the artisan and the peasant. The workers who contributed powerfully to the overthrow of the Orleans monarchy were still not a proletariat of a modern type and such representatives of this class as there were in France did not yet play an important political rôle. In their hatred of the financial oligarchy the wage-earners did inject a new social element into political conflict, but not yet from the standpoint of men who accepted the machine and all the attributes of an advanced economy. The blending of the new with the old, so characteristic of other spheres of French life at this time, was strongly marked too in the relations between classes.

What was significant was that, in an often confused way, the workers now challenged the sanctity of bourgeois property. They were not content with a mere change in régime which would leave the dominant oligarchy in place. They aspired to a social republic which would protect them from the rigours of the new industrial order and from the caprices of a market economy—both so strongly expressed in these years. It was for this that the Parisian workers spontaneously rose in June, 1848, and it was protect their very social existence that the bourgeoisie rushed to give their support to the violent suppression of the uprising. If social peace was secured by a military action of remarkable fury, a scar was left which never really healed and was to be reopened in 1871. For the present the repression served its purpose better than its authors and supporters knew; the working class was too demoralized and disillusioned to constitute a real threat for many years. The industrial revolution could thus proceed with only the informal resistance of workers who lacked even the right of trade union organization.

A major outcome of these years, then, was the consolidation of bourgeois property relations; they were tempered in the furnace of intense social conflict. But divisions within the French bourgeois which had their beginnings in the Revolution of 1789 and the deep political and religious divisions in French society, as well as the threat from below, made it impossible to establish the republic on a sound basis of parliamentary institutions. The overthrow of Louis Phillipe was followed by an interim of political turmoil and indecision ended only when Louis Bonaparte assumed the rôle of arbiter by establishing himself as a dictator.

I

The succession of economic events in these years may be briefly described. In their essentials they followed a course which was common to the other advanced areas of the world. After 1842 the railways brought a marked upward turn in economic conditions. The industrial revolution was making steady progress, especially in textiles, but now increased markets were opening up for the coal, iron and machine-making industries as well. As a result there was a growing demand for capital without an established habit of long-term investment or adequate mechanism to handle the flow. The over-investment and illiquidity which accompanied this as yet still modest effort in railway building would no doubt have brought about a financial crisis in any case. However, the first shocks came not from this most modern sector but from the troubles of agriculture and the influences which they communicated to the rest of the economy.

The first symptoms of crisis came as a result of the bad harvests of 1845 and 1846 which were general through much of Northern Europe. In the wake of the food scarcity came the phenomenon which Labrousse has called a crisis of an intermediate type.[1] What has to be observed, therefore, is the interlocking of the effects of the shortfall in the harvest with the commercial and industrial activities of the towns. Beginning in the rural areas, which normally had a surplus of grain for sale in the market, the effect was to reduce the demand for labour and the incomes of those peasants whose surplus in any case would be small. If the bigger producers gained in net income from the steep rise in prices and the fall in labour costs this was not sufficient to counteract the depressive effects of the loss of income to the smaller producers.

Within a comparatively short time the effects of the grain shortage hit the towns in the shape of higher prices. As bread grains made up the staple diet of the masses, and demand for them was consequently inelastic, wage earners had less income available for the purchase of other things. But the same applied to many peasants, with the result that the market for the commoner manufactured goods, notably textiles, contracted. Manufacturers, whether owners of factories or not, were obliged to cut production, with further depressive effects on the demand for commodities. Investment tended to fall off, the decline in incomes hit all manner of industries, including building. Correspondingly, a sharp reversal of business expectations took place. Emergency imports of food grains tended to draw down the gold reserves of the Bank of France, thus contracting the money supply.

Lack of transport facilities impeded the movement of grain from the ports or better provided areas to those which were suffering from famine. Hoarding and speculation in grain by big producers or dealers contributed to drive up prices, as well as to acerbate feeling among the hungry population. In some places unrest swelled into riots. Local authorities organized charitable distribution of food to the most stricken. Mendicity grew, much as it had done in the period before 1789, and many destitute people flocked to the towns in search of work or alms.

The very diversity of the economy at this time meant that there were very great regional differences in the nature and timing of the crises. These differences depended upon the nature of the agricultural production carried on and its ties with the market and upon the degree of industrialization which had been attained. Moreover, a crisis which severely affected one sector of the economy might leave some little disturbed, others, such as building, might quickly revive, while some local industries did not survive the crisis years or went into a rapid decline. In most coal-mining areas, again, the depression was more prolonged than in the manufacturing centres. Although the studies in the volume edited by Labrousse give a varied sample of the contrasts and parallels to be found in the various regions covered, a full and systematic study of the whole period of the crisis still remains to be undertaken.

II

The state of crisis created by the poor harvest was compounded with the effects of speculation and over-investment in railways. Although France badly needed railways, the capital demands which they made put a heavy strain on the inadequate financial system. Owners of capital were not used to placing it in long-term investment projects, others speculated on the assumption that share prices were going to rise or that they could realize on their initial gains. Thus some purchasers of railway shares became highly illiquid. Capital was in great demand in industry, with the result that manufacturers also tended to push on with fixed investment while running short of working capital, or they used it for speculative purposes. Gille has suggested that the burst of investment in the mid-forties may have drawn away capital which the large agrarian producers and landowners would otherwise have invested in the land.[2] Thus a possible connection may be established between the agrarian difficulties of 1846 and the preceding investment boom.

In any case, it may well be that the exhaustion of the industrial boom was itself a sufficient explanation of the crisis. Some industries were already suffering from a contraction of demand before the harvest failures, others were influenced by the export situation. Meanwhile, to arrest speculation the government obliged companies seeking railway concessions to possess 10 per cent of their capital. This caused a further immobilization of liquid funds and increasing credit stringency in the latter part of 1847. As many investors finally had to put their railway shares on the market to replenish their cash holding prices came tumbling down so that, instead of the expected gains, many made losses.

The Bank of France, with its gold reserves already depleted by an external drain in the previous year, now had to face an internal drain.[3] The rate of interest was belatedly raised and credit restictions became general. A number of provincial banks had to suspend cash payments and the *Caisse du commerce et de l'industrie* failed. This financial crisis had severe effects on some industries and commercial centres and seems to have been more or less independent of the harvest failures.

To whatever extent the agrarian and financial crises were separate or connected, and however diverse their effects on different sectors of the economy few sections of the population remained unaffected. In the rural areas, for instance, the harvest failure appears to have had a marked demographic effect. In particular, the birth rate, which had been falling only slowly under the July Monarchy, fell sharply and for good.[4] In many rural areas the harvest failures of 1845-6 seem to have been the final blow to the old equilibrium especially in the more densely populated areas with poorer soils, where agriculture was combined with petty industry. Hence a movement of population out of these areas to Paris or to the industrial and mining areas. This redistribution of the labour force, while aggravating the social problems of the big towns in the revolutionary period, contributed to the industrial growth and public works of the fifties: to the passage of the economy from an eighteenth century to a modern type.

The background to the February revolution was thus compounded of uncertainty and instability. Large numbers of people had, in the previous two years, suffered a real material loss. Peasants had seen their efforts unrewarded and others, completely ruined, left for the towns, hoping to find work just at a time when jobs were scarce. Declining rural industries, especially the traditional linen industry, received their final blow. Industrial depression and the cessation of building hit workers and entrepreneurs alike. Speculators and shareholders had suffered losses or had not reaped the handsome fortunes which they had expected. Business was constricted by lack of credit. Bankers were overcommitted in long-term investment. Railway companies, running short of capital, had to suspend construction. Many members of the bourgeoisie, as well as the working classes, tended therefore to blame the government.

The toppling of the Louis Philippe régime brought to power a government of political reform composed of middle class leaders who had not expected to obtain power and had no programme when they did. They confronted in Paris, as well as in a few provincial towns, a working class which expected the political overturn to be the prelude to social benefits. The inability of the new leaders to satisfy this demand because of its incompatibility with the claims of the bourgeois property-owners, led to the June days and the defeat of the Parisian workers. The threat from below was thus effectively dealt with by military means. However, this blow on behalf of property rights did not provide a basis for a firm government able to restore the conditions for business prosperity. Whatever the political reasons for the failure of the Second Republic, its inability to face the economic problems which it inherited, and which the Revolution aggravated, must be granted considerable weight in accounting for its early demise.

The Orleans monarchy had depended all along upon the support of a narrow and privileged oligarchy of bankers and financiers. It offered less and less to the disenfranchised majority of the bourgeoisie and disgusted many by its reliance on administrative methods to maintain its parliamentary majority, while a number of scandals touched some of those in high places. The wage-earners in Paris, not a factory proletariat but largely made up of skilled artisans working in small workshops, had meanwhile developed a strong and conscious opposition to developing capitalism. This meant that the workers were alienated from the bourgeois property system as well as from the political régime. They sought, that is to say, not political changes alone but a transformation of society which would recognize the right to work and end poverty and exploitation. Even before the Revolution of 1848, therefore, there were only tenuous bases for an alliance between the bourgeoisie and the workers of the kind which had brought down Charles X in the Three Glorious Days of 1830.

III

The Revolution was a signal for the complete paralysis of credit and for a crisis in the finances of the state. Without a programme, unable to offer real leadership, confronted with the exacting claims of the working class and without deep roots in the provinces the Provisional government failed to establish confidence in bourgeois democracy. The gesture to the workers in the shape of the National Workshops did not deceive them but alarmed the provincial middle class and peasantry. If the June days eliminated the threat of social revolution, pressing economic and financial problems remained. By freezing savings bank accounts and increasing the four main direct taxes by 4 per cent the government antagonized the middle class, who mostly held the former, and the peasantry and small tradesmen upon whom the latter bore most heavily. The discount houses closed their doors and credit was practically unobtainable. The big banking houses were themselves in difficulties owing to the illiquidity of many of their investments. However, the government had little choice but to fall back on the support of the bankers, the same oligarchy which had held a dominant position under Louis Phillipe.

One of the main results of the Revolution, in fact, was to strengthen the position of the Bank of France. It continued to discount high class commercial bills throughout the revolutionary crisis at a modest 4 per cent. The metallic reserves inevitably fell to a level at which cash payments could no longer be maintained. The regents therefore requested permission to grant its notes the status of legal tender without the obligation to redeem them in gold or silver and to issue notes of 100 franc denomination. It was hoped by these means to check the panic flight into liquidity which drained away the bank's metallic reserves into the private hoards of bourgeois citizens made nervous by the political crisis. As a corollary an increase in note issue up to a maximum of 350 million francs was also asked for. Meanwhile, in the provinces the Departmental Banks were in difficulties. They had also suffered from the rush for liquidity. Their position was also much weaker than that of the Bank of France for even in the best of times their notes had little circulation outside the immediate vicinity of the town and were not acceptable for tax purposes. The upshot was that the Bank of France took over the nine Departmental Banks and thus attained the position of sole note-issuing bank.

Even before these measures were taken the Provisional Government authorized the establishment of *comptoirs d'escompte* in Paris and a number of the principal cities.[5] Capital for these discounting institutions was furnished by the state and the municipalities—in the shape of bonds—and by private shareholders. Their purpose was to restore confidence and credit by enabling businessmen to discount bills unacceptable to the Bank of France but otherwise of high standing. The shareholders, to whom the entire profits were to accrue, were at first insurance companies, charitable organizations and speculators and, since the entire share issue was not taken up, the government had to increase its subsidy. In addition *Sous-comptoirs de garantie* were established for a number of trades which made loans on pledges of merchandise, commodity warrants and commercial paper. *Magasins généraux* were also set up which made loans on the strength of merchandise deposited with them or warrants for the same.

The new government was thus far from having disentangled itself from the grip of financial orthodoxy, especially as represented by the Bank of France. This institution, representative of Parisian high finance, enhanced its position very markedly as a result of the revolutionary crisis. During 1848 the Bank lent heavily to the state and to the municipalities of the big towns; it also lent on mortgage to heavy industry to enable it to execute orders in hand from the railway companies. It thus played a crucial rôle in re-establishing credit. For its part, the Provisional Government showed its anxiety to restore bourgeois society to its old equilibrium perhaps more emphatically, if less obtrusively, in this field than in any other.

If the Bank saved the state from bankruptcy it gained handsomely from the deal. It had secured a monopoly of note-issue and its notes, despite their inconvertibility, enhanced their standing. As soon as it could, that is before the end of 1848, it restored specie payment, though it was not legally obliged to give cash for its notes until August, 1850. In fact, taking into account, of course, that the denomination of the notes was sufficiently high to confine their use to business, they were preferred to specie. By absorbing the Departmental banks the Bank of France had reinforced its character as a national bank, permitting it to move closer to the position of a central bank through regulation of the credit supply by changes in the discount rate.

Doubtless the bourgeois property owners went through agonies in 1848: fear of social revolution, the threat of state bankruptcy, the risk of personal ruin. On the whole they survived, but the experience had been unpleasant and they tended to blame the republican government for the burdens which it had inflicted rather than to rally to its support for the blessings it had secured. The government also became what Marx called 'a harrassed debtor of bourgeois society'.[6] Unable to pay cash to the timid depositors in the savings banks it had transformed part of their deposits into state bonds; Treasury bonds had also not been redeemed and additional loans had been raised from the public. Partly by involuntary means, therefore, the number of rentiers had been markedly increased. A kind of uneasy alliance thus existed between the government and the bourgeois public. The republican régime conciliated the bourgeoisie without being able entirely to win its confidence. The great organs of the upper bourgeoisie remained reserved towards a form of government which, despite its efforts, did not offer all the guarantees of stability and security which, in the light of the events of the past few years, it deemed necessary. While some sections of the bourgeoisie looked back with regret to the days of the Orleanist monarchy, others endorsed in advance the assumption of full power by the Prince President.

IV

Already before the outbreak of the February Revolution unemployment had become a serious problem owing to the slowing down of constructional activity. A drift into the towns by peasants affected by the harvest failures aggravated the problem, which was alleviated to some extent by the setting up of *ateliers de charité*. The economic paralysis which followed the Revolution multiplied the number of unemployed several times over. The part played by the working class in the overthrow of Louis Philippe brought the social question to the forefront and the bourgeois liberals of the Provisional Government responded by making concessions. The most important was the establishment of the Commission composed of representatives of workers and employers which was to meet at the Luxemburg Palace. In the initial stages their discussion produced agreement about reforms, notably a limitation of the working day. At the same time, in a solemn parody of Louis Blanc's plan for the Organization of Labour, National Workshops were established in Paris. In practice the workshops were only a grandiose make-work scheme to keep the unemployed quiet, no doubt with the hope that, as a side effect, they would discredit the socialist supporters of the Revolution. Once the bourgeoisie felt sufficiently in command of the situation it allowed the Luxemburg Commission to fade into insignificance and then disappear and then took severe measures to dissolve the workshops and disperse those employed in them. After a series of clashes between workers and the authorities a general insurrection began in Paris on June, 1848, which was suppressed by armed forces and middle class volunteers under the command of General Cavaignac.

The defeat of the workers in the June Days was a significant turning point which ensured the bourgeois character of the Revolution. But, if the state was of a kind bound to uphold bourgeois property there still remained the question of determining how that could be done. Not only were the bourgeois supporters of the Second Republic divided about this, but the problems facing them became more acute. Above all was the need to restore business confidence and re-open the possibilities for profitable investment after several years of instability and uncertainty. Only partially successful in this task, the liberals, by their political ineptitude, cleared the way for the assumption of full power by Louis Napoleon, elected President under the republican constitution of 1848.

One of the major reasons for the economic standstill was the virtual cessation of railway building by the companies as they ran out of capital and could raise no fresh money. Had the government been financially strong, and opinion more favourable, nationalization might have provided a solution; it was in fact proposed by the Minister of Finance in May, 1848. However, the government lacked resources or credit, other than that which it had, or could obtain, from the bankers and financiers who were hostile to a measure which smacked of socialism.

Thus, while there was general agreement that the railways, and public works in general, would have to be re-animated there was less agreement about how this could be done. Pushed along by circumstances, the government of the Republic pursued a policy which was little more than a re-indorsement of that of its predecessor. That is to say, it accepted the principle of private ownership and finance, backed by guarantees from the state.

It was widely agreed that the state, through public works, had a rôle to play in providing favourable conditions for the investment of private capital. In this respect there was little change from the forties and Napoleon III only carried through in a more determined way what the republican régime had been doing more cautiously. The task of the latter was, indeed, of special difficulty because credit had collapsed and the companies were on the brink of ruin. The good harvests of 1847 and 1848, while they alleviated the food situation, had an unfavourable effect on the incomes of grain producers and dealers, thus curtailing the supply of savings. On the other hand, labour was in abundant supply and the prices of material had fallen; in fact the coal, iron and machine-building industries were severely depressed—which added to the urgency of dealing with railway construction.

The defeat of the Parisian workers, then the election of

Louis Napoleon, provided political conditions for the restoration of confidence. Measures taken in the banking field improved credit facilities and enabled business to begin moving again. All through the first half of 1849 influential voices in the legislature and in the press were calling for a resumption of large-scale public works, especially the railways. The prevailing note was against nationalization or statism but for budgetary aid and state support for the companies. Some railways had continued building, thanks to the law of 1842, and had thus contributed, more than the National Workshops, to holding up the level of employment.

However, the republican government was unable or unwilling to do more in the way of budgetary outlays; in fact credits were reduced considerably in 1850 and 1851 owing to budgetary stringency. Those public works, such as waterways, roads and ports which depended directly upon the budget suffered most from this parsimony. The ministers responsible for the budget held to the view that private capital would be encouraged by the restoration of state credit, which meant a small and balanced budget. If the economic outlook steadily improved from 1849 with the restoration of political stability the state did little to promote renewed economic expansion. It had contented itself with providing the basic political and social conditions for business confidence and pursuing an orthodox financial course in co-operation with the Bank of France. The bourgeoisie responded by increasing its holdings of state debt and by renewed interest in railways. As interest rates fell back from their crisis peak railway shares became increasingly acceptable. Everything pointed to a return to normalcy. Unemployment was being absorbed, share prices were rising, government credit had been restored, railway building resumed and the international currents were flowing towards a new phase of prosperity. However, recovery was by no means complete. The rate of new railway building was not sufficient to bring back full capacity working to heavy industry. The building trade still lagged, which meant the incipient threat of urban political discontent. And, as Louis Napoleon's mandate moved towards expiry—and under the constitution he could not be re-elected—the spectre of political uncertainty again raised its head. It is here that the secret of the *coup d'état* and its acceptance by business and the bourgeoisie seems to be found. Here too that the continuity with preceding policies as well as the precise point of difference, becomes apparent in the *économie politique du 2 décembre.*

Notes and further reading

1. See the collection of studies, mostly of the course of the crisis in different regions, in the work edited with an introduction by E. Labrousse, *Aspects de la crise et de la dépression de l'économie française au milieu du XIXe. siècle.* For a description of one region which had some mining and factory industry in the middle of the crisis years see 'La situation économique et social du département de la Loire d'après l' "Enquête sur le travail agricole et industriel" du 25 Mai 1848", by P. Guillaume in *Revue d'histoire moderne et contemporaine*, Vol. X, Jan-mars, 1963.
2. Gille, op. cit., p. 375.
3. On the Bank see works by Palmade and Liesse cited in the previous chapter and the chapter by Tudesq in Labrousse, op cit.
4. Ch. Pouthas, *La population française pendant la première moitié du XIXe. siècle* (Paris 1956) insists very strongly upon this point in his conclusions and also stresses that the crisis was the final blow to many rural industries.
5. This idea came from Emil Pereire, who helped to draw up the statutes for the Parisian institution, Cameron, op. cit., p. 126.
6. Karl Marx, *Class Struggles in France.*

CHAPTER VIII

The Political Economy of Bonapartism

FRENCH ECONOMIC DEVELOPMENT, 1851–1870

For almost two decades after the *coup d'état* of the 2nd December, 1851, the development of French capitalism took place within a distinctive political framework of authoritarian government.[1] The régime of Napoleon III differed both from the dynastic monarchies of the old régime and from the contemporary constitutional states, whether monarchical or republican in form. By virtue of the institution of universal suffrage it was ostensibly 'democratic', but the concentration of powers in the hands of the Emperor made it a personalized dictatorship of the kind established by Napoleon I. This dictatorship rested upon the control of the army and of a highly centralized bureaucratic apparatus, both of which were inherited from the past; in its early years it used these instruments to subdue its opponents and drastically curtail freedom of expression. Its ability to do this was, however, dependent upon the weakness of the opposition; that is to say the disillusionment and withdrawal from politics of the working class after the June Days and the dissensions and ineptitude of the republicans and monarchists.[2] Its success, however, required both the acquiescence, if not positive support, of the property-owning classes and the electoral big battalions of the peasantry. Several years of economic instability and political uncertainty and the fear of social revolution, briefly but vividly evoked in June, 1848, created a desire for order which presented Louis Napoleon with his opportunities. More than that, the bourgeoisie craved for a political environment which would protect their property and open the way for new profitable investments and business ventures. Too weak or disunited to project a régime of liberal democracy, it was prepared to accept a curtailment of civil and political rights in return for a prospect of peaceful material progress. This was the promise of the régime. The question is how far it fulfilled this promise and how far the economic growth with which the period has become identified can be placed to the credit of Napoleon III?

I

Louis Bonaparte was a political neophyte who found his place in history by reason of events which he had no part in making. His assets, apart from the prodigious one of his family name, were precisely that he had no links with the discredited politicians of the Orleanist period. Projected onto the scene from outside he lacked a definite social basis in France; he could not be said to represent a distinct class or economic interest and therefore could appeal to, and claim to represent, all. If this was his strength, the source of his political significance, it also defined the nature of his rule and makes it all the more difficult to grasp. Indeed, everything about it was contradictory. He arrived on the scene from nowhere, as a parvenu, with companions whose roots in the country were no firmer than his own, able, indeed obliged, to bring together a largely new team to carry on the government.[3] And, with the power which control of the state gave, he was able to endow other men, some also new, with economic privileges and opportunities for material gain which would not have come their way through the normal processes of the market-place. The régime had, at the same time, to find support within the existing social structure: one that was torn by all kinds of political, material and religious conflicts and dissensions. Had it not been for the depth of these antagonisms Bonaparte could not have taken power, but the fact that he had power did not mean that he could resolve them. On the contrary, he maintained his power on the basis of shifting coalitions of interest, making concessions first to one side then to another, until, by a process of erosion, many erstwhile friends had been abandoned or had become enemies. The lack of consistency to be found in the policies of the Emperor, therefore, derive from the very character of his rule.[4] To govern under such conditions required a shrewd and alert political instinct on the part of the dictator, but every mistake could be magnified in its consequences and weakened the basis of the régime. While in the early fifties Napoleon III possessed the necessary qualities in considerable measure, growing difficulties and his own failing physical powers undermined his régime in the following decade. This division conforms also with the economic pattern of the period.[5]

II

A number of the men who reached maturity during this period and played a prominent rôle in public life—in business, administration or learning—had, in their younger days, been followers af the Saint-Simonite cult. They suffered, no doubt, from the 'boredom' which seems to have afflicted the bourgeois youth during the uninspiring years of the Louis Philippe monarchy. Stirred by the possibilities of technological innovation and machine industry, they saw in the teachings of Saint-Simon a programme which gave men like themselves the possibility of re-organizing society, with the emphasis upon raising production and material welfare. Such a mixture of idealism and self-interest, as well as the accordance between the doctrine and the needs of developing capitalism, made it, in a sense, the ideology of industrialization in France at this juncture. At least, this it has been taken to be by a succession of eminent historians, some of whom presume that industrialization must have an ideology to break out of the confines of the old society.

The most influential Saint-Simonians, or ex-Saint-Simonians, were the Pereire brothers who founded the *Crédit Mobilier*, Michel Chevalier, who inspired the Treaty of 1860, and a number of others prominent in the business world such as Paulin Talabot. These men are credited with exercising an influence on Napoleon III and of belonging to 'a rather well-defined group'. Gerschenkron has attempted to explain the paradox of men identified with a socialist creed inspiring 'the fine spurt of industrial development which France experienced after the advent to power of Napoleon III'.[6] Hoselitz endorses this view and draws particular attention to the stress which Saint-Simon laid on credit institutions of a type which could release the productive forces of society and upon the central position of the banker. There is no reason to doubt that these ideas, formulated by Saint-Simon out of his own acquaintanceship with men, such as Lafitte, who had striven to create the type of credit institutions which France lacked, were fundamental in influencing Emil and Isaac Pereire. On the other hand, as Hoselitz admits, the *Crédit Mobilier* failed and while the old guard of bankers took over its institutional form, they threw aside the ideological garb given it by the Saint-Simonians.[7]

Not only is there cause for reflection in the failure of the Pereires, but there is also some need for caution in respect to the Saint-Simonian influence on the Second Empire. However clairvoyant Saint-Simon may have been in his writings and despite the evident talents of those who had been his followers, it may be that too much significance has been attached to the specifically Saint-Simonian influence on the policies of the Empire.[8] After all, the principles which he formulated regarding the rôle of 'industrialists' did not differ fundamentally from much of the teaching of the liberal school. It must have been apparent that if France was to catch up with England an increased social valuation would have to be placed upon the businessman. It was also very much in the objective position of the Second Empire that regardless of whether the Emperor had studied the doctrine, or was advised by men who had, the state should adopt the rôle of stimulator of the economy.

Enemies of the régime and of those it favoured, by using the term *la finance Saint-Simonienne* in a pejorative sense may have exaggerated both the homogeneity of the group and the specifically ideological component in its activities.

How far Saint-Simonism penetrated into the ranks of entrepreneurs, bankers, technicians and administrators during the period is difficult to determine. The burden of proof lies with those who maintain that it was influential. A more extended list of names of one-time Saint-Simonians in high places would not in itself be conclusive proof of the Gerschenkron-Hoselitz hypothesis. That does not mean, of course, that a few such men were not able to leave their mark on the early accomplishments of the Second Empire. But the impression must remain that the business world as a whole operated at a much lower level of inspiration and intellectual awareness of their rôle. Defence of property rights, freedom of enterprise—tempered by willingness to accept state support when it was believed to assist the balance sheet or to keep out foreign competition—and the sanctity of profits made a good enough ideology for most French businessmen in this period.

III

Without looking too closely at the antecedents or doubtful political methods of the Second Empire economic historians have been prone to regard it as having been a particularly appropriate political instrument for fostering economic development. There is no doubt that the economic life of France in this period cannot be understood apart from the policies applied by the state. Of course, in France there was a strong and continuous tradition of state supervision and promotion of industry and trade. While this had changed its form as a result of the Revolution it had by no means disappeared. If protectionism was its most obvious manifestation, the idea that the state could and indeed should intervene in the economy under certain circumstances had not been repudiated by the bourgeoisie as it had been in England.[9] It was widely accepted that the state should extend the opportunities for private enrichment and knowledge that it had favours to dispense meant that there was an active contest for them. Under Louis Philippe the main beneficiaries—except for the protected industries—had been a small circle of bankers and financiers who, until the beginning of the railway era, had mainly carried on business of the traditional kind. With the Second Empire the state comes to play a different rôle, more in tune with the technological and industrial needs of the time, and, while dispensing its favours predominantly to privileged insiders, offered to all the owners of mobile wealth the prospect of increasing it. It was this implicit appeal to the cupidity of the middle class and the better-off peasants which constituted the great strength of the régime; only, of course, because it did pay off. It was in the fifties and sixties that Guizot's '*Enrichissez-vous*' came true for large numbers of Frenchmen. Whether this should be ascribed to any particular economic virtues possessed by the régime is not for the moment in question; the fact is that its appearance coincided with the opening up of new possibilities of enrichment and widening of the investment market.[10] These were inherent in capitalist development and specifically in the favourable economic conjuncture which was an international phenomenon. In short, France began to take on more clearly the lineaments of an advanced industrial country than had been the case under the previous régime, at the same time as it experienced a financial revolution more spectacular if less far-reaching in its results.

The presence of the state in providing security for property as well as in actively promoting changes in the economy has to be underlined, but it must be also seen as determined by the bonapartist character which it possessed. It operated principally through private interest groups to whom it gave special privileges and support—access to means for appropriating part of the social surplus under favoured conditions. The emphasis, therefore, was not on industrial development but on those types of enterprise most closely related to the finances of the state, i.e. public works. Within the national context this meant railways and other means of communication as well as urban development and improvements, most of which were undertaken by private firms and for private profit. It is not surprising that much of this development had a hot-house character and offered innumerable opportunities for personal enrichment by doubtful means to the insiders, including members of the Imperial entourage.[11] Financial adventurism was the inevitable concomitant of the bonapartist political adventure.

IV

Louis Bonaparte assumed power at a time when trade was recovering from the crises of 1847-8 and the whole world economy was at the beginning of a long phase of expansion. The gold discoveries in California and Australia added rapidly to the monetary stock of gold of the advanced countries. Improvements in world communications stimulated the flow of international commerce. The spread of the industrial technologies of coal, steam and iron, and the adoption of new forms of organization, meant rising production and a steady growth in per capita incomes throughout Western Europe. The growing pressure of demand and the injection of new purchasing power into the system, facilitated by the increased output of gold, set prices on an upward course. The general environment in all the areas touched by advancing capitalism was favourable to enterprise. Profit expectations stood high, business confidence was strong and business of all kinds displayed a voracious demand for capital which the old methods could not adequately satisfy. Taken as a whole, then, this period was one of apparently boundless opportunity for enrichment. The new régime did not create the opportunities, they were given by the international conjuncture. What it did do was to provide French business with a favourable political climate to take advantage of them and actively to promote and facilitate the new forms of investment and acquisition.[12] Impersonal and market forces, much more than any personal qualities or ideas of Napoleon III or his associates, governed the course of economic change in France in the third quarter of the nineteenth century. Not that ideas and ideologies had no influence; but the economic conjuncture set the stage for their operation.

From the advent of the new régime, however, it was evident that it intended to break from the barrenness and parsimony of the Orleanist monarchy and to look from the narrow circle of bankers, financiers and lawyers to new layers of the bourgeoisie for support in its designs. Although the established names in high finance by no means dropped out of sight or surrendered their powers, secondary or less powerful figures were elevated to the front rank. At the same time, the government showed its determination to make full use of existing powers to exercise control over the economy and to take positive promotional action to stimulate prosperity. No doubt it needed prosperous conditions to justify its authoritarianism in the eyes of the middle class; it was a question of self-preservation. In France the principle of state action to promote enterprise was no novelty and the new ruler had at his disposal, in any case, a large and centralized bureaucracy with a tradition of intervention. There was no longer any possibility of parliamentary delays and obstruction. The government could thus make full use of the powers which the law already endowed it with, including the right to authorize joint stock companies (*sociétés anonymes*), and bring within its purview the whole province of public works, including the railway system. With these levers of command at its disposal it was able to play a positive rôle in creating more favourable conditions for the private capitalist and entrepreneur. If necessary it could use its powers to impose upon business what it thought was good for it, as in the case of the treaties of commerce. Undoubtedly the response which it evoked in business circles, was conditional support like that given to Napoleon I, rather than enthusiastic concurrence with all aspects of imperial policy. For the businessman the main virtue of the régime was that it assured him security and thus offered the prospect of more rapid accumulation. Hence, in 1852, under the umbrella of dictatorship, an atmosphere of business confidence was restored.

There thus began the first ascending phase of the régime which came to an end with the financial crisis of 1857. This period of boom witnessed its first, brilliant peaceful conquests. In these euphoric years credit gushed forth in unprecedented abundance. The conquests of the Second Empire were, indeed, to be built principally upon the wonders of credit and its fortunes followed those of the Bourse.[13] The new public figures it made were the heroes of finance and its great virtue was that it gave the investor a virtual guarantee that he could not lose and that his capital would increase handsomely in value.

V

The weakness of French finance before 1848 lay principally in the fact that it lacked institutions to attract the savings of the bourgeoisie into the large-scale projects of advancing capitalism. Consequently, instead of growing by leaps and bounds, capitalism in France tended to be slowed to a snail's pace, leaving the country as a whole still largely in the grip of an 'eighteenth century' economy of small units and archaic techniques. At least it can be said that the initiative of the régime of the 2nd of December helped to break this grip. But, of course, it was one thing to give the impulsion, or to favour new institutions, and quite another to bring about a thorough structural transformation in industry and agriculture.

Even in finance there was less novelty than at first sight appears. The Bank of France emerged from the trials of the Revolution of 1848 and its aftermath not only secure, but in a more dominant position than before.[14] It absorbed the Departmental banks during the financial collapse and thus secured a monopoly of note-issuing powers. During the crisis it had lent large sums to the state, municipalities and other public bodies as well as to private business. Its notes circulated more widely and enjoyed unquestioned credit even during the period of inconvertibility, which did not come to an end until the summer of 1850.

It was not until Louis Bonaparte assumed dictatorial powers that a political settlement acceptable to business, at least as preferable to uncertainty, was found.[15] Soon afterwards the charter of the Bank was renewed until 1867. At least the shadow of suspicion of complicity between this bastion of financial orthodoxy and the dictator falls on these events. The régime certainly needed the support of the financial world if it were to succeed in its projects.[16] To this end the Bank was authorized to accept railway shares and stock as collateral for loans and the bonds of the city of Paris were soon admitted to the same privilege. Meanwhile, by embarking on a policy of flexible discount rates, the Bank moved closer to the money market and to the rôle of regulator of the credit supply.

Like the Bank of France, the powerful merchant-bankers of Paris also emerged unscathed from the trials of 1848, ready to do business with the new régime however much they mistrusted it.[17] No doubt they preferred the laxer times of the Orleanist monarchy, but they recognized the inevitability of a strong state after the events of the Revolution. But, wherever their political sympathies lay, their traditional activities had brought them into close contact with the state. Moreover, their financial resources, actual or potential, were too great to be overlooked. They had already played a crucial rôle in railway finance and the *haute banque* in general, with James Rothschild its undisputed head, could not stand aside from the promise of an expansion of profitable business which the régime of the 2nd, December brought with it. Indeed, representatives of the old banking houses, bringing funds with them, found a place on the boards of the new institutions, including the *Crédit Mobilier,* which were their rivals.[18] The older houses, disadvantaged by their inability to tap the funds of the great mass of small investors by their traditional practices, were likewise obliged to adopt the techniques of investment banking or, as time went on, to work with the new institutions. As Landes has pointed out, the conflict between the Old Bank and the New has tended to be exaggerated. The Pereires had begun their career as protégés of the Rothschilds in the forties and, even after the resentment which James Rothschild felt for them after the launching of the *Crédit Mobilier*, the connection was not entirely broken despite the bitter rivalry which developed.

The Old Bank thus continued to play an important part in the financial history of France, adapting itself to changing requirements. With its secure position and unrivalled experience in raising public loans it served the Second Empire as it had done its predecessors. Its representatives were prominent in the financing of railways and other capital-absorbing projects of the time and continued to form the essential part of the financial élite of the capital. The régime could not have operated in the teeth of its hostility and was, in the late sixties, seriously embarrassed by its coldness.

VI

In most accounts of the economy of the Second Empire the accent is very heavily placed on the rise of new financial institutions and methods. The justification for this can be found in the important rôle which credit played in financing the large-scale projects with which the state itself was involved, and in the fact that it was through the overcoming of existing deficiencies in the field of banking and finance that the strides made towards the modernization of the economy were most obvious. Thanks to newly established institutions, and the adoption of their methods by other sections of the banking world, the savings of the middle class and frugal peasantry were tapped in a more adequate way than before. What might be called modern investment and banking habits began to spread. Under the Empire Paris assumed a central rôle as an international creditor second only to London. Changes diffused throughout the society, as well as those introduced into government itself, cannot be understood apart from the enhanced rôle of credit and financial institutions.

At the same time, the attention devoted to changes in the financial field may lead to exaggerated importance being attached to the new features introduced into the economy in the fifties.

The new financial techniques were almost exclusively geared to the needs of public works. The savings of the French rentier were being called upon to build railways, reconstruct the big cities, improve communications and open docks and harbours. As time went on, and the outlets for capital in this form diminished in relative scale in France, he was induced to place his money in similar projects in other European countries. In this way, as Cameron has pointed out at length, France played a prominent part in the economic development of Europe as a whole in the third quarter of the nineteenth century.[19]

The industrialization process required the creation of a substantial infrastructure which could only be financed through an organized capital market. The problem of railway construction posed the challenge in practice but in the thirties and forties the response had remained inadequate. No doubt the delay in railway building was not exclusively the fault of defects in financial institutions, but despite the rôle of the big banking houses, capital was not forthcoming on an adequate scale and required government guarantees to be forthcoming at all. It was not lack of capital, because the French bourgeoisie was relatively well-supplied with fixed property and liquid funds and the saving, or rather hoarding, habit, was widespread among the peasantry as well. The difficulty was how this property could be used as a basis for credit and how these spare funds could be placed at the disposal of the active promoters of economic change, especially those concerned with capital-absorbing enterprises, particularly the railway. The solution to these problems were worked out in the fifties by the establishment of new institutions and the adaptation of old ones. Within a few years the capital market assumed a new dimension and French finance became prominent throughout Europe.

The advent of Louis Bonaparte to full power by the *coup d'état* of 2nd December, 1852 gave the signal for a round of stock market speculation.[20] For the established financiers rising prices could only be the prelude to a subsequent fall; for the new régime, however, a fall in prices would have been disastrous. Hence the need to promote new institutions, led by men willing to break with orthodox financial practices, which could hold market prices on their upward course.

This, in brief, was the immediate background to the formation by the Perieire brothers, with the support of key figures in the government, of the controversial and much-discussed *Crédit Mobilier.*

The principle upon which the *Crédit Mobilier* operated was not new but it was the first institution in France to make it work.[21] In fact it was an investment bank, floated as a joint stock company, which was to raise additional capital both by accepting deposits and by selling stock. It thus offered an outlet for the funds of several sorts of prospective investor. These funds were then to be put to profitable use by buying the shares of, or otherwise investing in, other enterprises. The *Crédit Mobilier* was thus to become the *commanditaire* of all the new schemes which the régime was interested in promoting. As the company secured the confidence of the public it could place the shares of these concerns back on to the market and obtain the funds necessary to promote, or finance, additional projects. Whether or not the idea of investment banking of this kind was purely Saint-Simonian, it had certainly been canvassed by Enfantin and the school as a whole, and it was from this source that the Pereires had obtained it. It was an exhilarating idea, born of the confidence of the time, and appealing to the régime's need for material progress and visible signs of its beneficence. Through such an institution the whole of the French economy could be transformed, enterprises joined together into larger and financially sounder units, and the liquid funds of the bourgeoisie fructified to the financial advantage of all concerned.

However the first new institution intended to promote the credit expansion upon which the political future of the régime seemed to depend was the *Crédit Foncier.* This was intended to be an agricultural credit bank able to lend upon mortgage and release agriculture from lack of capital and peasants from dependence upon the village usurer. As it turned out it had negligible results in this direction and became instead one of the instruments for the financing of the grandiose projects for urban reconstruction which were among the glories of the régime. The *Crédit Foncier* was a creation of the government, which granted it a subsidy, appointed its governor and deputy governors and fixed the amount of its capital and the volume of loans it could make. The sale of its securities and the payment of interest were handled by government officials. But, although a government institution, it assumed a measure of autonomy. As with the

Bank of France, it was difficult to determine where the control of the state ended and that of private interests began.

The relations between the *Crédit Mobilier* and the state were different again. It was not established by the state, however much its promoters had the favour of the Emperor, but its objects corresponded closely with its requirements: to expand credit and promote prosperity. Throughout its life it took up state loans, as well as financing enterprises which were promoted by the Pereires and their associates; probably inadequately capitalized from the start, it was not surprising that it over-reached itself in several directions. Perhaps its ability to survive was more remarkable than its eventual reorganization.

The authorization of the *Crédit Mobilier* as a joint stock company was taken to imply semi-official endorsement and to fit in with Louis Napoleon's intention to develop the resources of the country.[22] It meant, equally, the hostility of the established financial houses and of James Rothschild the dominant figure in the financial world.

From the start the Pereires found themselves in an ambiguous position. They were favoured by the government but not altogether trusted by it, the stimulus which they gave to the stock market was welcomed in some quarters, but their activities were looked upon with suspicion in others. Judged from the standpoint of a developing capitalist economy they introduced useful forms of capital-raising and deployment. Yet the conception of investment banking, even without the speculation which infected the early fifties, was open to misuse and there is a good deal of evidence that the Pereires did misuse it. In essence they took a gamble on the continued increase in share prices and were thus prepared to borrow short and lend long—which was to leave their institution vulnerable to critics and exposed to the vagaries of public confidence. For success they needed an indefinite period of expansion and business confidence, a constant creation of new concerns and a flow of fresh capital into their hands. The justification would be found in the creation of new wealth, the eventual rise of real values to the fictitious heights created by speculation. If these hopes were not realized, however, the whole mechanism, at the best, would seize up.[23]

Some of these dangers were understood by the enemies of the Pereires, and their self-interest lay in successful rivalry with, but not the undermining of, the *Crédit Mobilier*, while adopting some of its techniques.

In its early years the *Crédit Mobilier* was closely associated with the boom and helped to sustain it. It paid handsome dividends and enjoyed the support of the public powers. However, its resources were by no means large enough to enable it to oust the established financial houses, nor could it live up to the ambitions of the Pereires. For one thing its direct effect on industry—manufacturing and mining—was slight. The firms in these fields were rarely organized as joint stock companies but mostly as partnerships or *sociétés en commandite* which obtained capital from local sources or through family and business contacts.[24] The main outlets open to the *Crédit Mobilier* thus lay in railways and public works in general, that is the privileged enterprises closely linked with the policies of the régime. And, failing a base in productive industry, the profits of the firm came inevitably from manipulations within the inflated structure of values which accompanied the boom and which it helped to sustain.

In the early years of its operation the *Crédit Mobilier* was not permitted to issue long term bonds, so that its investments were made from its own capital (held by shareholders) and deposits (subject to withdrawal). Its principal activities were in the sphere of railway finance; it made advances from its own resources and underwrote share issues. As a result of this the Pereires secured positions on the boards of many railway companies. In addition, similar services were undertaken for a series of other enterprises, most of which fell within the sphere of public utilities, including the big property development companies, and it went on to play a prominent rôle in the financing of foreign railways, which lay the Pereires open to the additional charge that they were encouraging capital to flow abroad to the detriment of French enterprise.

With the assumption of full powers by Louis Bonaparte by means of the *coup d'étât* of 2nd December, 1851, his hands were free to win the support of the middle class by restoring business confidence and of the workers by providing employment. To this end a programme of urban reconstruction was quickly put in hand in Paris and a number of the larger towns with state participation. A fresh impulsion was given to the main line railways, construction of which had lagged before

1848 and languished thereafter. Within five years the principal lines of the network were completed, thanks to a concurrence of the bankers, old and new, the railway promoters and technicians and the *grands commis* of the régime itself.[25]

This phase of railway construction was carried through within the legislative framework of 1842 which enabled the companies to obtain financial guarantees from the government. Now, however, much fuller use was made of these facilities, with the government only too anxious to see construction proceed rapidly. Safe in possession of a state guarantee of interest, the companies extended the practice of raising loan capital well beyond its former limits. Large amounts of stock were issued before share capital was fully paid up, much of it going to the shareholders themselves. Thus the companies were highly illiquid. They needed high share prices to attract more loan capital, which, in turn, meant high dividends. If actual earnings were not adequate to pay attractive dividends, then they might be paid out of money subscribed for stock—the interest on which was guaranteed by the state. This was arranged by the device of charging as many expenses as possible to construction costs and thus artificially increasing the returns on operations—a system which might reserve unpleasant surprises for the future. In this situation all parties had an interest in a continued climb in stock market values without which the confidence of the investing public might give way.

The justification for such practices was taken to be the results obtained. The trunk lines were being built and, this time under the pressure of the state, the companies were amalgamated into larger units; a tendency which certainly conformed with the character of railway transport and finance. The régime did not fear the large concentrations of power which amalgamation represented because it was itself deeply involved with the whole process. The building of the lines, by the demand created for materials and labour, stimulated wide sectors of the economy and hastened the transformation of industry along modern lines.

At the same time the railway network, this privileged form of capitalism, constructed partly at state expense, and with the state shouldering the risks, was to depend in the future upon state support to enable a return to be paid on the investment capital.[26] If the railways were a monument to the régime, like other monuments they represented a costly and in some ways a wasteful outlay. A quantitative estimate of their significance for the French economy would be useful; until it is made the presumption is in their favour.

VII

The great expansion of stock exchange business which took place in the 1850's was principally the result of the mobilization of capital for the railways. Joint stock companies were still subject to official authorization and comparatively few were formed. The great impetus was given within eight days of the *coup d'étât* in other fields in a decree authorizing a railway round the capital and a series of decrees and laws later in the year indicated that the régime stood solidly behind the railway. Concessions were now granted for 99 years, but the whole cost of construction had to be borne by the companies. It was this modification of the practice established by the law of 1842 which led the companies to raise the larger proportion of their capital as loans, assured as they were by the government of being able to pay a minimum interest of 4 per cent. These conditions applied to over 9,400 miles of line constructed or put in hand in the next five years and comprising the major part of the main trunk routes. Backed by various financial groups a number of new companies thus came into existence, or were formed as a result of the fusion of existing companies.

The outstanding feature of this turn in railway development was the firm state backing which was given, making possible a notable and necessary acceleration in the rate of construction. At last the economy was endowed with an impulse making for growth and change: the direct effects of construction which injected a new demand into the market for many commodities and absorbed much of the unemployed, or underemployed, labour available since the crises of the forties. This stimulus was particularly necessary for the iron and engineering industries. The railways created a large market for rails and hastened the transition to large scale production in coke-fired furnaces.

It was at last realized that the country could not be equipped with a railway network quickly unless a new impetus could be given to the mobilization of capital. Existing methods and institutions did not suffice. However, there was no sharp break with the law of 1842 except that the state no longer undertook to construct the 'infrastructure'. The establishment of the régime, and the lowering of the rate of interest to 3 per cent by the Bank of France brought out the savings of the investing public. It was only necessary to open the way for new or existing companies to tap this apparently abundant supply. With the new routes being opened up by large companies which received a government guarantee of interest their shares found a ready market. France was carved up into a number of railway regions by decision of ministers able to act without reference to a representative assembly. The concessions were made, naturally enough, to the great financial interests and with the support of technicians, administrators and contractors. Idle capital and the masses of unemployed could be put to work and a great new market opened up for the iron industry—too great, in fact, for its existing capacity and out-moded equipment to cope with. To overcome the shortage of rail iron which developed, under pressure from the companies, a breach had to be made in the tariff defences which gave the example for more far-reaching tariff changes still.[27]

Public works—the railways being the most notable and far-reaching in their consequences—were to be the most enduring monuments to bonapartism. But railways had to be built at all costs, as much, or more, for their immediate as for their long-run effects. Hence they were subject neither to the strict accounting of a state system open to parliamentary scrutiny nor to the full play of market forces. They remained, of course, a subject for stock exchange speculation. In this regard the most important thing was to pay dividends, because without dividends further capital could not be raised. On the other hand, the success of the railways was so important for the régime that they were shielded from the risk of loss. Dividends were hardly an index of efficient management because it was impossible to tell for sure whether they were paid from earnings or not. Increasing amounts of capital were swept into construction as new issues of shares and loan capital were placed on the market. As large a proportion of costs as possible was ascribed to capital outlays and some newly raised funds were no doubt used to pay dividends and interest.

Methods of this kind were by no means unique in the annals of railway building in other countries and it may be argued that their justification lay in the fact that France was at last being endowed with a network of main lines corresponding to economic needs. However, when carried to extremes these methods brought their own nemesis; by 1856 a number of lines were in trouble, having difficulty in obtaining the funds needed to complete construction. In the depression which followed the financial crisis of 1857 continued construction was threatened. In any case, with the opening of the main lines, the emphasis was bound to shift to others, for which a case could be made locally, or which could be said to be necessary to complete the transportation equipment of the nation but which, by their nature, were unlikely to yield a profitable return on capital. From this situation came the next landmark in railway history, the Franqueville conventions.

VIII

While it may be questioned whether the Commercial Treaty of 1860 with Britain was the most significant or interesting of the economic policy measures of the Second Empire, it has been the one which has evoked the most interest.[28] Not only was it a case of a deliberate change of fiscal policy after the style of that which had been made in Britain a decade or two before, but it was imposed by an authoritarian ruler against the wishes of many of his bourgeois supporters. While he was making political concessions to his critics, the abandonment of the traditional policy of high protection was only calculated, it would seem, to antagonize them.

The circumstances in which the policy was imposed adds some colour to the view that Napoleon III had a distinctive economic policy, influenced, perhaps, by Saint-Simonism. As has been seen, his state did, as it were, stand apart from contending economic forces. It could take a longer view than the profit-guided interests of the different sections of the economy. Napoleon was able to listen to advisors who took a more far-sighted view of the long-term interests of the national economy than did most of those who proclaimed that the country would be ruined if protection was abandoned. Then the régime also had its interests to safeguard, especially in relation to foreign powers. Its need to spread prosperity and contentment as a basis for its plebiscitary rule had been evident from the beginning. There is no doubt that by lowering tariffs Napoleon III hoped to stimulate material progress, after the initial dislocation; even this was to be smoothed by state loans. Thus, although the reduction of tariffs was, in principle, a liberal measure, in the context of bonapartist policy, it was not liberal in content. It was based on a recognition that national power was bound up inextricably with industrialization and it was intended to impel manufacturers into improving their technical efficiency in the cause of national power. In other directions, indeed, policy was interventionist rather than liberal.

If there is some reason to impute such motives to Napoleon himself, the main driving force for the treaty on the French side was Michel Chevalier, a free trader and ex-Saint-Simonite.[29] His standpoint clearly was that the treaty would improve the efficiency of the economy. However, in influencing members of the Cabinet he made considerable use of the political advantages of improving relations with Britain and, at this level, such arguments seem to have been decisive. Since politicians have to be convinced by political arguments, however, this does not prove the foreign policy motivation of the treaty, however much the improvement of relations with Britain may have been a factor in its favour.[30] In the country the argument ran rather along economic lines. The protectionist opposition laid much stress on the harmful consequences which it would have for French industry and agriculture. On the other hand, in the letter to Fould which preceded the formal announcement of the treaty, Napoleon III set out a manifesto of the régime's economic intentions.[31] In concluding the treaty and presenting it to the opposition as a *fait accompli,* Napoleon proclaimed that he thought he knew what was good for industry better than its owners did.While he had the political means to impose this decision, it was at the expense of increasing the mistrust of the protectionist manufacturers.

The treaty was in line with a series of measures taken in the fifties to lower tariffs on some raw materials and the unsuccessful attempt to remove prohibitions on other commodities in 1850.[32] It is evident, however, that at no time did Napoleon III or his advisors desire or consider it practicable, to impose a policy of free trade of the kind which existed in Britain. The most that they seem to have intended was to expose French industry to foreign competition on something like an equal footing, including enough tariff protection to bring about this hypothetical state of affairs. It was clear both to supporters and to opponents that the most highly protected French industries would be forced to equip themselves to world standards on pain of losing their home market, and thus their whole basis for existence. The French manufacturer, often satisfied with an assured market which gave him high profits from a modest turnover, and with costs considerably higher than his British or Belgian equivalent, would be forced to improve his efficiency or go out of business. Adjustments of this kind are never made without protests, but loud protests do not mean that adjustment could not be made. In any case, it was to be facilitated for those manufacturers who could establish a case with loans from the state.[33] Even so, not all adjustments were successful and many were painful. The political costs of the treaty at home seem to have been quite high; every economic difficulty or crisis gave the protectionists an opportunity to denounce the allegedly disastrous effects of the policy of commercial treaties. Before examining the evidence further, the exact nature and limits of this policy must be outlined.

It is clear that the notables of the French bourgeoisie as well as the landed proprietors considered protectionism as one of the foundations of the social order.[34] It took an authoritarian régime to bring French tariff policy near to the liberal programme. However, the tariff, although frequently discussed in the journals of informed middle class public opinion, was not the burning issue which it had been in England in the 1840's. For the majority of the population—peasants, workers in small scale manufactures, petty traders and shopkeepers—there was little danger from foreign competition or ambition to compete in foreign markets. As in less developed industrial countries the arguments of 'common sense' are stronger for protection than for free trade, no doubt those people who had opinions would have been in favour of the former.[35] Protection, furthermore, was the traditional policy of France and was re-enforced by Anglophobia. On the other hand, while there were some distinguished advocates of protection, economic opinion was mainly free trade in tendency and it was associated with liberalism and progress. French tariffs were open to many criticisms even by those who did not advocate complete free trade. Further, there were some business interests, notably in the wine, silk and luxury trades, and in the ports, who stood to gain from free trade.

The big battalions of protectionism were to be found among industrialists who had grown up with a feeling of inferiority in the face of English technical leadership. This applied particularly to the iron industry and to a large part of the cotton and woollen industries. Individual industrialists were very much influenced by circumstances in their own field and their ability to face foreign competition, whether at home or on the world market. They were thus capable of changing sides if circumstances changed. On the whole, however, opposition to a breach with traditional policy far outweighed the support for free trade in manufacturing industry.[36] As for agriculture, it is doubtful whether the peasants as a whole gained from protection or were much interested in it at this time, but the landowners and big grain producers believed they did and stood solidly behind it.

As finally adopted the treaty provided that French prohibitions on British goods should be abolished and British goods were to be admitted within two years at duties not exceeding 30 per cent and within five years at not more than 25 per cent.[37] In return almost all French goods were admitted into Britain duty free; lower duties were adopted for French wines and brandies; and no duties were to be levied on the export of coal. The French duties were to be converted from *ad valorem* to specific duties within six months. The working out of these clauses amounted to the creation of a new French tariff structure for British goods, and subsequently for those of other countries with which commercial treaties were concluded, the so-called 'conventional tariff'.

The outcry from French manufacturers did not deter the government from pursuing its course and carrying out the changes agreed upon. After ten months of negotiations the details were settled and, according to Dunham, 'in nearly every case, the French Government granted reductions in its tariff that greatly exceeded what England had expected and more than fulfilled the obligations incurred in the Treaty of January 23.'[38] Chevalier was realistic enough to understand, and the government accepted, that industry was entitled to state assistance in facing the expectedly keen British competition in the French market. While the negotiations had been continuing with the British, the *Conseil Supérieur de Commerce* held hearings in Paris at which the manufacturers could voice their fears.[39] This enquiry closed without the government accepting any obligations to industry, but, already in the previous year, when the treaty was germinating, a proposal for loans to manufacturers, believed to have originated with Chevalier, had been filed with the government. In August, 1860 a law on these lines was authorized which set aside the sum of 40 million francs available for loans to manufacturers at 5 per cent. A Commission was set up to administer this fund, receiving applications, making such enquiries as it deemed necessary and granting loans for purposes of re-equipment. Within less than a year 500 applications had been received and 200 had been approved, involving almost the whole sum made available. In the judgement of Dunham, while the amount involved was too small to have any noticeable effect on the industrial situation, 'there can be no question that the loans were of great service to a considerable number of manufacturers, and that they probably saved several of them from failure.[40]

In the next few years the French government made similar treaties with the main European trading nations, all incorporating, like the treaty with Britain, the most favoured nation clause.[41] The first was with Belgium, France's third most important trading partner, and, of course, an exporter of coal and manufactured goods in competition with Britain.[42] As the treaties came into effect Europe was launched into an era, not of free trade, but of lower tariffs. Essentially, most countries, like France, then had two tariffs: a conventional tariff applicable to the treaty partners, and a standard tariff, generally much higher, applied to the rest of the world.

French tariffs underwent further modification, notably by removal of tariffs on some important raw materials imported under French flag. In 1863 and 1864 duties on a number of commodities were reduced or abolished; export taxes, drawbacks, bounties and prohibitions, relics of mercantilism, also disappeared. In 1865, shipping and the shipbuilding industry, protected under the navigation act of 1793 and other laws which discriminated against foreign ships and shipping, lost most of their privileges. The evidence showed, in any case, that the great bulk of the trade entering French ports was carried in foreign, especially British, ships. As part of its policy of economic expansion in the fifties the government had already encouraged new shipping lines with loans and subsidies and it was principally through these means that it hoped in the future to safeguard the merchant marine. All these measures came under heavy fire from the protectionists in the *Corps législatif* and in the country at large. However, there does not seem to have been a strong and widely supported movement against the government on the protectionist issue. After all, the opposition came mainly from those who feared their privileges were in danger. As yet there was no threat to agriculture from foreign competition and some critics of the régime on general grounds were sympathetic to free trade.

Most scholars who have examined the effects of the commercial treaties on French economic development agree that they were beneficial. Lavasseur speaks of a revolution in the industries which had developed in the shadow of protection.[43] If some enterprises were eliminated with consequent hardships for the workers involved this was to be expected. Dunham's judgement is that the industries 'which had declared loudly that their immediate destruction would be the first result of a radical reform of the French tariff, survived and prospered exceedingly despite the Treaty with England and the Civil War in America. The stimulus of foreign competition forced them to enlarge their factories and improve both their machinery and their methods of production'.[44] After an examination of the balance of payments and the movement of industrial production Rist concludes that the Treaty did not bring about any general crisis in economic activity and that within two years the effects of the increased foreign competition had been counteracted.[45] French industry did this by improving its equipment and lowering its costs of production; on the other hand, concentration proceeded more rapidly with the elmination of the weaker firms. Kindelberger concurs on the whole with these conclusions.[46]

It is, of course, difficult to determine exactly what influence should be ascribed to the treaty in the complex of forces which shaped development in the sixties. For instance, the treaty came into effect when the balance of payments was adversely affected by abnormal grain imports. Then the

American Civil War profoundly influenced not only the textile industries but also some French export trades (See Appendices). Taken as a whole, the acceptance of the treaties was made easier by the continued upward trend in internal and world markets. But these were not the best years of the Empire. They were clouded by political disaster abroad and difficulties at home. Many sectors of the economy were undergoing changes which involved painful changes for some; the treaties tended to be blamed when the real reason lay elsewhere. These re-adjustments led up to the recession of 1867-8 which brought the most serious economic strain that the Empire had known. Meanwhile, the finances of bonapartism began to reveal disturbing weaknesses; the abdication of the Pereires was followed by the liquidation of some of the speculative property investments in the big cities. The days of easy credit had passed away. The improvisations of the early years were no longer tolerated. Orthodox finance came back into its own and staged a kind of strike against the régime as the expression of its disapproval.[47]

The chequered economic pattern of the sixties thus makes it difficult to appraise the treaties with assurance. Trade with Britain did grow considerably and France shared in the continued expansion of world markets. While there is reason to endorse the favourable judgement already referred to, in the absence of an adequate quantitative examination of the problem it is impossible to prove that the treaties had a major stimulating effect on the economy. They do not seem to have had any fundamental effect on the distribution of economic activities between industries. The main stimulus seems to have been received by the traditional industries : textiles and the products of the soil were most favourably affected by the growth of foreign markets.[48] The metallurgical and mechanical industries, while able to conserve their home markets, did not emerge as considerable exporters during the period. This suggests that the treaties had a less profound transforming effect than may sometimes have been assumed.

IX

Although textiles did not lose their predominance in the industrial structure or in the export trade, the more rapid growth of heavy industry and metallurgy reduced their relative importance in the economy. However, while these industries did grow more rapidly their specific weight was hardly great enough to warrant their designation as 'leading sectors'.[49] Nevertheless, it was in this period that the basic communications equipment, notably railways, was provided. Such constructional activities tended to pull coal, iron and engineering along behind them. Given the continued rôle of textiles, now undergoing more rapidly than before the process of geographical and industrial concentration already visible before 1850, this period is best seen as a transitional one.[50] The growing textile areas evoked expansion in other fields, including mining, iron and steel and machine-making. The initiative in growth, apart from these, until after 1870, came from railway construction—to which the new banking institutions could be added—not from manufacturing industry. Thus, if heavy industry was increasing its rôle it did so still in a complementary relationship with other sectors, not as one which was acting as the prime motive force in growth.

The railways and the other outlays under the rubric of 'public works' opened up a vast new market for iron, machines and constructional materials. Until the forties there were few firms in France in these fields operating on a large scale and with up-to-date equipment. Considerable investment was therefore required to keep pace with the new demand. At the same time the improvement in internal transport had its usual results in widening the market and encouraging specialization. More people were drawn into wage work in construction, industry, transport, distribution and services. Wage levels, as well as other incomes, showed a rising tendency and the secular upward trend in prices was favourable to enterprise. The urban population grew and social habits were changing, with greater emphasis on personal consumption among the middle class which was in character with the splendours of the régime. This was the time of much new residential construction, of the rise of the department store and of more sumptuous and expensive internal decoration.

From these changes in demand the development of the industrial structure can be largely derived. It meant, that is to say, not only an expansion of the producer goods industries requiring large capitals, advanced techniques and large number of semi-skilled or unskilled workers, but also the growth of consumer goods industries largely organized on traditional lines. It is true that these also underwent changes in organization and technique but only in a slow and piecemeal fashion. Artisan type production, small-scale organization, the predominance of commercial rather than industrial capital, and emphasis on quality and variety remained characteristic of many French industries.[51] In terms of price, of course, that placed many of them in the luxury or semi-luxury class: they sold to the middle and upper class, to people who prided themselves on their taste. But they also sold to tourists and visitors (*'articles de Paris'*) and to the export trade.

Growing prosperity did not, therefore, eliminate the old forms of enterprise; in some cases it might give them a new lease of life. There were, of course, small scale producers and shopkeepers who were driven out of business where the competition of new forms of enterprise was keen. But this effect seems to have been most pronounced in fields such as handloom weaving where the direct competition of urban machine industry was felt by rural producers.[52]

Another factor in the situation was that the weight of agriculture in the economy only decreased slowly. A large part of the internal market continued to be made up of low-income peasant households. These households were increasingly drawn into a market economy with the construction of railways and canals and the improvement of rural roads. Conscription helped to draw the peasants into the national life and evoke a taste for a higher standard of living. In favoured areas with good climate and soil and improved accessibility to markets agricultural incomes grew. In the less favoured rural poverty might drive people into the industrial areas in search of work. Building and constructional workers were recruited from the villages, although often on a temporary or seasonal basis. The great stability of rural France remains a feature of the period.

The growth of the internal market did not, on the whole, involve a striking breach with pre-existing conditions. Many commodities which entered into exchange never went outside the orbit of the local market town or, at the most of the region. In such conditions, small-scale, petty commodity production could survive. On the other hand, where the factory-made product showed its superiority in terms of price the petty producer or household production was doomed. By its nature, then, there was an irregular movement in consumption patterns and in demand, bound up, in turn, with the social composition of the population, as well as with income distribution and the rise in per capita incomes. This was the situation which confronted the French entrepreneur and to which he tended to adapt himself.[53]

X

Even in fields in which the machine and steam power were already established the French industrialist tended to display conservative traits. He continued to be impressed with the superiority of British production, unless experience had taught him otherwise. He was habituated to heavy protection of the home market, bringing forward an array of spurious arguments to support the claim that he and his workers would be ruined if foreign competitors were permitted to sell their products in France. Hence the outcry provoked in many industrial centres by the commercial treaties. In fact, by the fifties, the main industries likely to be affected by foreign competition—which meant competition from Britain and Belgium—were by no means infant industries. At least the more efficient firms in them were up to, or not far short of, world standards. In some cases, such as the silk industry—the principal export industry of the time—the business leaders were favourable to free trade. In others the great inequalities in efficiency meant that in the event of foreign competitors being able to compete more effectively in the home market the high-cost firms would have to re-equip themselves or go out of existence. The presence of many firms of this kind in industries which had well-equipped low-cost units suggests that where the owners of the latter pressed for the continuance of protection what they had in mind was the maintenance of monopolistic profits not the welfare of the national economy. It generally meant, too, that they were producing under conditions of decreasing costs and would not, as experience showed, have anything to fear from freer trade.[54]

The Second Empire maintained, or created, an environment favourable to the industrial capitalists. The working class was held in check, trade unions remaining illegal until 1864, with the worker an inferior party in the wage contract, subject in principle, to the régime of the *livret*.[55] Factory legislation was far behind that in Britain and was not effectively applied. There is no evidence of shortage of labour in the industrial districts and, although wages showed a rising tendency, for factory workers absolute levels were low. The entrepreneur was not subject to income or property taxes. The state did not interfere in his relations with his workers except to provide him with the support of the police if he should need it. By the legislation of the 1860's it offered him the possibility of making use of the limited liability company—thus rounding out a legal structure which was already heavily biased in favour of property-owners and employers. The state did not interfere with his business; the Inspectors of Manufactures were a thing of the past. But the state did assist him indirectly through its outlays on public works and the economic expansion which it promoted through easier credit conditions. In certain cases direct orders from the state, covert subsidies or privileges were enjoyed.[56]

The industrial entrepreneur, as distinct from the financier or commercial operator, attained a dignity under the Second Empire which had eluded him under the previous régimes.[57] No doubt most men in industry were more interested in economic power, their control over their enterprises and their importance as local notabilities, than they were in political influence.[58] However, the régime did elevate industrialists into its councils, men like Eugene Schneider, who became president of the *Corps législatif,* or Pouyer-Quertier, the self-made textile magnate who, a kind of Cobden in reverse, led the attack on the Treaty of 1860. If the circle is drawn wider to include the financiers, or men whose interests spanned over varied fields, it is evident that business had secured a more elevated position than ever before. A kind of 'industrial nobility', of whom the ironmasters were the prototype, had come into its own with the diminishing importance of landed property. Even when the régime imposed on industry a medicine for its own good which a substantial proportion of industrialists disliked, it tried to sugar the pill by drawing them into consultation and making loans available. In general, ministers displayed a deference to the industrial world quite unlike that of their predecessors and the régime showed how closely it identified itself with the industrial strength of the country in the great exhibitions which it sponsored.

XI

Textiles continued to dominate the industrial sector if measured by aggregate size, by their influence regionally, and even nationally, as a leading sector or *force motrice,* and by their rôle in the export trade. There is no pretence here to describe in detail the changes which they underwent during this period. Fortunately they are the one industry which has been subject to detailed examination by a recent historian.[59]

With the exception of silk, the French textile industries looked principally to the home market. Most textile products were protected by outright prohibitions on imports (which applied, for instance, to most cotton goods) or by tariffs at the rate of 30 per cent, until the treaties of the 1860's. Certainly the highly capitalized firms of the *Nord* and the *Est* had no need of such supports. Some proved it by pressing their sales in the British market itself. However, the textile industries, which were represented in many parts of France besides the main centres, displayed a highly variegated structure. Taken together with their associated industries, which extended from the large finishing plants to the hand-made lace manufacture, they are, therefore, extremely difficult to generalize about.

It is possible to discern certain distinguishing features of 'textile capitalism' which apply to the typical firms in the main areas. The rise of these firms coincided with the extension of machine methods. They were, and remained, family firms which had grown by the ploughing back of profits. By the mid-nineteenth century these firms had built up solid fortunes, conserved by careful marriages and forming veritable 'dynasties'. Within this general description considerable variety was to be found, both from one region to another and within the areas. In Normandy, for instance, the entrepreneur was still something of a merchant-manufacturer with large numbers of rural outworkers. His aim might be to build a fortune and then buy land and retire. In Alsace, on the other hand, the manufacturers formed a caste devoted to accumulation through business-like organization. While the Norman manufacturer kept machines in use long after they had been amortized and had become obsolete, those of Alsace were noted for their innovating zeal. They kept up with, and in some cases outstripped, their British rivals, remaining in the van of technical progress and adapting to changes in fashion. The manufacturers of Normandy, secure in the possession of a cheap rural labour force, concentrated on producing coarse lines for the low income market.

Reaching its apogee during this period was the textile area of the *Nord*.[60] Here, too, there was a hard-driving class of textile employers producing various sorts of yarn and cloth, making use of machinery and pioneering the use of steam power because of the lack of water power sources in the region. The region was also favoured by a large and growing population, part of which moved off the land into the growing textile centres. It was from factories here that came the light woollen cloths for the Paris fashion trade, an example of the willingness of entrepreneurs in the region to follow closely the changing needs of the market, thus enabling them to take advantage of the growth of incomes and the expansion of internal demand in the period 1840-70. But the products of Roubaix, Lille and Turcoing were able to carve out an important place in the world market as well.

The textile industries were undergoing a continuous process of change as techniques improved, tastes varied and markets expanded. In general, though the old artisan forms of production held out in specialized fields, the general drift was towards the centralized factory requiring large capital and a disciplined and dependable labour force. Some parts of the industry were unable to make the necessary adaptations, or entrepreneurs held out against making them as long as they could. All sections of the textile industry, but cotton and silk in particular, contained a high speculative element. Profits depended as much upon knowing when to buy raw material, how much to stock and when to sell the finished goods as they did upon the purely manufacturing side of the business. Here again the possession of reserves was a key to successful business.

Supply conditions and markets underwent serious disruption with the cutting off of raw cotton supplies from the United States as a result of the Civil War. The silk industry was also affected by diseases affecting the silk worm. The effects of these disasters coincided with the Treaties with Britain and Belgium and thus the opening of the home market to competition from foreign textiles for the first time. Protectionist manufacturers in the cotton industry blamed onto the treaties ills which were principally due to the cotton famine. The fluctuations in the raw material supply accentuated the speculative character of the industry, while the falling off in cotton production caused a switch to textiles made of other materials.

The Normandy industry suffered most from the crisis in the cotton industry.[61] It was more exposed to British competition and, since coarse cloths in which the cost of the material was an important element were its staple product, it suffered most from the increase in cotton prices. By early 1863 some branches were only producing 40 per cent of their normal output.

In Alsace the manufacturers were more far-sighted; they kept larger stocks of raw cotton because of their distance from the sea, their product was of a higher quality so that the price of the raw material was a smaller part of total cost and they were well supplied with working capital for such emergencies. In the *Nord* the industry was much more diversified so that there was a switch from cotton to wool and linen corresponding to that in consumer demand. At the same time, the principal firms in the area, however loudly they proclaimed their fears, were well able to cope with foreign competition after 1860. Business activity thus remained at a high level until 1867. The area had secured a dominant position in the French linen industry and accounted for about two-thirds of woollen cloth production. The industries of the region played a prominent rôle in the export trade, woollens being France's second largest export at this time.[62] Manufacturers in the region were decidedly oriented towards selling in mass markets and distant markets and technique and organization developed accordingly.

The silk industry, concentrated in the Lyons area, differed from the other textile industries in depending much more heavily on the export trade. Also, because of the nature of the material and of the product, it remained to a large extent dependent upon hand labour and skills. It remained the leading French export industry throughout this period and it became increasingly a user of imported silk.[63] It was, therefore, highly sensitive to outside events likely to interrupt the flow of raw material or curtail foreign demand. Control of the industry was in the hands of *fabricants* who did not own productive equipment but supplied raw material and working capital of *chefs d'ateliers* as and when they received orders, in turn, from merchant houses. Production of cloth was carried on in small workshops with four or five looms. The power loom was slow in making its appearance and, apart from a tendency for weaving to spread into the surrounding countryside and for the number of *fabricants* to decline, this part of the industry underwent little change during the period.

The main branch of the silk industry did not fear foreign competition and expected that the treaty with Britain would extend its markets, though there were some sub-branches, such as Saint-Etienne ribbon weaving, which were strongly protectionist. In the event the industry benefited from the treaty though how far it did so is difficult to estimate. 'We must be careful', notes Dunham, 'not to overemphasize the strength of the French silk industry and not to exaggerate its triumphs in England'.[64] A number of factors affected the industry unfavourably—difficulties in raw material supply, falling off in American demand during the Civil War, changes in tastes and foreign competition.

France excelled in many industries using textile yarns and cloths which were not individually of great aggregate importance but which together made a substantial addition to production and to the export trade. Most of these industries continued to be organized on the old lines or only slowly changed their character. They were dependent upon the nimble fingers of peasants working in their cottages as well as upon skilled workers in the back streets of Paris and other towns. There were so many varied patterns that it is impossible to generalize very far about these industries except to say that they survived.

More significant in the long run was the tendency in this period for the industrial structure to become rounded out with a diversity of industries. Some, based on new techniques, had not previously existed or only on a smaller scale. Others were being detached from the home or local production and going into larger establishments. Others again were subsidiary to more important industries or were only beginning to become important in their own right. Chemicals and non-ferrous metals would fit into the latter category. The growth of the sugar, chocolate and other edible products industries indicated the growth in consumer incomes.

As a country still largely agricultural, fluctuations geared to the harvest continued to play an important part in economic life.[65] But the industrial cycle was becoming more strongly marked in the sixties. Although the crisis of 1857 had not far-reaching industrial repercussions, a serious depression hit the main industries in 1867. Readjustments associated with the treaties with Britain and Belgium or with the disturbances introduced into the textile industries by the Civil War, were working themselves out. In particular, the financially stronger were gaining ground at the expense of the smaller and weaker firms. With this went industrial concentration and the extension of mechanization. By the mid-sixties a number of important sectors had become geared to conditions in foreign markets. The fall in cotton prices, a falling off in foreign demand coupled with bad harvests which forced up food prices, created a difficult situation, a kind of 'scissors crisis', which the protectionists again attributed to the treaty of 1860. In fact the source of the trouble arose from the shrinkage of markets at home and abroad and the curtailment of credit facilities which followed the unfavourable movement in the balance of payments. Coming after a period of expansion of production this brought inevitably a classic slump and depression. The cotton industry suffered more severely than it had done at any time since the late forties.[66]

XII

The rapid expansion of railway construction and other public works brought about a major technical change-over and re-organization in the iron industry in this period. The ironmasters established a strong and in some ways unique position in the French *patronat* which corresponded with the growing relative importance of heavy industry in the economy and the concentration of capital, and thus of economic power, which it involved. The formation of the *Comité des Forges* in 1864 may be taken as symbolic in this regard.[67]

Already before 1850 the growth in demand, which came principally from new users, had been largely met by the increased output of the technically better equipped and thus larger firms. But the balance towards the coke-burning techniques and thus the larger furnaces and foundries only swung decisively with the accelerated demand for railway iron in the fifties.[68] Indeed, home producers were for a time unable to keep pace with this expanded demand. On the other hand, a large part of the demand for iron arose locally from the needs of farmers, blacksmiths and small-scale metal workers and could continue to be met from the charcoal-burning section of the industry. Here high transport costs made for local monopolies, while demand was stable and could be highly specific regarding the quality of metal required. The general nature of the economic structure thus had a good deal to do with the slow rate of technical change in the iron industry in the first half of the nineteenth century.

At the same time, the ironmasters staunchly supported the protective system which guaranteed them against foreign competition in the home market. While protection did not prevent the larger enterprises from displaying technical progress, there is some warrant for the accusation that the iron industry, like others, tended to stagnate behind the tariff walls.

As is usual with an industry which depends on bulky natural resources, some of which are being used up while new deposits are becoming available, the relative weight of different producing areas was continually shifting. This tendency was reinforced by the decline of the charcoal section of the industry and the emergence of coal as a main locational factor. Simultaneously, the railways, while opening up wide markets for a standardized product, also made it possible to haul coal or ore much more cheaply than before. Under these conditions the most favoured areas, with good coking coal together with local, or easily accessible, supplies of ore, were likely to expand at the expense of others. However, routinism or lack of enterprise on the part of ironmasters could prevent full advantage being taken of favourable conditions where they did exist. Those in the *Nord*, for example, were slow to turn over to coke despite the existence of abundant coal resources in the area. However, this area went ahead rapidly after 1850. From the standpoint of technical advance and the development of large-scale, integrated plants, the Centre led the way. Lorraine, although favoured with extensive ore-fields, was still of lesser importance; it took the Gilchrist-Thomas process to make economical use of its phosphoric ores.

The famous Schneider works at Le Creusot expanded at a rapid rate and was highly prosperous under the Second Empire. It was a classic example of large scale operation and integration, employing 10,000 workers by the late sixties.[69] Here, and in a few other giant works, French enterprise showed itself capable of reaching the front rank by international standards. At the other end of the scale many small forges continued in existence. Even large producing areas, such as that of the Marne, displayed marked technical backwardness during this period. This area produced high quality iron for users who mainly operated on a small scale such as the Paris metal trades and the local cutlery industry. In addition, it suffered from the high costs of charcoal and difficulty in obtaining cheap supplies of coal. The scale and location of the furnaces had been determined by conditions which were now passing away. Production had been directed at markets which were stagnant and declining compared with those open to ironmasters elsewhere. Doubtless, therefore, this area would have had to go through a process of more or less painful re-adjustment even without the competitive spur of the commercial treaties. In the long run, as Dunham has shown, the ironmasters of the area did adapt to change and improve the efficiency, and presumably the profitability, of their firms as they did so.

The 1860's would in any case have been a period of reorganization, with difficult problems for the smaller firms and the less favoured areas. The changes in the economic conjuncture, especially the depression of 1867, further complicated the situation for an industry whose leaders had always been strongly protectionist. Hence the strong opposition to the treaties, which were made to carry the blame for difficulties which had their origin elsewhere.

In the iron-using industries, as in others, a great diversity in the size of the productive enterprise and its efficiency existed. Many were organized on the putting-out system or conserved an artisanal character, as they did, of course, even in Britain at this time. This did not mean that there was not scope for considerable division of labour within the industry or that they did not draw the maximum economy from the existing form of organization. Some depended upon highly skilled techniques transmitted from father to son which could simply not be simulated by the machine. In other cases, such as the manufacture of locks and padlocks, machine methods had been introduced and the artisan producers had been eliminated.[70]

What stands out from this brief description is the great variety of the productive units to be found and the continued predominance in many fields of domestic and artisan manufacture.[71] Some observers have tended to ascribe these characteristics to peculiarities of the French temperament, to the fact that employers as well as workers conserved their links with the soil and still had a peasant mentality.[72] However, the situation in French industry was by no means unique. Some of Duveau's observations, for instance, would apply just as well to many British industries outside the textile field and without much qualification to the industrial areas of Continental Europe. This suggests that the reasons have to be found in the nature of the social and economic structure and the process of industrialization as it worked itself out in each specific case. Instead of ascribing the pace of this process and its peculiarities in any particular case to one or two factors, such as entrepreneurship or the nature of the work force, a more rounded analysis has to be made in economic terms with the object of obtaining some quantitatively comparable results. In this respect, however, the study of nineteenth century French economic history is still at an early stage.

XIII

After 1851 the French capital market underwent some spectacular changes but twenty years later it was still far from being adequate.[73] Outside Paris and two or three large towns the banks remained local affairs, conservative and unable to attract large deposits or to act as levers of economic change. The peasants and farmers, despite the establishment of the *Crédit Agricole* in 1861, were as yet largely without access to modern means of credit. There were, it is true, now vastly more outlets for the small saver and the moneyed middle class than there had been under the Orleans monarchy. But still the main institutions for this purpose were operating on a large scale from Paris; they mobilized credit, but they did not make it available in small or medium-sized amounts for trade, industry and agriculture. The investment banks, after all, had few holdings in manufacturing and mining and did not play the same rôle in the financing of industry as did their

German counterparts. On the contrary, on the lookout for large, remunerative investments they went after foreign industrial investments, as well as state, railway and public utility investment which, abroad, as well as at home, was their staple business.

The finance of industry, therefore, was not transformed fundamentally, in this period. Despite the great increase in the use of the *société anonyme,* half the capital raised by them was in railways and a good deal of the rest in banking and finance, distribution and services.[74] Indeed, the pattern does not greatly differ from that in contemporary Britain. It is true, of course, that French industry could make use of the *société en commandite,* but even so, 'blind' investment in manufacturing must have been rare. As in Britain the joint stock company form was used by industry to effect fusions or to give continuity to a family firm rather than to bring in fresh capital.[75]

It was not until 1863 that the state abandoned its control over the formation of joint stock companies embodied in the Commercial Code. In the earlier years of the régime this instrument had been used to favour some concerns and to restrain the formation of others. However, it left companies subject to regulation: capital was limited to 200 million francs, the directors had to own, and retain, at least five per cent of the share capital and statutes and amendments had to be registered.[76] By the law of 1867 these provisions were superseded; administrative authorization was no longer mandatory for the formation of a joint stock company and limited liability was granted as a general right. Coming in the trough of the business cycle and inspired partly by the need to bring the French company law into line with the British, it brought about no financial revolution. French industrialists showed no greater alacrity than their British counterparts to take advantage of the wider facilities now granted. However, this liberalization of the law was definitely in line with the tendency towards concentration of capital and the emergence of a capitalism of large units.

Other changes were meanwhile taking place in the financial structure of French capitalism. Most important was the development of a credit network more closely tuned to the needs of internal trade and industry than the investment banks. At the end of the forties the French banking system still lagged very much behind the needs of business. The banking habit was scarcely at its beginnings even among the affluent middle class. Bank of France notes were of high denomination and cash was used for everyday transactions. Even in Paris discount facilities did not compare with those available on the London money market and in the provinces hardly existed.[77]

During the financial panic generated by the events of 1848 the provisional government established the *Comptoir d'Escompte* in Paris with the collaboration of the Pereires. A number of others were established in the provinces. The Paris institution flourished, taking on general banking functions and being chartered, in 1854, as an independent company, with its directors nominated by the shareholders. During the fifties its business increased considerably and it made good profits, but this was a result, not of a great increase in the volume of discounting, but of engaging in long-term lending and speculation.

Later in the life of the Second Empire important new developments took place in the field of deposit banking. Here the influence of the British model was very evident, but the fact that banks of this sort came on the scene so late is a good index of the relative weakness of the French financial structure. Success in deposit banking depended upon the willingness of the moneyed public to hold the major part of their cash reserves as bank deposits and the ability of the bankers to find profitable, but liquid, outlets for the funds entrusted to them.[78] In the speculative atmosphere of the Second Empire the temptation was to venture into long-term lending, either because the yields were expected to be higher, or because there were, in the absence of a highly organized discount market, inadequate short-term outlets. There were, therefore, few attempts at deposit banking in this period. The *Société Générale de Crédit Industriel et Commercial,* formed in 1859, had only a limited success, though it provided the example for some other banks of a similar type. A more portentous development came in 1863 with the formation of the *Crédit Lyonnais.*[79] It was no accident that a serious attempt to close the credit gap should be made in the great silk manufacturing centre which was itself undergoing considerable constructional activity and witnessing the rise of new industries. The new bank was born with the support of local business notables who felt the need for financial facilities not offered by any other institution. They also desired independence from the established financial interests and the state. Such ends could only be achieved by drawing in the spare funds of the moneyed middle class and even the small saver; this meant offering more attractive terms than could be obtained elsewhere. Like other contemporary institutions, therefore, it was tempted into long-term or speculative investments which a more experienced bank would have avoided. The *Société Générale,* an outgrowth of the anti-Pereire coalition of the *haute banque,* was authorized in 1864, but at this stage was an investment bank, after the style of the *Crédit Mobilier,* rather than a deposit bank.[80] In short, banks of the latter type, properly speaking, hardly existed, only their forerunners.

XIV

The success of the policies of the Second Empire in the 1850's was achieved by taking out a credit on the future. In the following decades the bills began to be presented at a time when external shocks and a waning of confidence in the régime in business circles at home reduced its room for manoeuvre. The fall of the Pereires and the dismissal of Haussman were symbolic of the change.

Even though the *haute banque* had established institutions with the form of the *Crédit Mobilier* its members never compromised with the spirit in which it had been founded. While the reconstruction of Paris brought fortunes to many, the single-minded aloofness of Haussman, expressed particularly in his financial methods, made him many enemies. Moreover, in opposing the privileged supporters of the régime its enemies struck against the power itself.

The *Crédit Mobilier* was concerned in all the economic activities of the bonapartist state, from financing the Crimean War to the rebuilding of the big cities. The promotional energies of the Pereires took them all over Europe in the search for profitable investments. Their ambitions grew with success and were not dulled by failure. The whole principle of their operations was that future income would be more than adequate to meet obligations.[81] But the capital tied up in fixed investment and projects which could only yield a return over a long period of time was so great a proportion of the whole that only speculation in shares and land values made it possible to maintain earnings. There was, therefore, a permanent need for fresh capital and for a constant increase in values to justify past ventures. In fact, the *Crédit Mobilier* only contributed indirectly to the process of wealth formation. It did not, in general, invest in industry, but in transport, public utilities, state bonds and real estate. Its success depended upon the continued general growth in wealth and income from which it could scoop up its share; and some of its investments financed unproductive outlays, such as the Crimean War.

The Pereires were closely enough bound up with the régime to share its successes, but they were not an integral part of it and they could be abandoned when it was in jeopardy. Their ambitions intensified the antagonism of their rivals. There was, for example, the episode of the Bank of Savoy. In 1862, Emil sought to obtain control over this note-issuing bank which could enable him to challenge the monopoly of the Bank of France, citadel of orthodox finance. The government refused to authorize this venture, which might have made possible the resurgence of the *Crédit Mobilier*. The following year it sought to double its capital without success. Permission to do this was granted, however, in 1866, by which time the institution had become increasingly illiquid. With the support of the rest of the financial world no doubt the *Crédit Mobilier* could have been saved, but by this time the Pereires had scarcely any friends and their influence in the government had appreciably declined.[82]

The troubles of the *Crédit Mobilier* came to a head with the difficulties of a property company, the *Société Immobilière,* involved in transactions connected with the reconstruction of Paris. The new capital raised in 1866 proved insufficient to cover the debts of this concern. A loan was therefore necessary and the Pereires asked the government to arrange this through the Bank of France. Taking revenge on the outcasts, with the support of the financial world of Paris, the Bank agreed to do so only if the brothers withdrew from the *Crédit Mobilier,* which they did. Whatever the sins of the Pereires, there is no doubt that they were forced out of the firm which th had created by a coalition of rival financiers who organized a bear raid on the shares of the *Crédit*

Mobilier, put pressure on the government and blocked every avenue through which they might obtain credit. In a sense, too, the ousting of the Pereires was a political act which was part of a drive by the orthodox financial capitalists against those features of the régime which they found objectionable. This took the form of an attack on easy credit facilities, *la finance saint-simonienne,* expressed not only in the enterprises of the Pereires—some of which did, of course, have serious weaknesses—but also in Haussman's reconstruction of Paris.

The attack on the Prefect of the Seine who had been put in charge of the transformation of the capital in the early days of the régime had also been maturing for a long time and in the same circles. The financial methods of Haussman, like those of the Pereires, comprised a gamble on the future. As Pinckney puts it 'he accepted the idea of spending in anticipation of increased revenues that the spending itself would help to produce. Long-term loans had no terrors for him.'[83] The immense constructional boom was made possible by long-term borrowing against future income, that is to say, municipal taxes. Subsidies also came from the state and the appropriation of land and the increase in land values which accompanied the rebuilding provided income both for the city authority and for a multitude of private individuals. However, in the sixties it became more difficult to borrow; the loan of 1860 was not taken up by the public on the scale expected and one-third was bought by the *Crédit Mobilier.*[84] In these more stringent circumstances Haussman resorted to different financial methods. Instead of financing the works from loans raised by the city and employing direct labour, contractors were employed who were able to issue bonds which, in turn, were accepted by the *Crédit Foncier.* By this means finance could be found without the approval of the city authority and without offering the bankers opportunity for commissions or other gains.[85]

Although some of Haussman's enemies suspected his methods some years earlier it was not until 1867 that the storm really broke in the *Corps législatif.* Haussman came under fire both from the orthodox financiers and from the liberal opposition in the press and before this body. Finally, in a great debate in February 1869, the attack became so serious and concerted that the government decided, and Napoleon reluctantly accepted, that the Prefect would have to be sacrificed. Haussman maintained that he did nothing irregular or illegal and obtained no personal profit from the transactions which he had authorized. He managed to remain in office until the early part of 1870, the appointment of Ollivier as prime minister being the actual occasion for his departure.

More than the fate of individuals was involved in these changes. They marked, in fact, the end of the financial practices with which the régime had been identified from the start; a victory for orthodoxy against the advocates of easy credit. No doubt, given the difficulty of sustaining credit and the growing hostility of the financiers to the régime—they had always been opposed to the interlopers, though they may have composed with them—the brakes would have had to be applied at some time. On the other hand it is possible that without the financial innovations of the fifties the economic development of France would have been very different and much slower than it was. Like similar statements it cannot be proved easily by quantitative methods. In any case, with the events of 1848 fresh in their minds, even those who most deprecated the expansion of credit no doubt preferred to see the workers of Paris on the constructional sites rather than on the barricades, particularly when, as has often been said, the new boulevards made the setting up of barricades impossible.[86] The quieting of revolution was only one of the virtues of easy credit. Through its means not only were the towns modernized and equipped with sewers and water supply to combat the cholera, but France was equipped with railways, ports, canals and similar paraphernalia essential for economic growth. With the experience acquired in the raising and deployment of capital and the organizations formed for the purpose French financiers penetrated many other countries and made Paris a great financial centre.

XV

During the great boom of the fifties the Pereires and other French financiers found their own country too small a stage for the specialized business in which they were engaged.[87] There was a limit to the number of railways, property developments and public utilities in France which could offer profit. A Europe starved of capital, but sharing in the prosperity of the time, displayed many such opportunities; hence it was not surprising that investment ran an extensive as well as an intensive course. It was easier to do the same kind of business in Vienna or Madrid as had been done in Paris than to turn to other forms of investment, even if they had been available, in France itself. The *Crédit Mobilier* form was emulated in Germany and other countries and thus brought out the funds of the local bourgeoisie and set going a process of credit expansion which, within a relatively short time, would cease to depend upon outside stimuli. In France itself it had brought about the definite establishment of the new banking techniques, leading to their emulation by Rothschild himself, both in France and outside. It made an important contribution to the implantation of the investment habit, offering the bourgeoisie as a whole more ample opportunities for enrichment than the collection of rents from real property.

XVI

The power of the existing or newly created financial groups connected with railway promotion and finance was a feature of the age. An impetus was given to large-scale business organization using the joint-stock company form of the kind inseparable from modern capitalism. It is true that the first steps in this direction had already been taken in the previous decade, but the process now went forward at a rapid rate and with the support of the state itself which provided, as it were, hot-house conditions for the completion of the process. However, it should be pointed out that this transformation hardly yet extended into the sphere of production: manufacturing industry was still carried on by the traditional methods of finance and organization. The new 'feudalism', which some contemporary critics denounced, was not yet securely based upon possession of the means of production. It derived its power on the one side from its ability to raise money from the public, thanks to the privilege of incorporation granted by the state, and to the financial guarantees and the monopolistic powers to operate a public utility obtained from the same source. Under the conditions of bonapartist economics, the régime also expected the railways and other public works to create conditions of prosperity and confidence upon which its own political health depended. Investment in these enterprises was at the same time a vote of confidence in, or gamble on, the régime.

When, following the financial crisis of 1857, the prices of railway shares and stock came tumbling down, the companies were forced to resort to the state for further aid and the régime, in turn, was just as much obliged to grant it. The problem of restoring confidence and permitting the building of the lines to continue could only be resolved by the government itself. It was complicated by hostility to the Pereires in the more traditional financial circles.

Thanks to the expansion of the post-1852 years railway building had gone ahead with only the minimum of state support worked out as each line was conceded; the miracles of credit did the rest. With the sobering up of the market, which became evident from 1856, the companies would be obliged, if left to themselves, to reduce the rate of new construction or, when the crisis struck, to suspend it altogether owing to the unwillingness of investors to buy stock. They knew, as did all informed people, that little of the construction then going on would issue in lines able to earn enough revenue to pay interest on the securities with which they were to be financed. In addition, some of the existing lines, in the changed business conditions, could not be expected to yield the profits anticipated in more buoyant times. Between 1857 and 1858, therefore, the understanding between the companies and the government underwent a significant modification which found expression in the Franqueville Conventions.[88] A distinction was made between existing and forthcoming concessions—the old and new networks—the profitable and the probably unremunerative lines. The former would be enabled to pay dividends approximately at the 1857 level but not more. Dividends were thus virtually frozen and the shares in the existing companies, exploiting lines generally profitable, attained virtually the status of fixed interest securities. The new lines, which were not expected to make profits, were to receive the excess profits of the old companies to enable interest and dividends to be paid. At the same time, the state gave a guarantee that it would maintain interest on the securities of new companies at 4 per cent. For the present, then, the state had no outlays to make and the principle that the excess earnings of the old network should meet the deficit of the new was not to come into effect until 1872. Of the six main line companies the Nord and the PLM made no use of the state guarantee, for the remainder the state guarantee did become operative during the 1860's. In the meantime, the companies went on building their new network, leaving the future to take care of itself. The state was too anxious to keep the economy moving to exercise a real control over the construction of the new lines and the companies, not subject to any check from market forces, had the assurance of state support in the future. It has thus been claimed that France was provided with many superfluous lines as a result of this agreement between the state and the big companies.

Certainly, apart from the outline of the main lines, which dated back to 1842, establishing Paris as the dominating centre of the whole system, there was no systematic programming of the railways. Short term financial interests and the needs of the régime itself were uppermost. If local political pressures were less obvious than under the Orleanist monarchy and were not permitted to hold up construction, they were undoubtedly still present. They were obvious enough, for instance, during the elections of 1857 and in the establishment of the lines of local interest during the sixties.

The justification of the policy as a whole lay in the fact that France was at last endowed with a railway system commensurate with the needs of the economy. During its construction the network had acted as a main motor force in continuing the process of industrialization and breaking down the barriers between one region and another. Without the railway, indeed, no national market—though the railway was not, of course, able to overcome entirely the tendency for markets to be local or regional in scope. Without it, too, no modernization of the industrial sector and no expansion of markets to permit continued urbanization and the improvement of methods in agriculture. The contribution which the railway made to the development of credit and the mobilization of capital is clear enough from the foregoing account. Thanks to the close association between the state and the private companies, holdings in the latter assumed virtually a gilt-edged status and became part of the portfolio of every prudent French rentier.

It would be too much to say that the railway brought a revolutionary transformation of the French economy or that it had the same effect in France as in neighbouring Germany, although its influence *at the time* on the economy was primordial. In this sense, therefore, there seems no reason to dissent from Marczewski's conclusion that 'the principal overall growth factor in these thirty years is railway construction.'[89] Nevertheless, in many ways, it tended to confirm rather than to break up existing economic configurations. In particular it confirmed the dominance of Paris and thus intensified the administrative and financial centralization inherited from the past. The metropolis grew, not only as a vast consuming centre, but also as a focal point of industry, witnessing, with the reconstruction and aggrandisement of the Haussman era, the growth of a new industrial belt.

XVII

For an authoritarian régime brought to power as a result of a conspiracy worked out with the complicity of the police and the army the Second Empire has come to possess a reasonably good historical image. Napoleon III has been accredited with various good intentions, if not exactly personal virtues; he has been seen as a social reformer, a pioneer planner, a frustrated internationalist and even a socialist.[90] In economic history, with its emphasis on 'growth', the tendency has been to underline the economic achievements of the régime and tacitly overlook its shortcomings.

As has been suggested at various points in this chapter, there are many aspects of French economic development in this period which remain obscure or need to be re-appraised, especially with the use of quantitative methods. However, while these tasks have been indicated, there is no pretension here to have begun to grapple with them. What remains to be done is to summarize some of the conclusions to which the foregoing account seems to lead and indicate more specifically what problems require investigation.

In view of the favourable economic conjuncture of the third quarter of the nineteenth century it seems likely that appreciable economic growth, necessarily involving qualitative changes in the financial and industrial structure, would have taken place under any form of government able to maintain civil peace. For the property owning classes the promise of bonapartism, above all else, lay in its claim to do precisely that: to provide a strong government enabling the bourgeois to sleep comfortably in his bed while his wealth fructified acceptably and in security. An authoritarian régime was no doubt less than ideal, but it secured the support, sometimes grudging, but often firm and complete, of most sections of the bourgeoisie during the miracle years of the fifties. However, the growing difficulty which the régime had in reconciling, or balancing between, conflicting interests and groups made much of this support increasingly conditional. Significantly, too, the dwindling political credit of the Empire coincided with the weakening of its financial credit.

The economic significance of what took place in this period can be defined from several different angles. As Perroux has suggested, it saw the supersession, at least to a perceptible degree, of the old-style family capitalism based on textiles by the capitalism of large units and modern techniques.[91] The view of the period will depend upon how much emphasis is placed upon the vitality of the old forms and how much upon the rise of the new. That the persistence of the former, and particularly the continued weight of agriculture, especially peasant agriculture, in the economy accounted for its later relative 'stagnation' seems to be clear enough.[92] But this was also a period in which the national market becomes more clearly defined, thanks principally to the railways and the improvements which took place in the credit system. However, without a deeper structural transformation the national market was bound to conserve features from the past and thus confirm some existing patterns. The nature of demand in a society made up to a large extent of peasant households and petty bourgeois, in which national economic integration was still only partially a fact, was bound to lay considerable stress on products of the old type and conserve a relatively stable shape. It thus influenced the structure of production in the same direction. In the same way, despite the new openings for profitable investment and the beginnings, at least, of the banking habit, bourgeois wealth continued, as before, to consist to a very large extent of land and house property.[93] Indeed, the relative prosperity of agriculture and the increase in urban site values which accompanied rebuilding added further motives to the old ones in favour of holding landed property. It would be a mistake, therefore, to assume from all the attention paid to the new credit institutions and forms of investment that the change in habits was more fundamental than was really the case. Rather there was, in this sphere as in others, a cohabitation of the new forms with the old.

Yet, at the same time, the period seems to have a very modern complexion, thanks to the rise of new financial institutions and the policy of the state. A state not afraid to spend and deliberately concerned with the promotion of economic prosperity—whatever its motives—is more in line with twentieth century concepts than with those of nineteenth century orthodoxy. Hence, perhaps, some of the grudging sympathy which the Second Empire has evoked.

What the balance sheet of state activity really was is difficult to say. Some things, like the tearing down of much of old Paris and its replacement by wide boulevards and fashionable shops, would obviously not have taken place without it. But such activity comported a degree of waste and absorbed resources which might have been put to other, more productive uses. Whether the change in régime was decisive in speeding up the completion of the railway network is not proven; nor is it possible to take the effects of the railways at their conventional valuation without further enquiry. That the beneficial effects of the Treaty rests also very largely upon presumption has already been suggested. The very involved complex of forces operating in the sixties needs to be more carefully examined. That French foreign trade leapt ahead at a much faster rate than ever before is clear enough (See Appendix A). This was attributable, however to the international conjuncture and to the fact that, as the most important industrial power on the continent, France, or rather French merchants and manufacturers, had every opportunity to expand their trade. Could they perhaps have achieved more?

Growing integration with the world economy was also displayed in other directions. French financiers, with the investors in their wake, looked to foreign horizons in this period to a markedly greater extent than ever before. At the same time, both in North Africa and further afield the beginnings of a new economic imperialism can be discerned. There seems no reason to doubt, though more proof would be desirable, that expected profit rates or returns—and actual yields over time—were higher abroad than in France.[94] Was this a result of a surfeit of capital at home keeping down the profit rate or of an institutional bias in the capital market? Combined with this is the question why there was not more investment in industry since it is clear that, in many fields at least, French costs of production, because of less intensive mechanization, higher fuel and transport charges, were above those of foreign competitors? As in the case of Britain, the short-run trends in foreign investment corresponded with those in the domestic economy. But the fact that both forms of investment moved together does not really prove that there was not a conflict between them.[95] French industrialists seem either not to have wanted to borrow on the capital market or not to have been able to because the dominant institutions were not interested in industrial investment. In the same way, French agriculture was able to make little use of available capital both through lack of demand or creditworthiness and lack of appropriate institutions.

State initiative might have done more to channel investment flows. Despite its modest loans to industry in the sixties, however, the state was principally interested in large-scale projects which would influence general prosperity and enhance its prestige. In fact it was not deliberately promoting industrialization or the re-allocation of resources but undertaking public works upon the success of which its political existence seemed to depend. And it did this with a short range perspective, taking little thought for the ultimate financial reckoning. A full balance sheet of its activities would have to take this into account. In the sixties, when bills had to be met and early gambles proved to be less successful than had been hoped, the régime lost credit; but it may have been as unjustly blamed for difficulties in the sixties, which arose from circumstances over which it had no control, as it was praised for the prosperity of the fifties.

The fifties, therefore, show up as a period of accelerated extensive and intensive growth, with some falling off, but still continued expansion, until the end of the Empire. However, the progress of the industrial revolution was notably uneven in France; in some areas and industries there had been an unmistakable structural transformation, but large parts of the economy remained substantially unchanged. The balance of the economy was still affected by the contribution which a relatively backward agriculture continued to make to total income.[96] Even the marked growth in exports was based upon an expansion in textiles and natural products; silk retained its lead, textiles as a whole remained predominant and the heavy industries made relatively little contribution (See Appendix F). Such structural changes as did take place seem, therefore, to have been connected more with internal demand, which as suggested, continued to a considerable extent on the old pattern.

Thus the French economy entered the last quarter of the nineteenth century, which was to see a change in the international conjuncture, with some, but only some, of the attributes of an advanced industrial society. On a relative scale it had lost ground to its German rival. The demographic trend which had become established by the middle of the century was on the whole unfavourable to rapid growth and change. In short it had attained, in the third quarter of the century, unprecedented prosperity and a higher rate of investment and real income, but it did so as part of a general expansion of the world economy and with only a partial transformation of the economic structure. The take-off hypothesis, which seems at first sight to be confirmed by the surge forward in the fifties, the completion of the main railway network and the appearance of large credit institutions, is belied by an examination of these deeper trends.[97] The economy had grown, the bourgeoisie had become richer, mobile capital had come to predominate over landed property and was widely distributed among the extensive petty bourgeoisie; the industrialists in large-scale industry had achieved a social stature which brought them to the level of the *haute banque*, concentration of control over the decisive sectors of the economy had meanwhile grown and class lines had become more sharply marked.[98] In a land of diversity and contrasts, with the most advanced techniques and organization as well as the archaic co-existing, French capitalism had taken on a distinctive form which it was to conserve into the mid-twentieth century.

Notes and further reading

1. In addition to the economic histories cited in previous chapters, see the general surveys of the period by modern authors, which have summaries of economic developments. In particular, Marcel Blanchard, *Le Second Empire* (Paris 1950) and J. P. T. Bury, *Napoleon III and the Second Empire* (London 1965).

2. On working class reactions, including pro-bonapartist sentiments, see George Duveau, *La vie ouvrière en France sous le Second Empire* (Paris 1946), Introduction; an indispensable work for the mass of material it contains on industrial conditions but less satisfactory on interpretation.
3. The regime brought its new men but also depended heavily upon those who rallied to it from other camps. In the administration and in the localities among the notables the *coup d'état* did not mark a sharp break with the past.
4. Karl Marx's classic, *The Eighteenth Brumaire of Louis Bonaparte* (various editions), conserves its interest, not only as a sociological analysis but also as a description of the regime in its early stages which brings out well its contradictory nature and its need for economic successes. 'Industry and commerce, i.e. the business of the middle class, are to be made to blossom in hot-house style under the "strong Government" ', Kerr edition, trans. De Leon, 1914, p. 156.
5. The *coup d'état* of 2nd December, 1851, is taken as the beginning of the bonapartist period; the Empire was not proclaimed for another year. For some purposes it is no doubt preferable to end the period in French economic development in the 1880's, but the role of the bonapartist state has been taken to justify the adoption of the political divisions. See succeeding chapter for other possible turning points.
6. Alexander Gerschenkron, *Economic Backwardness in Historical Perspective,* pp. 23, 191.
7. Ben. T. Hoselitz, 'Entrepreneurship and Capital Formation in France and Britain since 1700', in *Capital Formation and Economic Growth,* Moses Abramovitz, ed. (Princeton 1955), pp. 307-8; like other writers he is particularly interested in Saint-Simon for his influence on the new credit institutions. Landes has pointed out that he exaggerates the differences between the new bankers and the old, David S. Landes, *Bankers and Pashas in Egypt* (London 1958), p. 50, note 3.
8. It must be admitted that the weight of opinion is strongly against the more sceptical attitude adopted here and all the works used attribute considerable weight to Saint-Simonism in influencing prominent individuals, including the Emperor, and the policies of the régime itself. Perhaps too much weight has been placed on particular individuals such as the Pereires and Chevalier; their policies were supported by others not so influenced. The former Saint-Simonians, too, were not always on the same side, e.g. Talabot supported the Rothschilds against the Pereires.
9. See Fohlen, op. cit., note 47, Ch. VI.
10. 'Never had money flowed so rapidly or in such torrents from the Treasury into the pockets of private citizens and thence back again into government loans—a merry-go-round that swelled the banks with business and brought joy to middlemen and brokers'. Octave Audry, *The Second Empire* (trans. A. Livingstone, New York, 1940), p. 69.
11. It was part of the '*fête impériale*' that the Court should spend

freely and that some of those in the know should enrich themselves personally. 'Morny est dans l'affaire' was a good recommendation for any investment.

12. Régine Pernoud, a critic of the Second Empire for its gaudy display, wastefulness and disregard for human values (the 'ideas' of Napoleon III remained largely good intentions), places to its credit the endowment of the property-owning bourgeois with something of the dynamic mentality of the capitalist entrepreneur, *Histoire de la bourgeoisie en France,* Vol. II, pp. 564-5 (Paris 1962). She attributes this to the influence of the disciples of Saint-Simon.
13. Those attracted to the new forms of investment were also placing their money on the regime. As a foreign journalist put it: 'The purchase of property in France at the present time may be regarded as the purchase of a probability, and its market value will depend upon the general impression as to the chances of duration of the present regime; but it is a matter of guess'. *The Spectator,* 22nd January, 1853.
14. Andre Liesse, *Evolution of Credit and Banks in France* (Washington, 1909), pp. 81 seq.
15. Louis Girard, *La politique des travaux publics du Second Empire* (Paris 1952), p. 81. With some exceptions, he suggests the financial world was not exactly in complicity with the *coup d'état,* but, though many bankers would have preferred a monarchy, they recognized that a political change was due and found Louis Bonaparte more re-assuring than any alternative in view.
16. The Bank of France was governed by an oligarchy drawn from the narrow circles of Parisian bankers, Jean Lhomme, *La grande bourgeoisie au pouvoir* (Paris 1960), pp. 106 seq. The first Rothschild to obtain a seat, Alphonse, did so in 1855. On the policy of the Bank during these years see André Plessis, 'Essai sur les profits de la Banque de France sous le Second Empire', *Histoire des entreprises,* No. 10, November, 1962. As might be expected, Plessis finds that the primary aim was not to make profits (though it did that) but to hold a strategic position which enabled the regents to 'maintain the position of their own firms and develop their own profits', p. 5. The bankers needed to maintain public confidence in the note circulation (memories of the *assignats* had not been effaced) and thus they sought to maintain a liquid portfolio.
17. The financial history of this period has been more fully covered than most other aspects. There is a brilliant outline in Guy P. Palmade, *Capitalisme et capitalistes français au XIXe. siècle* (Paris 1961). David S. Landes has elucidated the relations between the Pereires and the Rothschilds and described the role of the merchant bankers and their rivals in 'Vieille banque et banque moderne', *Revue d'histoire moderne et contemporaine,* 1956, and in *Bankers and Pashas in Egypt* (London 1958), Chs. I and II.
18. Landes, Vieille banque . . .', p. 216.

19. Rondo E. Cameron, *France and the Economic Development of Europe* (Princeton, 1961).
20. See especially Girard, op cit., Ch. 1, L'économie politique du 2 décembre.
21. As Landes, Hoselitz, Cameron and others have pointed out the principle of the *Société Générale du Crédit Mobilier,* to give it its full name, had been known and to some extent used, for twenty years. See their works already cited. The best concise account is Rondo E. Cameron, 'The Crédit Mobilier and the Economic Development of France', *Journal of Political Economy,* LXI, 1955. He considers that 'it seems clear that in the absence of some stimulus such as the *Crédit Mobilier* provided, the members of *la haute banque* would have been much slower to adopt the new policies of industrial promotion'. However, it did not promote *industry,* properly speaking.
22. An intention expressed in the speech to the Chamber of Commerce of Bordeaux—the fourth largest city—which was much noted at the time. Napoleon expressed his social and economic policy as follows: 'I wish to restore to religion, morality, and opulence, that still numerous part of the population which, though in the bosom of the most fertile country in the world, can scarcely obtain the common necessities of life.

    'We have immense waste territories to cultivate, roads to open, ports to dig, rivers to render navigable, a system of railways to complete; we have opposite Marseilles a vast kingdom which we must assimilate to France; we have to bring all our great western ports into connection with the American continent by a rapidity of communication which we still want; lastly we have ruins to restore, false gods to overthrow, and trust to be made triumphant.' *Annual Register for 1852,* p. 259.
23. 'Le Mobilier, excellent stimulant à la hausse, n'offrait pas de garantie en cas de crise. Le papier des entreprises auxquelles il donnait son crédit devenait à son tour son garant du crédit du Mobilier. Dès que viendrait la baisse, le portefeuille déprécié de cette Banque d'affaires devait faire tomber ses cours. Les Pereires ne pouvaient être utilisés par le régime qu'en enfants-perdus', Girard, op. cit., p. 116.
24. Claude Fohlen, 'Sociétés anonymes et dévéloppement capitaliste sous le Second Empire', *Histoire des entreprises,* No. 8, Nov. 1961.
25. See Girard, op. cit., for the fullest account.
26. Pernoud, op cit., p. 567.
27. According to Girard, the iron industry was not able to adapt itself quickly enough to the surge in demand for railway iron, transport facilities were inadequate and orders were badly allocated. In November, 1854, Emil Pereire threatened to break off construction on the *Midi* if importation of rails was not permitted. He had his way and other companies were also allowed to import rails at a reduced rate of duty on the grounds that this would keep down prices. Op. cit., 142-6.
28. On the negotiations leading up to the Treaty and its effects the standard work is Arthur L. Dunham, *The Anglo-French Treaty*

of Commerce of 1860 and the progress of the Industrial Revolution in France (Ann Arbor 1930).

29. It has been suggested, however, that the germ of the idea originated with Persigny, a long-standing friend and supporter of Louis Bonaparte. See Gordon Wright, 'The Origin of Napoleon III's Free Trade', *The Economic History Review,* Vol. IX, 1938-9.

30. Political historians may stress too heavily the political motives while economic historians may overlook them. In this case a reconcilation between political and economic considerations was not difficult. One student concludes that 'The evidence seems to show that all the important persons by whose activity the treaty came into existence were influenced to a greater or less extent by considerations of foreign policy. In any case, however, no interpretation of the facts can make it appear that foreign policy was in any degree subordinated to the dictates of commerce.' Walter B. Harvey, *Tariffs and International Relations in Europe, 1860-1914* (Chicago 1938).

31. Fould, Napoleon III's minister of state, was a member of a Parisian banking family. The essential passages in the letter ran as follows: 'Before developing our foreign trade by the exchange of products, our agriculture must be improved and our industry freed from all internal obstacles. . . . To encourage industrial production all raw materials indispensable to industry must be freed from all duties and it must be lent the capital which will assist it to perfect its equipment. . . . The minister of Public Works will have carried through as promptly as possible the canals, roads, railways . . . and will work to reduce rates by establishing fair competition between canals and railways.

    To summarize: abolition of duties on wool and cotton—Reduction by stages of duties on sugar and coffee—Improved means of communication—Reduction of rates on the canals—Loans to agriculture and to industry—Substantial public works—Suppression of prohibitions—Treaties of commerce with foreign powers—Such are the bases of the programme to which I pray you to draw the attention of your colleagues who should prepare without delay the projects and laws destined to realize them'. First published in *Le Moniteur Universal,* 15th January, 1860.

32. Thus, after the Universal Exhibition of 1855, imported articles on show could be sold on the home market, whether prohibited or not, on payment of a 22 per cent duty. The government's attempt to abolish all prohibitions in 1856 was abandoned owing to the vigorous resistance of the protectionists. See Eduard Levasseur *Histoire du Commerce de la France,* Vol. II (Paris 1912), pp. 290-1. This showed that free trade reform could only be carried over the heads of the *Corps législatif.* A short account of tariff policies is in Frank A. Haight, *A History of French Commercial Policies* (New York 1941); see also Hugh O. Meredith, *Protection in France* (London 1904).

33. This had been proposed in the draft treaty, presumably the work

of Chevalier, the main influence on the Emperor, drawn up in 1859. See Dunham, op. cit., Appendix.

34. 'Pour l'ensemble de la bourgeoisie française ralliée au 2 décembre, le système douanier figurait entre les piliers de l'ordre défendu et sauvé', Blanchard, op. cit., p. 123.
35. Cobden, of course, thought 'common sense' spoke in contrary terms.
36. For the line-up of opinion see Palmade, op. cit., pp. 194-6, who points out that at least a part of the economic élite was now ready to do battle with the most advanced industrial country.
37. Dunham, op. cit., pp. 98 seq.
38. Dunham, op. cit., p. 139
39. Dunham, op. cit., Ch. VII passim.
40. Dunham, op. cit., p. 160.
41. That is to say, 'The signatories agreed that any reduction of duty of importance granted by one of them to a third country would be conferred upon the other and that no prohibitions would be applied which would not at the same time be applicable to all other countries', Haight, op. cit., p. 37.
42. As an important exporter to France Belgium feared that her goods, which competed with those of Britain, would be excluded from the French market. Negotiations began in May, 1861. See Levasseur, op. cit., p. 297, pp. 784-6.
43. Levasseur, op. cit., p. 304.
44. Dunham, op. cit., p. 141, and for a fuller and more nuanced summing up, 362-7.
45. Marcel Rist, 'Une expérience française de libération des échanges au dix-neuvième siècle: le traité de 1860', *Revue d'économie politique*, LXVI, nov.-dec., 1956, p. 937.
46. Charles P. Kindelberger, 'Protected Markets and Economic Growth', in *Factors Affecting the United States Balance of Payments, Congressional papers*, pp. 160-1, and *Economic Development in France and Britain* (Cambridge 1964), pp. 282 seq. In the latter Kindelberger suggests that it is a mistake to think of the treaty as a 'sharp discontinuity. . . . Economic growth supported by investment in railroads, Paris buildings, ports and public works, along with increasing exports, helped tariff reductions as much as the tariff reductions completed the transition from handicrafts to the machine and the factory, or from charcoal in steel making to coal', p. 283. However, economic growth does not bring about tariff reduction of itself; in the context of the Second Empire the treaty was, as Levasseur called it, a commercial *coup d'état,* which introduced *new* factors into the situation.
47. *La grève du milliard,* Girard, op. cit.
48. Jean Coussy, 'La Politique commerciale du Second Empire et la continuité de l'évolution structurelle française', *Cahiers de l'Institut de Science Économique Appliquée*, série P., No. 6, December, 1961, pp. 35-7. He concludes that the new commercial policy probably had the effect of widening the markets of traditional sectors of the economy. The share of '*produits naturels*' in the

export trade rose from 37.3 per cent in 1860 to 45.8 per cent in 1865 and 49.1 per cent in 1870. He claims that the attachment of the agricultural population to the Empire arose from the fact that it widened their markets at home and abroad. Kindelberger dismisses this essay rather abruptly. See trade statistics in the appendices to this chapter.

49. Rostow's view of the French take-off is now no longer tenable. See Jan Marczewski, 'The Take-off Hypothesis and French Experience', in Walt W. Rostow, Ed., *The Economics of Take-off into Sustained Growth* (London 1963). His statistics show that in general the industries which grow fastest have a low specific weight, p. 123.
50. Claude Zarka, 'Un example de pôle de croissance. L'industre textile du Nord de la France', 1830-1870', *Revue économique*, No. 1, January, 1958. See especially pp. 76 seq. Zarka combines his thesis with that of Labrousse on the 'intermediate' nature of the French economy in this period.
51. Duveau's classic study brings out the continued importance of this type of production, also the tremendous variety of forms which it took. The work is invaluable for a study of French industry during this period.
52. It is on these grounds that Zarka explains the abundance of labour power available to the textile industry in the Nord, op. cit.
53. It has something to do with the stereotype which emerges in the writings of Landes and other exponents of the entrepreneurial explanation of French economic trends.
54. Rist, op. cit., pp. 950-1.
55. By legal provision dating from the First Empire, all workers were issued with a *livret* and an employer was not supposed to hire a worker who was not supplied with one duly filled in by his previous employer. The law of 22nd June, 1854, re-enacted this provision but, according to Duveau, the *livret* was regarded with indifference by workers and employers alike, though the law was not repealed until 1890.
56. Notably in the case of the industries connected with armaments. The metallurgical and shipbuilding industries were especially favoured as a result of the change-over to the armour-plated steam-powered warship. Important contracts were passed at the time of the depression of 1857, again in 1860 after the treaty with Britain and in the recession of 1867, which helped industry to maintain production and profits. See Franklin W. Wallin, 'French Naval Conversion and the Second Empire's Intervention in Industry', in *Studies in Modern History in honour of Franklin Charles Palm* (New York 1956).
57. Palmade, op. cit., p. 166 seq., Lhomme, op. cit., Léon 'L'Industrialisation en France', op. cit., p. 183.
58. Lhomme, op. cit., p. 131.
59. Claude Fohlen, *L'Industrie textile au temps du Second Empire* (Paris 1956), from which some of the following points are drawn.
60. Zarka, op. cit.
61. Dunham, op cit.

62. Levasseur, op. cit., p. 772 for details.
63. Dunham, op. cit., Ch. XIII Passim.
64. Dunham, op. cit., p. 279.
65. Labrousse, *Aspects de l'évolution économique et sociale de la France et du Royaume-Uni,* Vol. I, p. 267.
66. Fohlen, op. cit., for an excellent account of the 1867 depression in textiles; see also, Zarka, op. cit., pp. 90 seq.
67. For *les rois du fer,* see Palmade, op. cit., pp. 168 seq.
68. See Dunham's account, op. cit., Ch. IX Passim.
69. Schneider-Creusot comprised 15 blast furnaces, 160 coke ovens, 85 steam engines with a total of 5,500 h.p. Schneider had made the business highly profitable; in some years of the sixties dividends were at 20 per cent. Duveau, op. cit., p. 158.
70. Duveau, op. cit., p. 160.
71. See Duveau, in particular, for emphasis on the complexity and variety of the industrial structure. He expressed the problem concisely in the following passage: 'Tantôt on met trop fortement l'accent sur le caractère artisanale de la vie ouvrière pendant le Second Empire et on néglige d'enregistrer le dynamisme qui se manifeste dans l'évolution industrielle; tantôt, et c'est le cas le plus fréquent, on s'interesse presque uniquement à la grande manufacture et on oublie l'artisan, l'ouvrier des campagnes. Nous disions au début de ce chapitre que, sous le règne de Napoléon III, il y a cohabitation de deux systèmes de production et la France apparaît de plus en plus, quand on entre dans le détail de la vie industrielle de cette époque, comme un pays dans lequel s'entrecroisent les courants les plus divergents.' Op. cit., p. 229.
72. Duveau is prone to do this and it seems to be one of the weaker sides of his work.
73. See the works by Palmade, Landes and Cameron already cited.
74. Fohlen, article cited note 24.
75. Fohlen, op. cit.
76. Georges Ripert, *Aspects juridiques du capitalisme moderne* (Paris 1951), pp. 62-3; Lhomme, op cit., p. 173.
77. For some retrospective glimpses of this and other features of the nineteenth century financial structure see J. S. G. Wilson, *French Banking Structure and Credit Policy* (London 1957).
78. It was apparently easier to inveigle the French saver into buying a share or a bond in some enterprise of which he knew little than to persuade him to entrust his money to a banker down the street. The rapidity with which peasants and petty bourgeois learned the language and tricks of the Bourse, however, astounded contemporaries.
79. Jean Bouvier, 'Aux origines du Crédit Lyonnais: le milieu économique et financier au début des années 1860', *Histoire des entreprises,* No. 6, November 1960, and *Le Crédit Lyonnais de 1883 a 1882—Les années de formation d'une banque de depôts* (Paris 1961).
80. For the background to this institution see Bernard Gille, 'Introduction aux Procès-verbaux de la Réunion Financière' in *Histoire des entreprises,* No. 9, May 1962.

81. 'L'Empire et la finance saint-simonienne avaient toujours éscompté l'avenir. Et l'avenir de 1852 était le présent de 1868. . . . L'Empire n'arrivait pas à sauver les Pereires, et cependant le régime semblait indissolublement liés à toutes leurs imprudences; des irregularités commises en espérant un rebondissment du crédit, le public ne voyait plus qu'elles.' Girard, op. cit., p. 371.
82. Girard, op. cit. La chute des Pereires.
83. David H. Pinkney, *Napoleon III and the Rebuilding of Paris* (Princeton 1958), p. 54. Haussman was appointed after the first works had been put in hand because 'he shared the official views on finance. He was to do for Paris what the Pereire brothers and the *Crédit Mobilier* hoped to do for industry—by long-term borrowing against future income he would provide the means to perpetuate the construction boom in Paris', pp. 180-1.
84. Pinkney, op. cit., p. 187. Haussman's projects were constantly running into trouble as a result of rising costs.
85. Pinkney, op cit., p. 192 seq.
86. Not only the width of the streets but also the direction in which they ran and the location of barracks and police stations were determined with a view to putting down a popular insurrection. Régine Pernoud, op. cit., p. 556.
87. These aspects have been exhaustively covered in Rondo E. Cameron, *France and the Economic Development of Europe, 1880-1914* (Princeton 1961) and are summed up by him in 'Le développement économique de l'Europe du XIXe. siècle. Le rôle de la France', *Annales—Economies, Sociétés, Civilisations,* Vol. 12, No. 2, avril-juin 1957.
88. See Girard, op. cit., and Kimon A. Doukas, *French Railways and the State* (New York 1945).
89. Marczewski, op cit., p. 129.
90. A selection of historians' views has been made by Samuel M. Osgood, *Napoleon III: Buffoon, Modern Dictator or Sphinx* (Boston 1963).
91. François Perroux, 'Prises de vue sur la croissance de l'economie française, 1780-1950', in *Income and Wealth,* Series V, ed. Simon Kuznets (London 1955). 'Ces deux capitalismes ont eu de nombreaux contacts: d'ensemble, ils se sont rapprochés, sans pourtant se confondre. Le premier ['de caractère producteur et familial'] est ennemi des formes brisantes de la concurrence libérale: il reste attaché à des structures et à des valeurs peu compatibles avec l'industrie anonyme. Le second ['financier et spéculatif'] est dressé contre les valeurs et les structures traditionelles, mais doit bien les ménager officiellement pour en tirer le meilleur parti à ses fins propres', p. 60. This provides a glimpse of the complexity of the relationships between the different segments of French capitalism.
92. It is difficult to measure the 'weight' of agriculture in the economy, especially in view of the shortcomings of the statistical data. Marczewski, op. cit., gives the following figures for *physical product*:

Period	*Physical product at constant (1905—1913) market prices in millions of francs* *Agriculture*	*Industry*	*Total*	*Agriculture as % of product (approx.)*
1835/44	6,601	2,446	9,047	73
1845/54	7,290	3,115	10,405	70
1855/64	8,217	4,091	12,308	67
1865/74	8,713	5,339	14,052	62

from Marczewski, op. cit., Table 10.
Perroux, op. cit., gives the following figures for *net product*

	1835	1847	1859	1872
	(*millions of francs at market prices*)			
Agriculture	5,200	6,050	8,730	9,540
Industry	2,550	3,900	5,800	6,750
Commerce	770	990	1,400	1,600
Liberal profs.	300	316	360	518
Services of buildings	400	700	900	1,045
State	1,050	1,630	2,210	2,720

93. Private Wealth, from Perroux, op. cit., p. 63:

	1835	*1853*	*1878*
		(*in millions of francs*)	
Land (propriété non batie)	36	58.8	88
Buildings	13	19	35
Industrial property	3.3	6	13
Agricultural property	3.7	5.5	9
Valeurs mobilières	4.5	10	50

94. Cameron, op. cit. As he points out 'in view of the large capital losses through inflation and repudiation after 1914 . . . France would be better off today if all or most of the exported capital had been invested at home', p. 504.
95. As Cameron argues, op. cit.
96. One of the other overheads was a relatively immobile and an under-educated population. In 1870 one in four men getting married and 40 per cent of the women signed the register with a cross.
97. Marczewski, op. cit. Passim.
98. Duveau points to this as an industrial phenomenon; urban reconstruction also separated the classes physically, with distinctive workers' quarters taking the place of the vertical division (income declining as the stairs were climbed) found in the older areas, Pinkney, op. cit. The depths of the antagonisms thus created were to be shown in the Commune.

APPENDICES TO CHAPTER VIII

APPENDIX A

FOREIGN TRADE OF FRANCE
1850–1870 (General Trade)
(in millions of francs)

	Imports a	*Exports b*
1850	1120	1435
1855	2160	2167
1860	2657	3148
1861	3085	2660
1862	2899	3050
1863	3237	3526
1864	3408	3921
1865	3528	4087
1866	3545	4281
1867	4031	3934
1868	4258	3721
1869	4009	3994
1870	3498	3456

Source: Annuaire Statistique: Résumé rétrospectif.
IMPORTS a: All merchandise arriving from foreign countries and colonies by land or sea, including high sea fisheries.
EXPORTS b: All merchandise leaving France regardless of origin.

APPENDIX B TABLE 1

FOREIGN TRADE OF FRANCE 1850–1870
*IMPORTS a
(in millions of francs)

	Food	*Raw Mats.*	*Man. Goods*	*Total*
1850	131.4	618.5	40.8	790.7
1855	486.1	1032.1	75.9	1594.1
1860	395.3	1443.1	58.9	1897.3
1861	842.5	1487.5	112.3	2442.3
1862	613.9	1433.1	151.6	2198.6
1863	541.2	1741.0	144.2	2426.4
1864	506.6	1866.6	155.0	2528.2
1865	498.6	1971.4	171.8	2641.8
1866	494.8	2091.6	207.1	2793.5
1867	825.1	1971.7	229.7	3026.5
1868	950.9	2115.7	237.1	3303.7
1869	707.5	2173.7	271.9	3153.1
1870	802.2	1766.6	288.6	2857.4

Source: Annuaire Statistique
* SPECIAL TRADE: All merchandise from foreign countries and colonies available for consumption including withdrawals from warehouses.

APPENDIX B TABLE 2

FOREIGN TRADE OF FRANCE 1850–1870

*EXPORTS b

(in millions of francs)

	Food and Raw Material	*Manufactured Goods and Postal Packets*	*Total*
1850	321.9	746.2	1068.1
1855	477.8	1080.1	1557.9
1860	848.5	1428.5	2277.1
1861	745.2	1181.1	1926.3
1862	882.4	1360.3	2242.7
1863	1152.1	1490.5	2646.2
1864	1219.1	1705.1	2924.2
1865	1413.6	1674.8	3088.4
1866	1464.9	1715.7	3180.6
1867	1295.5	1530.4	2825.9
1868	1305.9	1484.0	2789.9
1869	1435.0	1639.9	3074.9
1870	1376.9	1425.2	2802.1

Source: Annuaire Statistique

* SPECIAL TRADE: All goods of French origin leaving the country, plus re-exports, admitted duty free or having paid duties.

APPENDIX C

(in millions of francs)

French Exports to

	Britain	*Belgium*	*U.S.A.*
1847-1856 (ann. av.)	279.7	115.3	194.7
1857-1866 (ann. av.)	694.3	199.3	166.7
1867	907.0	255.0	156.3
1868	878.5	271.7	125.7
1869	909.6	295.0	192.9
1870	860.5	310.8	306.9

French Imports from

	Britain	*Belgium*	*U.S.A.*
1847-1856 (ann. av.)	126.9	139.2	135.6
1857-1866 (ann. av.)	459.6	230.7	165.6
1867	578.2	380.9	140.9
1868	580.4	354.1	149.6
1869	560.2	315.81	174.5
1870	525.4	272.0	217.6

Source: Annuaire Statistique

APPENDIX D

PRIVATE SAVINGS BANKS

	Deposits (in millions of francs)	*No. of Books*	*Average amount per Book (francs)*	*Books per 1000 Habitants*
1850–	134.9	565,995	218	16
1852	254.4	742,889	340	21
1854	271.6	865,478	313	24
1856	275.3	936,188	294	26
1858	310.5	1,042,205	297	29
1860	377.3	1,218,122	309	34
1862	424.2	1,379,180	307	37
1864	462.1	1,554,151	297	42
1866	528.9	1,748,944	360	47
1868	633.2	1,971,523	321	52
1870	632.2	2,079,141	303	58

Source: Annuaire Statistique: résumé rétrospectif

Deposits fell drastically during the 1848 Revolution and did not exceed the 1847 figure until 1861.

APPENDIX E

THE FIFTEEN PRINCIPAL FRENCH EXPORTS

(*value in millions of francs*)

	1846			*1869*	
1	Silk cloth	147	1	Silk cloth	447
2	Cotton cloth	140	2	Woollen cloth	268
3	Woollen cloth	109	3	Wines	261
4	Wine	46	4	Table ware etc.	180
5	Table ware	28	5	Silk	156
6	Prepared skins and hides	27	6	Prepared skins and hides	99
7	Linens	26	7	Clothing etc.	84
8	Paper etc.	21	8	Tanned hides	81
9	Pottery, glass, ceramics	21	9	Refined sugar	81
10	Clothing etc.	18	10	Cheese and butter	81
11	Madden	12	11	Cotton	64
12	Metal wares	12	12	Cotton cloth	75
13	Horses, Mules, Cattle	11	13	Cereals	70
14	Refined sugar	11	14	Brandies and Spirits	56
15	Cotton and Wool yarns	10	15	Horses, Mules and Cattle	53

Source: E. Levasseur: *Histoire du Commerce de la France,* Vol. II p. 772

CHAPTER IX

The Making of a Modern Economy

STABILITY AND GROWTH IN THE FRENCH ECONOMY, 1870–1914

IN the first phase of the history of the Third Republic a certain form of capitalism, derived from the institutions and innovations characteristic of the nineteenth century, reached its maturity in France.[1] This was, at least in appearance, a period of international peace and social stability in which the principles of economic liberalism still held sway. The principal economic actors whose decisions made the French economy what it was were profoundly affected by the immediate and prevailing evidences of material progress and stability. At least until the growing tensions, domestic and international, of the last pre-war years, they were, on the whole, convinced that these were conditions destined to last.

In this period the competitive forces of the market were scarcely impaired. The rôle of the state in economic life remained a minor one. The age of bourgeois dominance continued, despite the growing strength of trade unions and the socialist movement. Individual private property, the virtues of thrift, the rightness of profit and a return on savings, the injustice of taxes on income or property, and the inexpediency of state expenditure which disturbed the allocation of income determined by the market-place—these were the foundations of social order and orthodox thought. There was less pragmatic adjustment to circumstances than in Britain, less scope for an alternative which recognized the need for state intervention than in Germany. The tradition of Colbertism, though by no means dead, was never less potent than at this time.

To speak of the French bourgeoisie is to evoke a class constituted under very special historical circumstances which have been examined earlier in this work. Its origins under the old régime, its projection to social power in the course of a revolutionary upheaval, gave it a close involvement with the state. Private property, its foundation-stone, was not exclusively, or even predominantly, held in the form of business assets, though, as the nineteenth century wore on, this did tend to become more and more the case. The point is that it was not in origin a commercial and industrial bourgeoisie and its centre of gravity only moved slowly towards business and the ownership of industrial capital. By nature it was an open class and the growth in national income promoted into its ranks a growing host of less affluent property owners who acquired the same outlook, and set themselves the same aspirations, as those already in place. These were the famous *nouvelles couches sociales* who came into their own under the Third Republic.

As this is primarily an economic history these references to social changes are only intended as a bench-mark in pursuing the main task of this volume. The nature of the bourgeoisie, its ideology and outlook, contributed in no small measure to the peculiar physiognomy of the French economy, as has already been seen. Its behaviour under the changing technical and economic conditions of the late nineteenth and early twentieth centuries has now to be examined in its diversity and contradiction. In a work of this kind definitive conclusions are not, however, to be expected. The most that can be done is to explore the main specific features of the French economy, tentatively proposing some explanations for them and revealing, in the course of the enquiry, what seem to be the open questions which require further, more detailed investigation.

This period opens in misfortune: a calamitous military defeat and the burden of a war indemnity on the nation and the capital city, the rumblings of social revolution, uncertainty about the future shape of political institutions. The final balance sheet of bonapartism must include its responsibility for the war and its effect on the national economy.

The debacle underlined the relative industrial weakness of France. It also exposed the unfavourable demographic trends and, through its effects on mortality and on the birth rate, it accentuated them still further. Germany's road to industrial power was now marked out and, by the same token, the stature of France was diminished. That is not to say that the

Third Republic renounced the effort to remain a European great power, more, a world power. French nationalism was acerbated by the war and by the penal clauses in the Treaty of Frankfurt. The tendency towards protectionism and economic nationalism was strengthened. Generally, however, the rise of Germany was seen more in its military than in its economic aspects at this time; more conscious effort and resources were put into military preparations than into dealing with internal tasks of economic development. Consciousness of the economic factor was slow to develop. On the other hand, patriotic Frenchmen could not forget that defeat had deprived their country of part of its national territory. Alsace was a prosperous province with an advanced textile industry; the rich iron ore deposits of Lorraine, which played no part in the drawing of the new frontier, were to become the basis of a modern steel industry which might have been French. The peace treaty, moreover, imposed a heavy war indemnity and until it was met German occupying forces would remain on French soil. In addition, by clause II of the Treaty of Frankfurt France was obliged to grant most favoured nation treatment to Germany in perpetuity and, although this was on a reciprocal basis, it was an undoubted, and unwelcome, curtailment of tariff autonomy.

The new régime was thus confronted with serious economic problems even while its own fate hung in the balance; not until 1875 was the republican form of government finally decided upon. It also inherited the bitter after-effects of the Commune and of the repression which followed it. Whatever the nature of the Commune itself there can be little doubt that its supporters had been principally drawn from the working classes and that it was upon them that the repression which followed it therefore fell. Class relations remained strongly marked by this experience, just as they had done after the June days of 1848; the bitterness left behind is difficult to gauge, but it went deep and long endured. The free development of working class organization was held back and trade unions remained illegal. Politically and socially the Third Republic found it difficult to integrate the growing class of wage earners; that it did so less successfully than other countries is largely an inheritance of the events of 1871.

Despite the defeat and the partial occupation of the country the credit of the new French government stood high both with the international bankers and with the saving public at home. It therefore proved possible to raise the capital sums exacted by the Treaty of Frankfurt more rapidly than the German government had expected. Patriotism played a part, but the loans were also a good financial proposition for the creditors, especially the bankers. The recuperative powers of the country turned out to be greater than had been expected. This was perhaps not surprising; reconstruction booms after wars are a general rule. France, after all, was a prosperous country. The war had not been a total war and the brunt had fallen on Paris and the northern departments. The disturbance to trade, especially foreign trade, and to industrial production, though severe, was not prolonged. In any case, the period up to 1873 was one of the most prosperous which Europe had ever enjoyed; reconstruction therefore took place under the most favourable conditions.

The initial problems of the new government took the form of a need to restore confidence and organize the big loan operations required to meet the indemnity. New sources of revenue thus had to be found. For the old enemies of the free trade Emperor it seemed to be the opportunity they had been waiting for. Thiers, always an eloquent defender of protection, was head of the government and the protagonist of the textile manufacturers, Pouyer-Quertier, who had campaigned to the end of the Empire against the treaties, was his Finance Minister. The attempt to use the obvious need for increased revenue as the means to move towards higher tariffs, including those which would fall on raw materials, proved to be a failure. Resistance to protection of this kind remained strong and the agriculturalists did not as yet feel threatened by cheap food imports. Most of the proposed duties were thus abandoned and, although the Commercial Treaty with Britain was denounced it was, after the fall of Thiers, re-established. For all practical purposes the first decade of the Third Republic was lived out under a tariff policy which differed little from that of its predecessor.

The increased revenue was found by increases in the old direct taxes and in the excise duties. There was strong opposition to the proposal for a progressive income tax, an obvious source of revenue in such circumstances; but the income tax was resisted until the end of this period. With internal activity rapidly restored, however, the taxes imposed proved sufficient to bring in a revenue surplus. The Third Republic was born under the sign of severe financial orthodoxy, which, despite later accusations of extravagance, remained its canon down to 1914. Taxes falling on income and property were as far as possible avoided and in intention, if not always in practice, ministers maintained a Gladstonian respect for balanced budgets.

The restoration of normal economic activity was rapid and the burden of the indemnity was borne with relative ease. Frenchmen brought out the savings which they had accumulated during the preceding period of expansion. Prudently they seem to have laid aside from their gains in that time of financial wonders a store of specie or notes as a reserve against the kind of bad times which they remembered from the 1840's. There were, in addition, foreign titles which could be mobilized. The loss of territory, serious as it was to patriotic sentiment, diminished the aggregate national power of the nation but did not leave the remaining population any worse off. Private property rights in the lost territory, including those in the railways and public services, were respected and compensated for where necessary. The payment of the indemnity came partly from credit, from the existing reserves of the population and from a levy on current production in the following years extracted through taxation. A very complex network of transactions, bringing considerable profits to the big creditors and financial intermediaries, was involved. The indemnity not only introduced many humbler Frenchmen to the novelty of paper titles to wealth but it also brought money into the coffers of the financial institutions. The payment to Germany, in turn, required a capital transfer through the balance of payments which was facilitated by the boom and perhaps aided the recovery of French trade and industry.

Meanwhile, ever since the beginning of the war the country had been using an inconvertible paper currency which represented Bank of France lending to the government. Further issues had to be authorized in the reconstruction period and the Bank of France put into circulation notes of small denomination: 5 and 10 francs. This paper currency was a dereliction from orthodoxy imposed by the stringencies of the time and steps were taken, as soon as order could be established in government finances, to curtail borrowing from the Bank of France and make possible convertibility of the notes. Full convertibility was restored from the beginning of 1878 and it may be said that this date represents the final liquidation of the direct financial consequences of the war. Monetary troubles were not, however, at an end. France was on a bimetallic standard and was thus concerned with the problems which flowed from the appreciation in the price of gold which was characteristic of the period. However, for economic development the effect of changes in the price level and the relative stability of the monetary unit were of greater importance.

I

Whatever part economic weakness may have played in the military defeat of 1870-1, the result of the war, and the growing economic power of the new German Empire which followed it, signified a major change in the international position of France. France no longer held the first position on the European continent economically or demographically. French industrialization may be said to have had its origin in the eighteenth century, but the pace and extent of German industrial growth from the eighteen fifties raised up a new and implacable rival. By comparison the economic performance of France appeared less dynamic and inherited defects and archaisms stand out more sharply. In terms of aggregate economic power and wealth, however, France retained second place on the continent down to 1914; in industrial terms she was third in Europe and fourth in the world; not exactly a stagnant backwater. As a world financial centre Paris was second only to London; with great acquisitions of overseas territory in the period France held second place as a colonial power. It was largely the rapid economic growth of Germany and the United States, and the use made in these countries of the latest and largest in industrial technique and business organization, which diminished the stature of France. By comparison everything in France tended to be on a smaller scale (the Eiffel tower was a defiant gesture that it was not necessarily so) and, in material terms at least, France lagged behind these youthful giants.

Taken as a whole, however, this was not a period of stagnation or entirely of inadaptation in the French economy. The slowing down in the eighties and nineties was common to all the advanced economies. In the last few years before the First World War industrial growth was rapid.[2] France retained her position relatively to most other countries, unmistakably a country of advanced industrial capitalism: a wealthy country and an international creditor. If the standard of comparison is the advanced business sector in Germany or the United States harsh criticisms may be made of many habits and institutions in France. On the other hand, the kind of criticisms which can be made of British economic performance and business zeal in this period are virtually interchangeable with those which can be made for France.[3] France may be considered as an old industrial country with an inherited structure which was resistant to change and blocked fuller adaptation to the technical and organizational conditions of the twentieth century.

A major problem for the student of the French economy in this period, therefore, is that of understanding why it did not grow more rapidly or carry out more fully the kind of structural transformation which, from the standpoint of economic growth, was both desirable and possible. From this point of view it may be useful to speak of the 'retardation' of the French economy as long as the term is used with caution: growth was taking place but it fell short of what was required to bring the economy into line with the best results achieved elsewhere.[4] Evidently in some spheres of life, including industry and business, the peaks were attained. It is the general level, the persistence of large areas of underdevelopment—whether looked at geographically or sectorially—which, at least with the advantage of hindsight, is open to criticism.

The passage of time, especially the recuperative powers which the French economy has shown in the nineteen fifties and sixties, enables this problem to be seen in a new light. The danger of seeing it in the narrowing sense of national stereotypes has been revealed. A certain one-sidedness is apparent in some earlier treatments.[5] Some aspects now need to be reworked with closer attention to practical alternatives and to quantitative estimates: what proportion of French entrepreneurs were conservative or bound by routine and what general effects could their behaviour have had?

Events have, of course, shown, in the most disastrous way, through waning political power, military defeat and enemy occupation that French capitalism carried over inherent defects from its nineteenth century past. The nature of these defects has, if possible, to be determined. At the same time, more recently, the economy has revealed unsuspected reserves of strength, a potential for growth and adaptation which casts doubts on the old stereotypes. These developments tend to suggest, therefore, that there was no inherent reason why, in the late nineteenth and early twentieth century, growth should not have been more rapid and the structural transformation of the economy more complete. In the last analysis there was, perhaps, a lack of will to make the necessary changes for social reasons bound up with the old structures themselves. The task of historical explanation remains; there is no pretence here to have made more than a modest contribution to a continuing enquiry; at least it becomes more difficult to accept some of the facile explanations proferred in the past.

II

The historian who seeks to examine the economic forces in the history of the Third Republic becomes increasingly conscious of the weaknesses of French historiography in this field. He finds no master-work of empirical studies upon which he can draw for essential facts, little but raw and inadequate statistics, though a new school of quantitative history promises much, few monographs on industries or commercial problems or scholarly biographies of business leaders.[6] It must be said that there is little evidence of lively enquiry and research into the economic history of this period. With such a paucity of material it might be thought that any kind of synthesis would be premature and doomed to superficiality; indeed, to some extent so it must. Little more can be done here, then, than to follow out the main lines of enquiry and investigation pursued in the earlier chapters. It will, it is hoped, be evident what lines of research can be followed up with most profit as a result of the hypotheses tentatively put forward. In any case, some kind of framework for further work is required which incorporates, as far as possible, what is most valid in the work already done by scholars in France and elsewhere.

As for earlier periods, the broad outline of economic development might be considered as a complex interplay between the forces making for change and growth embodied in the techniques and productive relations of modern capitalism and the inertia and resistance of the inherited structures making for stability and continuity with the past.

Once the approach is no longer encumbered either by search for a 'take-off' or an industrial revolution analogous with that which took place in Britain, or with inflexible stereotypes of entrepreneurial behaviour or national character, the specific processes of growth and change to which the French economy was subject may be analysed more objectively. That is not to deny that the very lack of such a marked turning point, a concentrated process of change biting deeply into inherited structures and transforming them, however it may be explained, is of considerable significance for the understanding of French economic development. Nor can it be denied, of course, that in particular areas of the country rapid industrialization did occur at various times in the nineteenth century. In a sense then, France experienced a series of localized 'industrial revolutions'. In these areas there were industrial towns, an urban proletariat, all the social and technological problems of an industrial revolution. These were sufficient to enable the French economy to grow steadily throughout the century. On the other hand, the rise of these industrial centres was spread out over time, only a minority of the population was drawn into them, and the increased production which they made possible did not sharply affect the aggregates of national income and output in any particular period. Nevertheless this cannot be seen as a strictly evolutionary process. France was experiencing, even if in a piecemeal fashion and strung out over time, all the consequences of *the* industrial revolution. The economy as a whole was being transformed by the advance of machine production, steam power, the railway, the creation of a national market and the spread of urban patterns of living. This was industrialization in the French way.

Steadily, then, the economy had been assuming the lineaments of a modern, advanced country. Old industries were destroyed or transformed, new ones rose to importance. To an increasing extent capital was being accumulated in 'mobile' forms rather than as real property. The industrial and commercial segments of the bourgeois grew stronger as they accumulated capital and built themselves an accepted place in society. With this went the growth of impersonal investment and the rise of a system of deposit banking. In a still mainly agrarian society the weight of the urban population increased, indeed did so in excess of its proportional size. The numbers of wage earners grew; among them the factory and mining proletariat assumed a larger and more distinctive place. Factory industry extended itself at the expense of the older productive units, however resilient they remained. Giant enterprises emerged as large as any to be found in Europe. Given the heavy and inert weight of the old structures—the tenacity of peasant agriculture, the capacity for survival of artisan industry and the continued tendency for the country to be fragmented into separate local and regional economies in many of which the industrial revolution made no mark—the transformation of the economy remained incomplete. The revolution did not triumph as swiftly or as thoroughly as it did in some other environments. Even where it did conquer, the advanced outposts of modern industry remained marked by the prevailing social and cultural as well as economic environment. Hence a specific physiognomy which distinguishes French capitalism from its counterparts in other physical and cultural settings.

Some explanations have already been suggested for these peculiarities in previous chapters. No doubt, especially after about 1900, the French economy did begin to adapt its structure more fully to the requirements of modern capitalism. The effect of the accretion of many partial or localized changes was bound to have an aggregative result which precipitated qualitative changes. One side of this was the growing rôle of heavy industry and the rise of new industries. Another was the growing class-consciousness of the industrial proletariat expressed in trade union struggles and electoral strength. The new modern iron and steel industry and coal mining enterprises, the signs of concentration and monopolization in a number of spheres of business, the establishment of modern banks and financial institutions, the extension of new techniques and large-scale organization into industry, the new attention paid to colonial expansion and the continued export of capital were all evidences of deeper tides of change. These new phenomena, corresponding to those found in all the advanced countries at this time, have to be noted and explained by the economic historian as evidences of a new stage in the development of capitalism in France as elsewhere. In the longer historical span the old forms were bound to succumb; for the moment, and for some time afterwards, they continued to display considerable resilience in France, but that should not prevent the historian from pointing out what was new and changing even if, as yet, it has not become a dominant feature of the situation.

III

In the early twentieth century the French economy was distinguished by the size and resistance to change of its agrarian sector compared with other advanced countries, especially Britain. This was the result of the revolutionary land settlement which made possible the continued existence of a substantial peasant sector.[7]

A drift from the land had already attracted attention in the 1860's. From 1870 to 1914 there was a continuous steady decline in the proportion of the population dependent upon agriculture for its livelihood and in the contribution which it made to total national product. The agricultural depression of the eighties was accompanied by an accelerated movement into the towns and talk of a 'rural exodus'.

The main trend is clear enough; its more detailed statistical corroboration rouses numerous difficulties owing to the shortcomings of the data and variations in the definitions used.[8] More refined statistics, such as those of crop yields or labour productivity, can only be used with considerable reservations. When efforts are made to establish relationships between changes in agriculture and those in other sectors of the economy still further difficulties arise and causal statements can only be made with caution.

To the economist pre-occupied with the desirability of growth agriculture unquestionably occupied too prominent a place in the economy. It tied down many people who might otherwise have been absorbed into more productive pursuits instead of producing little more than their subsistence needs in agriculture. The country remained basically self-sufficient in foodgrains and most other agricultural products which could be cultivated in temperate regions, and variety of soils and climate made it possible to cultivate a wide range of marketable crops. However, owing to the weight of the peasantry in the agricultural sector, there were too many small, capital-starved and technically inefficient units, many of which continued to be run more for subsistence than for the market. Only in a few areas were modern methods widely practised. In technical efficiency, the use of fertilizers and crop specialization, and thus in net yields, French agriculture fell behind that in other parts of Western Europe. The result of having a large and unprogressive agrarian sector was thus to keep national per capita income below what it might otherwise have been.

Peasant farmers, producing little surplus for sale in the market, were, in turn, able to buy little from it. The internal market for manufactured goods was correspondingly restricted though it had undoubtedly been growing. Moreover, as will be seen, the existence of a large peasantry tended to have unfortunate effects on population growth and labour mobility which may have put a brake on industrialization and held back per capita incomes. In every way, then, the inherited weight of antiquated and not fully capitalist rural structures constituted a major force acting against more rapid change and growth. That is, if we consider the picture from an exclusively economic point of view. Certainly it was not, perhaps could not, be so considered in the nineteenth century; in the final analysis non-economic factors tended to conserve a system which stands condemned in terms of economic rationality. It should be remembered, however, that even in Britain various real or imagined virtues were attributed to peasant agriculture and voices were raised in favour of bringing back to social life a class which, for all practical purposes, had ceased to exist. In Britain such views were put forward by opponents of the large landed estate. In France the preservation of the peasantry was seen as a barrier to social revolution; revolutions began in the towns and the large estate owner, as well as the bourgeois, saw in the wide distribution of landed property a safeguard for his own property.

If the economist sees the inefficiency which went with the preservation of peasant ownership, the social historian tends to stress the great variety of the French rural scene, its continued importance as the frame of existence for a substantial part of the population. There were pronounced regional contrasts, some arising inevitably from differences in climate, soil and topography. Others had cultural roots in a Latin,

Germanic or Celtic past. In times when communication and contact between one area and another were sparse these differences were further heightened in response to political events and the diverse impacts of nineteenth century economic change. Where towns and railways extended the market for agricultural produce, the old village economy would dissolve more rapidly than where it retained a relative isolation throughout the century, as was the case in less favoured parts.

There was, by the 1880's, a well-defined regional pattern which corresponds to that of French agriculture to this day. There were areas of large estates, farming for the market and already specialized, using fertilizers and machinery and requiring a hired labour force. In others the small farm unit predominated, whether its head was a peasant proprietor, a tenant or a *métayer*.[9] Such units, though needing to market some crops to meet taxes or essential expenses, could exist almost as self-sufficient units or, at least, obtain most of their needs by exchange which hardly went beyond the confines of the village. On this kind of holding methods of cultivation remained largely traditional; there were few, if any, reserves and it was a struggle to keep out of debt let alone find capital for improvement even if the peasant had been dissatisfied with inherited practices. Even the smaller units were not, of course, entirely impervious to improvements which slowly filtered into the village or followed the turnover of the generations.

The larger holdings accounted for a considerable proportion of the marketable produce, especially grains and livestock, and in some areas the large farm predominated. Where the peasant produced a cash crop, as with the vine, marketing and production tended to be concentrated in few hands. In some cases there might be scope for the more prosperous peasant to become richer and to educate his sons for a middle class, urban life. The outstanding characteristic of French agriculture, however, was the existence of a multitude of small peasant or tenant holdings, a division of property which gave access to the land as owners, tenants or *métayers* to a large proportion of the rural population. This division, indeed sub-division, of landed property, more than the still substantial importance of the larger estate, attracted the attention of outside observers and was a matter for self-congratulation for many Frenchmen of the middle class. It was certainly this characteristic of agriculture which was of the most economic significance.

The bulk of the peasantry led a by no means idyllic existence: incessant toil for small rewards was the lot of even those with land of their own.[10] To the vagaries of the harvest were added, for most, the fluctuations of market demand. The well-being of the peasant household depended upon prices over which it could have no control and probably also upon the demand for the labour of its members in agriculture or in industry. The penetration of market relations into the village was no new thing in this period, but now it was going on more widely and it went deeper than before. A steady disintegration of the old rural ways and ties was now in progress. As in all peasant societies, differentiation between the peasants became more marked as market opportunities were enlarged. Those with draught animals, having capital reserves, able to keep their holdings together or add to their size in the flux of inheritance and marriage and cope successfully with the twin problems of technical change and marketing could improve their position. They could undertake more specialized production, employ wage labour, increase the surplus available for sale, afford fertilizers and better tools and implements and accumulate still more capital to buy or rent more land. Small landowning peasants might be pleased to rent them their own plots. The successful peasant, growing prosperous by farming for the market, was exposed to new risks and unforeseeable changes, as happened, not only with the wine-growers, but with the cultivators of plants used in the manufacture of dyes.

No doubt there always had been a rural proletariat. Here again, the penetration of market relations more fully into the village accelerated already existing trends. Many holdings were, in any case, uneconomic; divisible inheritance tended to make them more so. To the landless were added the semi-landless who had to find some paid work or be forced back to barely a subsistence level. The decline of rural industries, or inability of the small-holder to adapt to production for the market, obliged others to seek wage-work. Whether there would be a demand for labour in the village depended upon circumstances; agrarian change might reduce the demand, the agricultural depression certainly kept it down while population continued to increase, if only slowly. By comparison with the perspectives offered in the village to the landless and the lower ranks of the peasantry, life in the towns and mining villages tended to appear more attractive, to the women, perhaps, even more than to the men. The persistent drift from the land was enlarged into the 'rural exodus'; the increase in population went, the main contingents of the peasant army stayed put and fought as best they could under often disadvantageous conditions.

IV

Between the large, prosperous farmer or wealthy peasant producing for the market and the landless labourers or peasants with too little land to support themselves and their families stood the numerous group of owner-occupiers who stamped the agrarian sector with their special character. This peasant mass neither employed much regular wage-labour nor savoured the thought of working for wages on anything more than a temporary basis. It clung to its supposed but illusory independence even though it meant small returns for much work. Where extra labour was required it was often supplied by members of the extended family: sons of other peasants who would one day inherit land or perhaps acquire a plot of their own by marriage or purchase. This sums up what is meant by saying that there was access to the land; not everyone had it but many might get it some day in the normal course of things. Working for wages was thus a stopgap, even when it took the villager far afield: he might hope to come back when he had made a little money to marry and set up home. Not all, of course, did come back. On the other hand, some spent their whole working lives in the city and then came back; some cultivated their plots at weekends, others had them cultivated for them by brothers or tenants. The claim for early retirement in the public services is said to stem from the peasant background of many of the recruits.

The significance of these trends in retarding the establishment of a permanent urban wage-labouring force need hardly be underlined; nor need the resemblance with conditions in other less-developed countries where the worker-peasant is a familiar social type. There seems, then, no need to evoke a peculiar French temperament to explain such characteristics.

More properly are they to be associated with the situation of a peasantry and rural society in contact with the market but not wholly absorbed by it. The land was still seen as essential to life itself; it offered at least some security against the vicissitudes of life which man himself made. As for work for others, especially manual work, that was something regarded as a painful necessity in certain cases but to be avoided where possible.[11]

The modern roots of this structure and the outlook which went with it are to be found in the Revolutionary period. From that time onwards the peasantry was to be a basic social fact, unable to exert a coherent will as a class, a battleground of conflicting interests and yet too numerous to be ignored by any contender for political power. The votes of the peasantry had brought Napoleon III to power. Under universal suffrage no politician who wanted power for himself or his party could afford to appear to be against the peasantry. Since the peasant had become a property-owner, deeply attached to his property, other property-owners saw in him an invaluable ally. Since the mass of the peasants were toilers, not employers, and suffered from the money-lending and commercial capitalists, the working class movement tried to win their support too.

The fuller and more rapid development of industrial capitalism in France could hardly come about unless the agrarian sector could be placed upon a more efficient basis; but this was scarcely seen at the time. In any case, it was not practical politics to adopt such a policy; it could only take place as the result of a slow process of attrition, one in which state policy acted as an impediment rather than as a positive assistance. The tacit agreement of all parties, whether of the left or of the right, to conserve the peasantry, as well as the peasants' tenacious efforts to survive, can be held to explain a number of the fundamental features of the French economy in this period.

Peasant agriculture could itself have been made more efficient given a more positive state policy in respect to education, credit facilities, cooperation, the marketing of agricultural products and re-arrangement of land holdings.[12] Such a policy was almost entirely lacking or was pursued halfheartedly. The peasant was left to adapt to changes in the market as best he could and with unfortunate results for many. Adjustment to the market was difficult without reserves, without technical knowledge and some ability to plan ahead. The peasant knew well enough the value of money and might be a shrewd bargainer and a thrifty manager: but this was not enough to make him a successful business man. One essential condition was the existence of a ready market for a cash crop which he could produce economically on a small holding. Unless cash receipts could be counted on the peasant had no alternative but to produce the basic grains he needed for household consumption whether or not the soil and climatic conditions were favourable.

As a result average yields were low; the small or moderately sized peasant holding tended, even in the early twentieth century, to be something of an autarchic unit, producing a large part of the household's needs. Where this form of agriculture predominated it was in the grip of a vicious circle which impeded specialization. With little or no opportunity of selling a large surplus of a cash crop the peasant had little chance to accumulate the capital which would have enabled him to invest in better tools and implements, use more fertilizers and better seeds in order to become a specialized producer. Where such conditions did exist differentiation went ahead faster, naturally, and the peasant was exposed to changes in fortune which, to him, were just as arbitrary as those inflicted by harvest fluctuations. Sometimes this drove the peasants to mass protests. The more specialized producers suffered most from the diseases which affected the mulberry and the vine.[13] The market for some industrial crops disappeared overnight as a result of technical change. The peasants had not yet learned to demand guaranteed markets and guaranteed prices—which were, in later years, to introduce new inflexibilities and waste into the system.

In the meantime perhaps the unfortunate experiences of the wine, madder and silk-worm producers strengthened the peasants' unwillingness to change and experiment. But whether they liked it or not the peasants were drawn increasingly into a market economy which was not merely national but world-wide in its scope; the stronger peasants—and the farmers on the larger estates—were affected most of all by these trends. They were thus exposed to the severe falls in world prices which occurred in the eighties as a result of competition from overseas producers made possible by lower transport costs. The pressure hit cereal growers most of all; many of them were large tenant farmers so the blast was felt by the estate owners too when leases came up for renewal. The spearhead for the protectionist drive came from these sections, not from the mass of the peasantry, and it merged with the cries for protection which the industrialists raised at the same time. Industry, or most of it, had never been reconciled to the commercial treaties and was thankful to find allies among those who had hitherto been indifferent or hostile to protection. Although a large part of the peasantry produced little or nothing which was sold in competition with foreign imports, it could be moved by a nationalist call and diverted, incidentally, from policies which might have been of more positive assistance to it.

Even though agricultural regions had a higher rate of population growth than the average for urban areas, it continued to be lower than in comparable European areas. Few Frenchmen left their native land in this period compared with the millions of emigrants from Germany and Italy but many joined the 'rural exodus'. As a result, the proportion of the rural population to the national total steadily fell; the rural areas lost, in effect, their natural increase to the towns but they continued to hold over half the total French population down to the First World War.[14] In the last few years of peace some 55 per cent lived in the rural areas and agriculture accounted for over 40 per cent of the active population. These were high figures compared with the other industrial countries.

After the recovery from the depression the productivity of labour in agriculture steadily improved. This may indicate that the 'rural exodus' had drained off surplus population and that a further shift of manpower out of agriculture would have had further beneficial results. It is a hypothesis which cannot be proved in a situation composed of so many shifting variables. Productivity per male employed seems to have fallen off when the movement from the land was at its height, but this may have been because it co-incided with low and falling prices and slackening demand.[15] When the price situation improved the tendency was towards increased productivity and some check to the movement of rural population.

Perhaps because of the lack of a positive agricultural policy sponsored by the government, French producers were slow to take advantage of the growing demand for dairy produce, vegetables and fruit arising from the other industrial countries. To do this would have required a serious marketing effort—co-operation among producers, credit facilities, an organization for grading, packing and marketing the produce—of the kind which took place in Denmark, to some extent with the aid of French capital. In fact, little was done, except in the case of certain high quality products and specialities, renowned but too expensive to make much impression on the international market. The failure to develop an export market for agricultural products can hardly be laid at the door of the peasant. The costs and risks involved meant that the stimulus had to come from the state or from large-scale private enterprise: neither showed interest and great opportunities were lost.

V

The agricultural crisis which began in the mid-seventies and became acute in the following decade was a crisis of falling prices which affected most of all those peasants and farmers already dependent on the market. In the nature of things the peasant who produced mainly for his household or local demand did not stand to lose much, if at all; indeed, he might gain from lower prices and, if some members of the family did wage work for others, real income might rise. Even when income from one source disappeared, as happened to many as a result of the phylloxera epidemic, other sources of income might remain as before. Only the most commercially-minded peasants had abandoned all attempt at self-sufficiency in the basic foods. There is reason to believe, therefore, that the depression could have had little deleterious effect on the real income and welfare of the substantial middle strata of the peasantry. The pinch was felt most acutely by those farming for the market. Many at the bottom of the village social scale, with little or no land and dependent largely on the demand for labour, at last decided to sample the benefits of urban living.[16] But who can be sure what the decisive factors were in such decisions? The facilities offered by the railway network, the attractions of town life, the new opportunities offered by public employment as well as business may have been as potent a cause as any disturbance arising in agriculture.[17]

The rural exodus was deplored on a variety of social and moral grounds, but they lacked economic substance. Seen in relation to the problem of economic growth it was a healthy sign which ought to have been encouraged. In practice nothing of real consequence was done either to arrest it or to facilitate it. If rural interests deplored it, urban employers were ensured of a supply of labour. Nothing could have been done about it without clashing head-on with prevailing concepts of economic liberalism and arbitrating between these conflicting interests. The safest political position was to do nothing. In the devising of pragmatic measures the politicians of the Third Republic displayed little initiative or ingenuity.

These movements of population caused problems in areas most affected by the loss; as these were mostly the most disinherited, stagnation and backwardness were aggravated. In the better endowed regions the redistribution of population was probably beneficial.

In any case, the malaise in French agriculture revealed by the depression was deeply seated; it arose from the inheritance laws and the distribution of landed property and thus the existence of too many small-scale and inefficient units. If this was understood it was hardly expedient to say so; peasant votes were too valuable. These problems, as well as the reluctance to face up to them, were to persist long after the depression had been overcome and forgotten.

In fact the only policy to which the depression gave rise was the return to protection, notably the Méline tariff of 1892.[18] The claim that this 'saved' French agriculture rests on very flimsy grounds. There is little doubt, on the evidence, that the extent of the agricultural crisis was greatly exaggerated for purposes of special pleading by the large land-owners and farmers who led and supported the protectionist movement. This small minority of the agricultural population, the most affected by the depression, was well-organized and extremely vocal. Together with the industrialists, who probably had even more to gain from protection, they campaigned energetically and effectively for the abandonment of the commercial treaties and for higher tariffs to cover agricultural as well as industrial products.

The alleged benefits of protection are not easy to discern.

The home market price of the main grains seems to have been raised by just about the amount of the tariff; the difference was divided in some unknown proportion between landlords, farmers and grain dealers. The mass of the peasantry, selling little or no grain and not competing with foreign producers, had to pay more for a large range of imports; it gained little or nothing. A flood of cheap grain and other foodstuffs onto the French market was avoided, if it were ever likely. Had an influx of cheap foreign produce been accepted the electoral costs might have proved very high. In economic terms a painful but perhaps salutary re-adjustment would have been imposed upon the agrarian sector strictly by market means. High cost producers would have gone to the wall or been obliged to switch production to more rewarding lines or find new markets. Some concentration of production in larger and more efficient units might have occurred and more peasants, squeezed out of agriculture, would have had to find work in the towns. But all this is speculation. As it was, partly cushioned by protection, agriculture, despite the renewed prosperity of the 1900's—which tended to re-affirm the old structures—was only partially re-adjusted to modern requirements before 1914. Many of the archaisms of the peasant sector were preserved; politicians neither had the courage to perform a surgical operation by positive acts of policy nor a desire to see it effected by the market forces to which they gave lip service.

That is not to say that agriculture was not in a greater state of evolution and flux than at any time since the Revolutionary period. The remnants of the landed nobility, as well as the large bourgeois proprietors, found that landed property was drawn more closely into the meshes of a market economy. This imposed the need for more efficient estate management, sometimes the turning over of more land to non-agricultural uses. These landowners were themselves being brought more closely into the business process as shareholders and members of the boards of business companies formed under the legislation of the sixties.[19] Closer ties were established with the bankers and industrialists in social life, in the political parties or through inter-marriage.

In agricultural matters, however, the progressive character of the larger estates should not be over-estimated; some owners clearly saw in protection an alternative to the large outlays on modernization which would otherwise have been required to meet foreign competition. Opportunities for the enterprising peasant or farmer able or willing to specialize for the expanding market were offered by transport improvements and growing real incomes. A slow but steady rise in the general efficiency of agriculture was apparent; but in neighbouring countries it went on more rapidly and perhaps more uniformly. Meanwhile, at the bottom of the rural scale a large proportion of the peasantry continued to toil for niggardly material rewards, badly housed, without adequate sanitation or water supply, postal services or medical and educational facilities. At its lowest point the French rural environment was not far removed from that of Southern Italy or Eastern Europe. To lay the blame exclusively on the peasant would be, to say the least, unrealistic. It may be added that the problem remains to this day in some parts of France.

It is important to note, in concluding this discussion of agriculture, that its specific weight in the economy was steadily declining and its relative decline appears most sharply in the final peacetime years. Thus, although agriculture successfully pulled out of the depression in the 1900's it was precisely at this time that manufacturing industry and tertiary activities concentrated in the towns embarked on an even more rapid expansion. As a result there was a quite remarkable fall in agriculture's contribution to national product.[20] The so-called 'balance' in the economy was on the change, a trend which must be accounted a healthy one unless some mystical virtue is attributed to the existence of a large rural sector with low average incomes and a less than proportionate pull on the national market. This relative decline of agriculture can more properly be taken as a sign of more rapid modernization of the economy as a whole, a process still impeded by the excessive commitment of manpower and resources to agriculture. Self-sufficiency, and whatever social benefits flowed from having a large peasantry, were bought at a price: a lower average real income than might otherwise have been attained.

VI

As has been seen, in the 1880's the alleged needs of agriculture were thrust into the foreground of the tariff debate.

In fact industry's clamour for protection had never died down and the intellectual arguments for protection were presented in textbooks and lecture courses as well as in propaganda form.[21] Under the system of commercial treaties inaugurated in 1860 France was not properly speaking a free trade country; industry still had a degree of protection though agriculture had practically none. Treaty partners were only accorded the advantages of a lower, conventional, duty than that payable on imports from other countries. To return to full protection, however, required the restoration of tariff autonomy, as might be said, by denouncing the treaties in force.[22]

The protectionists had never admitted defeat and the downfall of the Empire offered them the opportunity they had been looking for. Thiers, a confirmed protectionist, seized the need for increased revenue to meet the post-war financial burdens as an occasion for raising tariffs. To this end the commercial treaties with Belgium and the United Kingdom were denounced in 1872 and a new convention was negotiated in the following year. However, the fall of Thiers led to the repeal of this convention, the required revenue was raised by new internal taxes and the situation reverted in all essentials to what it had been in the closing stages of the Empire.

The trend in business circles during the 1870's was towards support for moderate protection and the substitution of specific for *ad valorem* duties.[23] The tariff of 1880 established a higher general tariff as a basis for subsequent negotiation; otherwise, apart from the almost complete abandonment of *ad valorem* duties, the situation remained unchanged. The signs of a protectionist reaction had become visible in other continental countries following on the intensified international competition of the 1870's, but it was not until the following decade that the clamour for protection reached serious levels in France.

After 1882 the economy suffered from a general depression. The price fall of agricultural products became especially serious with the larger owner-occupied and tenant farms suffering most. Why did agricultural prices fall? Obviously there was a connection with the changes which were then taking place in the world market and from which France had been comparatively insulated in the seventies. But it is doubtful whether the fall in prices rose directly from an increase of agricultural imports into the home market. It is much more likely that it was communicated to agriculture through the depression in industry. Intensified competition in the home market impelled industrialists to fall back upon their traditional remedy for crisis—higher protection—and the claim could be made more plausible if it were linked with a demand for agricultural protection. More plausible and also more effective because of the voting power of the rural constituencies. At this time, too, wine-growers were suffering from the effects of the phylloxera; sugar beet producers were suffering from the effects of over-production. The other main sufferers were the wheat-growers and wheat was a main source of cash income for many small producers. The difficulties encountered in the marketing of other crops may have induced producers to put more wheat on the market and weakened their position as sellers of this commodity. If factors on the demand side associated with the industrial depression and these supply conditions suffice to explain the downward price trend for wheat, it is hardly likely that it could be remedied by protection. On the other hand, although there were not large inflows of foreign wheat, the low prevailing world price could depress the home price as long as the market was protected only by transport costs. More especially, when the harvest was below average in yield farm incomes would not receive the compensation of a steep rise in price. Perhaps this was the key to the agricultural support for protection.

In time, presumably, larger quantities of cheap foreign food would have entered the French market even if this had not happened on any scale at the height of the agricultural depression in 1888 and 1889. In appraising the return to protection this also has to be taken into account.

The emergence of Jules Méline as the champion of the case for agricultural protection dates from his time as Minister of Agriculture in 1883-5. His victory came with the tariff law which bears his name passed in 1892. Méline did not initiate the tariff reform campaign, his social connections were with business rather than with agriculture of which he had no practical knowledge; he has thus been represented both as the saviour of agriculture and as a charlatan. The personality of Méline and the details of tariff history do not concern us here, but some estimation has to be made of a step which marked a turning point in the fiscal history of the Third

Republic and perhaps in the history of the French economy.

The assessment of the effects of protective duties is never easy because they can seldom be clearly distinguished from that of many other influences on the situation. It is perhaps safe to say that these effects are generally overestimated both by the supporters of the duty in question and its opponents; this was probably the case with the Méline tariff. The debate on protection was pursued with great ardour on both sides from the end of the eighties. The existence of depression was a strong argument on the side of the protectionists as was the adoption of higher tariffs by other countries. The appeal to the peasants was highly demagogic; the solicitude for agriculture was expressed in no form other than one which, at the same time, offered even greater benefits to industry.

The law as passed in 1892 provided in fact for general protection and was the basis for a series of subsequent revisions culminating in another major tariff law in 1910. France had not returned to protection because protection had never been completely abandoned, but it now became declared policy. The commercial treaties of the 1860 variety were allowed to lapse and tariff autonomy was resumed.* However, the country did not and could not have attained self-sufficiency. Continued industrialization and rising incomes dictated ever more complete immersion in the international division of labour. Even food imports continued to increase. If industrialists obtained a sheltered market for some products, protection did not save the dyestuffs industry, prevent dependence upon imported machine tools or keep out a wide range of imported manufactured goods. Where protection was effective did it permit the maintenance of profits and encourage investment in more advanced technical equipment or simply cushion inefficient producers against the effects of price competition? Can the shortcomings of French industry be blamed upon the tariff? But Germany and the United States were both highly protectionist, while free trade Britain showed symptoms of inadaptability not unlike those visible in some sections of the French economy.

The inconclusiveness applies equally to agriculture. The fall in agricultural prices continued after the imposition of the tariff, suggesting that causes other than direct competition from foreign imports were involved. On the other hand,

* Except as limited by the Treaty of Frankfurt.

it is claimed that the price fall would have gone further but for protection; it is possible, but not certain. If it was the case then French consumers had to pay more for their food than they might otherwise have done and resources were kept in agriculture which might otherwise have been transferred elsewhere. As it was the rural exodus continued for, as has been argued already, protection could make little practical difference to those sections of the peasantry from which the migrants mainly came.

Agriculture had to wait for its real recovery until the closing years of peace when the economy as a whole experienced a phase of expansion. In the meantime it made some readjustments of a kind common to European agriculture as a whole: a shift from the cultivation of foodgrains to the production of meat, dairy produce, vegetables, fruit, eggs and poultry. Such a trend corresponded to the growth of urban markets, the steady rise in consumption standards, the effects of higher incomes; it has not been demonstrated that this change was brought about by protection. It is true that France remained largely self-sufficient in foodstuffs, including cereals, despite these changes, unlike Britain and Germany. Whether this was an advantage, even on strategic grounds, is another matter; many Frenchmen no doubt believed that it was and accepted the price which had to be paid, although they were careful not to put the issue to the electorate in that form. Moreover French population was growing at a slow rate so there was little pressure on the food supply.

It would be acceptable to all concerned to say that the Méline tariff slowed the pace of change, that it tended to conserve the existing social structure as far as it was effective as a protectionist instrument. Its appeal was directly nationalist and conservative and it rallied the support of those who had most to fear from change. That it did not prevent change, even the sort of change which enthusiastic or opportunist advocates suggested that it would prevent, is evident enough. The view that French agriculture would have been doomed to disaster without it 'cannot be tested or proved.'[24] In any case it depends what is meant by disaster. Without protection it would certainly have contracted much faster than it did; for some this would have been a disaster. But contraction does not necessarily mean disaster either for those left in agricuulture, for other sections of the economy or even, after the first pains of adjustment had been overcome, for those obliged to move out of it. One is reminded of the millions of emigrants from other countries, not from France, who made entirely new lives on the other side of the world in this period.

Finally, the protectionist reaction took place under middle class leadership and would not have been possible without the support of industry. Apart from the active support of the landlords and farmers organized in the influential *Syndicats agricoles,* the impression must be that the peasant mass followed blindly a measure from which it derived few if any benefits. Augé-Laribé has argued this case persuasively and at length; what agriculture required was a positive policy: irrigation and drainage, better roads, education and research, not the illusory benefits of the tariff.

After the expiration of the commercial treaties the French government continued to offer a lower tariff than the maximum to countries which offered similar privileges to French imports, but did so on an annual basis instead of for a term of years.[25] By a law of 1897 the government was authorized to raise or lower tariffs by decree, subject to subsequent parliamentary sanction.[26] The major tariff law of 1910, which deputies would have made more severe than the government was prepared to accept, increased minimum rates on metals and machinery and revised the classifications and nomenclature used in the tariff schedules to bring them into line with technical changes in industry. Maximum rates were of the order of 18 per cent of current values but most of France's trading partners enjoyed the minimum rate.

VII

As in the previous period, France lacked powerful export industries which could have imparted a more dynamic quality to the economy as a whole. Foreign trade grew steadily and modestly, reflecting the fluctuations in the international conjuncture with a marked depression in the 1880's.[27]

The composition of French foreign trade was that of an old manufacturing country with a high standard of living. Among imports textile raw materials predominated; there were also large imports of other industrial raw materials, notably oil seeds and nuts, rubber, skins and hides and wood. Owing to the national weakness in fuel production there were considerable, and vital, imports of coal and coke. Imports of machine tools, printing machines, typewriters and sewing machines—giving a net import balance in this category—again indicated a presumed weakness, this time in industrial production.

However, France was a great exporter of certain types of manufactured goods. There was a substantial merchandise trade balance with neighbouring countries, testifying to the success of French exports in the sophisticated, high income markets of Western Europe. In addition the many tourists from these and other countries who visited France purchased a large but unknown quantity of French-made goods not distinguishable in the figures.[28] Exports to distant markets, especially the less developed and raw material producing countries, were at a low level and there were substantial trade deficits with the Argentine, India, China, Brazil, Japan and Australia which supplied France with important raw materials.

From this it will be seen that French exports showed a definite pattern and reflected the industrial and agricultural structure of the country. Staple exports, apart from wines and spirits, were manufactured specialities, mainly of textiles; that is they came from the old established manufacturing sector; silk, wool and cotton in that order by value. The main markets for these products were found in the advanced countries of Western Europe and North America. On the whole they were goods of good quality, relatively high priced, some of which fell in the luxury class: they appealed to the better off consumers with discretionary purchasing power. Such products, and even more some of the other commodities which figured on the export side, were subject to the vagaries of fashion: to a large extent, however, the fashion trends were set in Paris, from which many of them came. The high prestige of French goods of this class was one of the reasons why so many foreign tourists visited the country. They generally took home with them such articles as clothing, jewellery, furniture and souvenirs of various kinds, more often, no doubt, the product of the small workshop than of the large factory.

It was characteristic, then, that French industry failed to exploit the growing markets in the new countries in which cheap, standardized goods sold best: the sort of markets in which the British, and then the German, exporter excelled. In fact, France's trade deficit with these areas was met from the proceeds of trade with the highly industrialized countries, just the opposite to what happened in the case of Britain. Given the nature of French industry, this seemed to be a rational adaptation to the international division of labour even though it tended, in the long run, to accentuate traits in French industry which were unfavourable to change and also to adaptation to the trends in world trade.

On the basis of these trade patterns French firms could be accused of neglecting foreign markets, certainly of not seeking out markets in the new countries. On the other hand, those which did participate in foreign trade—and for many in the large export industries it was an indispensable part of their turnover—their behaviour seems to have been rational enough. By sticking mainly to tested lines and tried markets near at hand a growing volume of business could be carried on with the minimum of risk and without the need for large outlays on new capital equipment or the prospecting of new products. The emphasis was on the continued production and excellence of products in which a reputation had been established over many decades and for which a strong consumer demand had been created. Although it was not strictly true that French exports were based on luxuries, they were the kind of goods which sold mainly in the high income urban markets of the civilized world.

As has been pointed out, agriculture lost opportunities for developing a profitable export trade with the other industrial countries. Here the blame can be squarely laid on the big producers, especially those of Northern France, who tended to stick to grain, beets and potatoes when they might have turned over to meat and dairy products for export. Wine exports were hit by the phylloxera as well as by foreign tariffs. The trade in horticultural products developed in the Midi was again mainly of a luxury kind.

The weaknesses of foreign trade were reflected in the poor performance of the shipping industry.[29] Of course, much French trade went overland and shippers did not have the advantage of an important bulk export as British shippers had in the case of coal. In relative terms the mercantile marine did not improve its position in this period despite government supports; probably lack of a long-distance outgoing trade was a major factor in its mediocre performance.

On the other hand, tourist expenditures in France were an important source of income throughout; they played an essential role in the balance of payments and they supported a whole range of activities in France itself. Many of these—hotels, restaurants, entertainment—were in the tertiary field. Tourist expenditures could not have the same effect on the economy as, say, the same volume of expenditure by inhabitants of the developing countries on industrial products from France. The demand for services, investments in hotels and casinos, may be considered of a lower economic significance than demand for calico and steel girders and investment in textile mills and steel plant. Whether this is so or not may be left to the judgement of the reader.

The other major items in the balance of payments derived from France's role as an international creditor. Unfortunately measurement of these items depends upon estimates and there is thus room for difference of opinion about their size and rôle. It is agreed that on the average the earnings from past investment at least covered the net annual addition to French holdings abroad. It seems likely, however, that they did more than that and that these earnings made a contribution to deficits arising elsewhere in the balance of payments. Probably to some small extent, then, the French economy was cushioned by earnings from past investment and was in a 'rentier' position *vis-à-vis* the rest of the world.[30]

Although export trade was of relatively less importance than in the case of other advanced European countries, there can be no doubt that the French economy was deeply involved with the international market. Some sectors of industry depended to a vital extent upon imported raw materials or foreign markets, or both. Foreign coal and coke imports were indispensable for the iron and steel and other industries. The tourist trade, with its wide ramifications in the domestic economy, was a valuable source of foreign exchange. As will be seen more fully later, an elaborate apparatus had been built up in connection with France's position as a creditor nation, and foreign bonds were widely distributed among French savers.

VIII

The structure and problems of French industry in this period reflected very closely the influence of changes in the world market and the new trends in technology and business organization common to all the advanced countries.[31] It is of some significance that the standard of comparison for judging the performance of French industry tends to shift from Britain to Germany, or even the United States; the implication of much recent writing is that it should have grown faster or have displayed more fully the traits appearing in the leading foreign industries. As far as the conditions of international competition were concerned it does seem that, by the end of the century, French businessmen had shifted their fears from Britain to Germany, especially as German industrial power was associated with worldwide political ambitions which conflicted with French interests.[32] Both German and American businessmen moved in a social environment and, more specifically, faced market conditions, which were very different from, and noticeably more favourable than, those confronting their French counterparts.

Large sections of French industry underwent little change in technique or structure during the whole of this period. Stability in the product and the ways of producing it corresponded to a stability in demand and consumer taste. This accounted for the continued vitality of the old forms of artisan production and small-scale organization in consumer goods industries,[33] but some industries organized on a factory basis did not behave very differently. It was in these fields that quality and individuality in the product were likely to be a major factor in its saleability and in which, therefore, hand skills and even a workmanship which rose close to artistry found a place. Here there was not much place for the machine, or it was not allowed to dictate the nature of the production process.

Especially in the earlier part of this period the French consumer market—notably the urban petty bourgeoisie and the better off peasants—was not much influenced by modern forms of salesmanship and publicity. The demand for household objects seems to have reflected a traditional esteem for durability and the desire to maintain certain conventional standards. Thus bed linen might be assembled before marriage and be expected to last a lifetime. Furniture and utensils were bought once and for all; they were expected to last and be passed on by inheritance. Many articles of clothing were still made within the family or, in the case of the middle class, might be procured from small dressmakers. The peasant family, to an even greater extent, would make many of its own requirements or continue to obtain them locally from artisans who worked in the traditional way.

There was, of course, nothing unique or even particularly remarkable about this state of affairs, which was general throughout continental Europe at this time and had not disappeared before 1914 even in North America.[34] It was less obvious in Britain because there was no peasantry to speak of and because urban patterns of living had exercised a longer and more pronounced effect on consumption patterns. In France, however, given the social structure, it was to be expected that the nature of the market should permit the older forms of industry not only to survive but to flourish. It was especially true, of course, of the high quality and luxury articles; but by no means only for them. The weight of these industries in the export trade, or as an attraction for foreign visitors, and the prestige which they enjoyed—and continue to enjoy—may lead to some exaggeration of their importance. Clearly the mass of the population could not afford articles of this class. Nor does their existence prove that there was some inherent love of quality and workmanship in the French nature. Machine-made products were conquering one field after another: the nature of the market, perhaps more than any other single factor, can explain why they did not do so more thoroughly before 1914.

Many types of production were, in addition, not yet susceptible to mechanization or standardization or, until a large and uniform market was known to exist, the capital outlay involved did not seem to be worth the risk. In other words, the transformation of some lines of production by machinery was hardly likely to come about until there had been a general process of change affecting incomes, styles of life and consumption patterns: i.e. the growth of urban living.

Small-scale production and antiquated hand methods thus survived, not only in cases where the high quality of the product justified it, but also in industries which employed cheap and unskilled labour. Some French industries of this kind were unbeatable for quality, if not for price, and the standards which they set no doubt influenced larger sections of the artisan industries. The numerical importance, too, of small enterprises, each having only a small number of workers but comprising, in the aggregate, a large proportion of the labour force, together with the fact that many of these workers still used the old complicated craft skills, certainly helped to give French industrial capitalism its specific physiognomy. This was an aspect of the incompletenes of industrialization which can be explained without imparting praise or blame. In time advancing technology and changes in the market would alter the picture, destroying or radically changing many of the old trades.

However great the weight of these small-scale industries using little or no modern machinery, the most significant trend of the second half of the nineteenth century and the early twentieth was undoubtedly the rise of heavy industry and the continued advance of machinery and steam power.[35] There were, in France, highly industrialized areas comparable with any in Western Europe in which all the features of modern large-scale industry were to be found. In iron and steel and engineering, in some branches of the textile and chemical industries, as well as in some of the new industries based upon applied science, there were French firms of world class and some which were world leaders in particular processes or products. Advanced forms of business organization and modern financial and managerial practices were to be found; the problems of large-scale organization were being encountered and overcome.

In a sense, therefore, there were two industrial sectors: a traditional one dominated by the small-scale unit and largely dependent upon human muscles and hand skills, and a modern sector based on the large factory and with a labour force conditioned to the requirements of machine production.[36] In practice such a distinction turns out, as it must, to be blurred at the edges and too definite conclusions should not be drawn from it. For one thing, the older-established factory firms had taken on some of the characteristics of the traditional sector: they had settled down to routine production for a given market. Such behaviour was not, of course, possible in the kind of industries which could not exist other than on a large scale and with constant attention to technical efficiency. However, it may well be that the peculiarities of the French environment influenced the behaviour of entrepreneurs in these fields, too. It was not merely that the outlook of the other sort of entrepreneur rubbed off on to them, but also that the heavy specific weight of the traditional industries and agriculture in the economy created the 'objective' conditions to which they were, to some extent, obliged to adapt since they could do little, individually, to change them.

IX

That section of industry which, for want of a better name, may be designated as 'traditional' was, by its nature, predominantly concerned with the production of consumer goods. Although there were areas of concentration determined by other factors, nearness to the consumer market constituted the principal locational pull, hence their importance in the larger towns, especially the capital. Paris was itself a great consumer market, a show place for the products of the quality industries and an industrial centre.[37] Despite the growing attraction which it had for engineering and miscellaneous industries organized on factory lines, it continued to be a stronghold of the small master and the skilled artisan. The rise in incomes and the growth of the market encouraged further division of labour, the splitting off of industries from a parent branch rather than an increase in the size of the firm.

The modern sector was made up of heavy industry and the manufacturing industries using machinery and steam power; the former had taken over from textiles as the chief growing point in the economy in the latter part of the nineteenth century. These were the industries of highly developed capitalism: they used large amounts of fixed capital, machine techniques and an articulated system of division of labour within the productive unit. Inevitably they required a committed labour force, an industrial proletariat of a completely modern type. Organized on a large scale, subject to a greater or lesser extent to the pace imposed by foreign competitors, such enterprises posed new problems of industrial management and control. While some were still family businesses, they were taking on a joint stock company form for purposes of legal convenience if not for economic reasons. The need for a directing body of decision-makers, for a hierarchy of command, for the establishment of specialized departments staffed by experts, was in the logic of the development. Whether or not French business lagged behind in these particulars is not easy to say with any confidence.

In practice it would be difficult to say where the traditional sector ended and the modern one began. It was a shifting dividing line as more processes became susceptible to mechanization. In some fields where new techniques were being introduced the initial capital required for entry might not be large, in others, such as the production of electrical equipment, financial backing was essential from the start.[38] Traditional enterprises might become transformed into firms of a modern character; the family businesses of Peugeot and Bréguet changed their products in accordance with technical and market developments.[39] Some of the old-established textile businesses seemed to resist all change.

Modern historians and economists have passed many stern judgements on French enterprise and the French entrepreneur and have created a stereotype of complacency and routine. No doubt there were firms able to exist for generations which would in other countries have been forced to the wall. There were sheltered industries in which firms were able to continue to produce with antiquated methods abandoned long before in other places. Many entrepreneurs tended to accept a fixed level of demand, were willing to live and let live with competitors producing at higher cost and looked forward to an early retirement when they had accumulated enough capital to live out the rest of their lives as respected rentiers. It is said that the entrepreneur was not highly thought of and that the best talents were directed into other spheres of endeavour. Systems of accounting were said to be primitive and business capital was not distinguishable from the personal holdings of members of the family. That such characteristics were widespread in France is no doubt true; how widespread they were is a matter for empirical enquiry which has not yet been systematically carried out. We have to depend, then, on an assessment of mainly qualitative evidence. Mostly this consists of implied comparisons between particular examples of entrepreneurial behaviour and a norm established probably from the example of entrepreneurship in some other country. But the spectacular growth of a uniform market, one unhindered by traditional survivals, on the lines of the United States did not, and could not, happen in France. The possibilities opened up by the development of the Ruhr did not exist in France, at least not on the same scale. The lack of a great export industry which could have led the way in a more thorough industrial transformation of the country cannot be blamed exclusively upon the entrepreneur. Sufficient has been said about the environmental and structural conditions out of which he emerged, and with which he had to contend, to make an explanation of French economic development primarily in terms of entrepreneurial behaviour seem naïve.

In any case, a modern sector was being built up in a way and at a rate which would not have been possible if all French entrepreneurs had conformed to the stereotype. In the establishment of a modern large-scale steel-making industry and the growth of engineering and allied industries in the period before 1914 technical innovation and organizational and entrepreneurial qualities of a high order were required.[40] The iron-masters seized with commendable rapidity the opportunities presented by the Gilchrist-Thomas process for using phosphoric ores in the converter.[41] On the basis of their foresight large scale integrated plants of the most up-to-date kind were constructed on the Lorraine minette fields which remained in French territory. This was a quite remarkable story of industrial expansion, the creation of what was virtually a new industry capable of producing in the necessary quantity—and range of qualities—what had become the basic constructional material of modern economic life. No little stimulus was received, as in other countries, from the needs of the state for war material, particularly armour-plating and heavy weapons, which taxed the resources of even the largest firms. The firm of Schneider-Creusot showed itself particularly successful in this regard and could hold its own in competition with foreign rivals.

The revolution in steel-making accomplished with the use of the new technical processes required a re-location of the producing centres together with a process of concentration both in plant layout and in financial control. The industry moved definitively into the phase of the giant firm; oligopoly took the place of competition. It was apparent that the heavy capital outlays and risks involved in an industry of this scale rendered the competitive free-for-all quite obsolete.

Some regulation of the market was inevitable. The interests involved were wealthy and powerful; combined together they would be more powerful still. With thoughts of this kind in mind almost all French iron and steel firms were joined together for policy purposes in the famous *Comité des Forges.*[42] Its power, real or potential, the association of the iron and steel industry with the manufacture of war material and the secrecy which surrounded its operations has given this body a more sinister reputation than it perhaps deserves. In any case it signified that large-scale capitalism was incompatible with unchecked competition; its foundation was symbolic of the new era of organization.

The older areas of iron production diminished in importance as local resources of iron ore were exhausted; the Centre and the North continued to be centres of heavy engineering and metal-using industry, much of the material used being brought in from outside. The new steel-making plants grew up on the really productive coalfields (North and Pas de Calais), on the sea coast where imported high-yield ores could be conveniently brought in and, of course, on the Lorraine ore fields. The larger firms extended their operations to the three main centres of the industry as they were concerned both with producing steel and with fabricating it; regional competition was thus curtailed or prevented altogether.

The continued process of concentration imposed by technical considerations required enormous outlays of capital; in turn this imposed the need for further integration as firms sought control over supplies of ore and coal and pushed into the engineering field in order to reduce costs, ensure outlets for their products and spread heavy capital outlays over a larger volume of turnover. Although the major firms in the industry were controlled by a few powerful families, notably the de Wendels and Schneiders, the new conditions required injections of capital from other sources. Joint stock companies were therefore formed and the big steel firms became closely tied to the banks. Confronting powerful foreign rivals, having to be prepared for further heavy investments to keep up with technical change, the giant firms husbanded their financial resources, building up large liquid reserves while keeping dividends to shareholders at a low level. Such a policy came in for some criticism; a certain conflict of interest between directors and shareholders was inherent in the situation. Even holding accumulated reserves in the business was not enough to meet the voracious demands for capital of the steelmakers. Additional stock issues had to be made and the leading steel magnates established intimate contact with the world of banking and finance. A new, more modern face was being given to French capitalism by the upsurge of the steel industry between the 1890's and 1914. It was in this field that the new problems of business administration and control were posed most sharply.

Although France was the second country in known iron ore reserves before 1914, the metallurgical industry was inevitably handicapped by the shortage of good domestically-produced coking coal. The Lorraine steel industry, for instance, became a tributary of the Ruhr coalfield and there were, in fact, close links between German industry and the French Lorraine ore fields and between French firms and German coal. The accidents of political geography prevented the complementarity of Lorraine ore and Ruhr coal from being fully established, especially in view of the mutual suspicion which marked Franco-German relations through most of this period. It did not prevent the de Wendels from conserving their interests, and their political concerns, in both countries.

The character of the iron and steel industry in the older established centres remained strongly marked by their heritage from an earlier time. There is little doubt, however, about the general will towards modernization displayed by the big firms, despite the third generation men who were in control of them. The conditions of the industry imposed their own inescapable logic: it was a choice between expansion and concentration or stagnation and disaster.

By 1900 it can be said that the industry had assumed its modern form. At its peak stood the already proven *Comité des Forges* which concerned itself principally with relations with the government, the price of iron and steel and the situation in foreign markets.[42] How much influence it exerted on the government is difficult to say since its operations were naturally cloaked in a veil of discretion. It was one of the strongest pressure groups working for the return to protection. It was naturally interested in the military and naval arms programme and in foreign affairs. By the 1900's it was flanked by a number of *Chambres syndicales* representing various branches of the industry. Its members were represented on many official and unofficial bodies and it was able to co-ordinate their policies and activities. The general tenor of its influence was, as Eugene Schneider himself once explained, designed to bring about a stabilization of the market and the rational allocation of contracts among the principal firms in order to secure for each of them the maximum continuity of operation.[43] This need was a corollary of the heavy overhead costs characteristic of the steel industry; if met it would enable profits to be kept up by eliminating competition, cutting out plant duplication and spreading costs more evenly over the available volume of orders. Whether this is regarded as 'economic malthusianism' or a rational and excusable practice will depend upon the vantage point of the observer. Some critics of the British iron and steel industry in this period would claim that it did not go far enough in this direction.

The iron and steel industry, by virtue of the immense capital aggregations which composed it, was drawn more closely into the political arena and into contact with financial institutions than most other industries. Its profits were closely bound up with government decisions on armaments, railways and public works, foreign loans and alliances. It pressed hard for a protectionist policy and in politics was strongly nationalist and conservative despite the fact that some of its members had close business ties with their opposite numbers in other countries, including Germany.

The growing productive capacity and plant integration characteristic of the industry brought producers up against the problem of finding markets for such semi-finished products as plates, girders and springs. Once again competition proved unpalatable to all concerned; producers of these articles came together in *comptoirs* which shared the market between members according to their capacity and ensured that orders were fulfilled by the nearest plant in order to keep down transport costs.[44] This further rationalization of the market, assisted no doubt by protection, also contributed to stabilize prices and keep up profits. Although the marketing organization of the French industry did not reach the same pitch as the German it was considerably in advance of the situation prevailing in Britain. In the metallurgical industries, at least, full rein was being given to the tendencies inherent in large scale capitalism while technical change took place steadily and output increased.

Possibly a more detailed examination would reveal significant defects in the French heavy industries; they would scarcely be of the kind for which French industry has typically been blamed. The leaders of these industries seemed to be taking their models from Germany and the United States. If they did not do even better it was largely for reasons beyond their control: the cost of fuel, the nature of the market. Within these limitations they appear to have been acting in line with the technical and organizational demands imposed by large scale operation.[45]

Despite the overall inability of the coal industry to meet home market demand and the disadvantages which flowed from the dispersal of the coal measures and their geological disposition, sections of the industry, notably in the Pas de Calais, came up to international standards of efficiency. Here, and in some other fields, there were large pits using modern methods and equipment, but many small, high-cost pits were kept in operation in the smaller coalfields. The areas of modern mining, especially in Northern France, showed all the characteristics of capitalist industry. The typical industrial landscape, the close-knit mining community virtually without a middle class, the company town which had been built around the pit-head and the slag heap; in externals there was little difference from the corresponding communities in Britain, Belgium or Germany.[46]

In the new fields development had been rapid. Exploitation was in the hands of a few firms which needed large capital to be able to stay in business. In structure, then, these sections of the French coal mining industry were more modern than much of the industry in Britain. The Anzin company was, at this time, with its annual output in 1884 of 2.3 million tons, the largest coal mining enterprise in the world. In the Moselle, a smaller field which underwent rapid expansion in the years before 1914, there were also large modern pits. Part of the coal output was directly controlled by ironmasters; the Wendels produced 2 million tons of their own on the eve of the war.

In the coal industry there were, then, signs of large-scale, highly capitalized enterprise alongside some archaic survivals. There remained, of course, a large deficit in fuel supplies which had to be met by imports from neighbouring countries. To what extent this shortage of fuel had a retarding influence on French industry is a matter for controversy; it can become a convenient explanation for characteristics which have their real origin elsewhere.[47] No doubt industries which required large amounts of coal were handicapped if they had to pay more for their supplies than foreign rivals. Had there been more abundant supplies of good coking coal the change-over from charcoal to coke in the making of iron would no doubt have been more rapid and the industry as a whole would have been stronger; not every country is fortunate enough to have a Ruhr. The failure to make use of coal by-products in the chemical industry does not appear to be explicable solely, or even mainly, in terms of the supply of the material. A similar weakness appeared in Britain where coal was abundant, cheap and of high quality. As already noted, French shipping lacked the advantage of a cheap bulk export; indeed, much coal was imported into France by sea, mainly in British ships and thus to the advantage of its main rival. On the other hand coal was often used wastefully in Britain, notably in the iron and steel industry, while in France an incentive was given to efforts to conserve it, to make use of waste heat and gases generated in steel-making and other processes, to use the lower grades in the manufacture of briquettes and to develop alternative sources of power, though before 1914 it must be said that this had not gone very far.

X

A steady overall tendency towards the modernization of the French industrial structure was discernable from the 1890's. Larger units, using more powerful machines, were characteristic of the producer goods industries which were in the vanguard of this movement. In production as a whole, therefore, the weight of the output of the producer goods industries grew proportionately to that of the consumer goods industries.[48] The latter, which had a considerable degree of protection against foreign competition and which worked often for a local market and for a stable demand, grew in line with the growth of national income. In these fields there was little incentive for producers to change their ways. Even some of the newer industries tended to follow a similar pattern at the start; technical innovations, such as the motor car, did not necessarily lead to heavy capital outlays in the initial stages and might create a new demand for high-class, artisan labour. It was, as has been seen, chiefly in heavy industry that the new trends in technology and business organization were most strongly marked.

The iron and steel industry, and its prolongation in engineering, was the heart of the more advanced, modern sector of the French economy. If the representative plant in this industry was not as gigantic as that in Germany or aggregate production so high as in Britain that can be explained in terms of the market—which was growing less rapidly, was less uniform and was not accompanied by a large export trade—and the raw material and fuel supply. Although there were differences in detail, there was no doubt that this period was notable for the fact that in the course of it France also acquired a modern capital goods industry.

The growing relative weight of the mining and metallurgical industries was a symptom both of continuing industrialization and also of the transition to new forms of capitalism. This was a capitalism of large units, of the joint stock company with its division of ownership and control, of 'big business' having close ties with the banks. It was a capitalism which required at least a national market and tended to seek markets further afield because of the continuous increase in the volume of fixed capital investments. It produced under conditions of increasing returns where competition was thus inherently unstable. Concentration became a dominant trend and a small number of large firms came to occupy each field, or, at least, to set the pace for the rest.

Changes in the same direction took place, as will be seen, in the field of banking as well. It had also become apparent in distribution. Alongside the traditional outlets which, needless to say, were to continue to multiply and dominate in most lines of retail trade, there appeared the department store and the chain store. The early history of the former belongs to the Second Empire; by this period they had secured an accepted place in the urban landscape and the main Paris department stores were already well established. By the end of the century a number of regional chains had appeared in grocery retailing. Developments of this kind were a reflection of the extension of the market and the need for new sales techniques which accompanied the rise of big urban consuming centres. Whether the final product passed to the consumer over the counter of a large store or a small one-man shop it was increasingly likely as 1913 approaches that it had been preceded by publicity in the press or by placard and was sold pre-packed or under a brand name. Parisian entrepreneurs had been among the pioneers of the department store; in other forms of large-scale retailing and in the techniques of marketing the nature of the social structure, and thus of the market, slowed down innovation. Until there was a larger, more uniform demand from a population of town-dwellers much retail trade was likely to conserve its old forms. But products such as chocolate, soap, aperitifs and toiletries were already creating their brand images in the minds of consumers.

From the large-scale integrated steel plant to the branded aperitif bottle the French economy was thus moving into the twentieth century on the same lines as the other advanced countries. It still conserved, and was to retain for decades yet, features which reflected the conditions of a century before. The structure as a whole, and its overall rate of growth, were thus the combined result of the interaction of the newer, more rapidly growing sectors with the more slowly changing, traditionally-oriented parts of the economy.

XI

The growth of a national system of deposit banking was one of the outstanding developments in the French economy during this period which marked the transition to modern large-scale capitalism. The building up of the national networks was a prolonged process and the penetration of the habits which they sought to engender into the pattern of French living took even longer. The banking habit, particularly the use of the cheque, for long remained less widespread than in Britain.

The great deposit banks, of which the *Crédit Lyonnais,* one of the pioneers, has been studied in most detail, tended to confirm some of the existing traits of French capitalism as well as to direct it onto a new course.[49] They differed both from the English joint stock banks and from the German credit banks although, inevitably, since the general functions which they fulfilled were similar, they had much in common with those institutions. They were affected by the specific features of the environment in which they took shape, by the traditions of French finance and especially by the experience of the *Crédit Mobilier* and similar institutions in the immediate past.

French society, because of the weight of the urban petty bourgeoisie and more prosperous peasants, had a relatively large number of modest savers as well as the wealthy families of the *haute bourgeoisie.* This had already been demonstrated in the financial history of the previous régime and in the alacrity with which this wide saving public subscribed to the public loans needed to pay off the war indemnity. A considerable number of people were familiarized with paper titles to wealth and the operation of the capital market, even though banking institutions of a modern type had yet to win their confidence. The rising generation of bankers had thus to find a way to overcome the suspicion of banks in the minds of this mass of savers if they were to realize profits from the many opportunities for investment which appeared to exist but were not being grasped by existing institutions.

With the improvement of transport and communications and the growing integration of the national market, the material conditions for branch banking networks were present from the 1860's. It was these conditions which were seized upon by men like Henri Germain, the presiding genius of the *Crédit Lyonnais.* Their main task, then, was to attract the capital of the middle class savers, win their confidence and establish a solid reputation for probity in financial dealings; to do this they had to offer facilities superior to those otherwise available. In fact, there was not very much competition from other agencies; the services which they proceeded to offer had either not been required very much before or had not interested the established banks. Once the new institutions began to attract customers' deposits the search for secure and profitable investment outlets became their main concern. Success or failure in this regard was crucial; it determined whether or not public confidence would be maintained and deposits grow, or whether it would decline, with the danger of falling victim to the first crisis of confidence. As new institutions, the French deposit banks did not grow up with a developing economy; they had to establish a place in an already active and sophisticated economy, hence the burden which was thrown on the investment side of their activities.

The continued growth of the economy was, however,

generating a demand for a larger volume of credit. Established industry on the whole was not in the market: it supplied most of its own finance for expansion or could obtain what it required through the traditional channels. In these circumstances the banks might have decided to launch new enterprises in industry, becoming industrial investment banks somewhat after the German model. Indeed, in its early years the *Crédit Lyonnais* did engage in such promotional activities, notably in the case of the ill-fated chemical company to use the fuchsine process; this proved a costly and almost disastrous experience and it was not repeated.[50] The alternative was to lend to entrepreneurs who could give some kind of collateral security. Firms in this position seldom sought outside finance for fixed capital investment; as in Britain the tradition of industry was against it. The business which the deposit banks did with industry in France, therefore, consisted principally of granting short and medium term credit secured on the firms' working capital and the personal guarantee of their owners. In sum, then, this represented no more than an extended discount business which was, by its nature, confined almost entirely to already established businesses; the lending policy adopted by the new banks, sound as it was from a banking standpoint, tended to confirm existing structures rather than introduce a dynamic element into them.

This characteristic of French banking did not spring so much from the aversion of bankers to long-term investment as to the lack of demand for it from industry. The alternative was for the bankers to become industrial entrepreneurs themselves or try to find newcomers to industry to whom they could supply financial backing. Since, hardly surprisingly, they were not prepared to do this they could but look outside industry, and even outside France, for long-term borrowers. Indeed, there was already a well-established tradition of foreign loans and men with the connections and experience who could be made use of.[51] As the banks succeeded in tapping a larger volume of funds and came into contact with wider layers of savers so they became interested in the large-scale borrower: railways and public utilities, foreign governments. It was not so much that they invested their own funds in this way as that they persuaded their clients to do so, making use of their name and reputations and the branches which were bringing them into contact with savers all over the country. For the banks this was a lucrative business; it no doubt offered greater returns in a shorter time and with far less risk than would have been involved in direct industrial investment. In effect, the banks acted on a commission basis for the large borrower, usually a foreign government or an enterprise located abroad.

Lack of industrial investment is said to have been a major defect of the French economy in the nineteenth and twentieth centuries.[52] It is difficult to see how either entrepreneurs or bankers can be blamed, however, for pursuing policies which brought them acceptable returns for minimal risks. The banker had to find ways of keeping up current earnings in order to pay dividends to shareholders and interest to depositors. For this reason he preferred to deal with a few large-scale borrowers rather than a large number of smaller ones. He also preferred the gains of an issuing and promotional business, regardless of the ultimate use to which the capital raised was put, rather than the uncertain yields from participation in industrial finance, particularly as he had little chance of obtaining a share in the profits of established business. Who can say whether a more venturesome policy, with a longer time horizon and a more patriotic bent, would have speeded up the industrialization of the French economy?

As it was, the rise and extension of branch banking in the hands of a small number of powerful networks brought about no investment revolution; rather did it confirm and strengthen existing tendencies, both in finance and in industry. On the other hand, the bankers were able to tap the wider sources of savings arising from economic growth through their regional or nation-wide branch systems. It gave them strategic command of a multitude of small capitals which, when brought together, placed unprecedented financial power in the ruling oligarchy of a few banks. At the same time it fitted in with established investment habits: the passivity of the rentier saver was encouraged. The latter left his spare funds with his branch bank and followed the advice of its manager in making his investments; he, in turn, followed the directions of head office in Paris. The rentier sought security and the prospect of a good return. Where and how his interest and dividends were made did not concern him in the least, that was the beauty of the system. He reposed confidence in his financial mentors and measured their performance in the financial columns of his daily newspaper. On occasion, of course, he was grossly deceived and he was plunged into panic and despair.

The most spectacular case of this kind, though there were others, came with the crash of the *Union Générale* in 1882, which some historians have taken as a turning point in French financial history. The story will only be told here in its briefest outline. As happens so often in such cases, this bank was very much the child of one man; Eugène Bontaux, who had a lengthy experience with the railway companies of Central Europe and who, like others more fortunate, seized the opportunities presented by the existence of a vast saving public. But his public was of a special kind. The *Union Générale* was the bank of the catholic and legitimist aristocracy and middle class, mostly of the Lyonnais region, favoured by the Church itself; it was a kind of challenge to the predominance of Protestants and Jews in the French financial world. In the prosperous years from 1878 to 1882 the bank flourished and Bontaux's star rose high with his supporters, if not with the sceptics and his rivals. As a result of his past experience, the investments of the bank were directed towards his old stamping grounds in Central Europe. As with the other banks, high-yield outlets were required to maintain the volume of deposits and enable it to pay attractive rates to shareholders and depositors. But Bontaux's investments turned out disastrously, though this was not apparent as long as the boom lasted. In 1882 the bubble was pricked; mismanagement came to light, risky and doubtful investments were exposed and the *Union Générale* collapsed to give the signal for a general crisis and liquidation, especially acute in Lyons, bringing heavy losses to other firms including the *Crédit Lyonnais.* The boom years were at an end and the French economy entered a phase of severe depression which did not really end until the late 1890's.[53]

The responsibilities of Bontaux are difficult to assess. He maintained that his downfall had been engineered by a conspiracy of his enemies. He remained a hero for the anti-republicans, although many had lost money in his banks. It is certain, however, that his firm had committed itself so heavily in illiquid investments of a controversial nature that it was highly susceptible as soon as speculative optimism gave way to a panic flight into liquidity. Unlike the *Union Générale,* other firms had read the signs of impending storm from the middle of 1881 and had begun to take measures accordingly; by thus safeguarding themselves they closed the credit tap at a time when investors were already fully committed and made the crisis certain. It is unlikely that they did this with the deliberate intention of ruining Bontaux and his supporters.

In short, the excesses of credit and the artificial stimulus to production which went with them were bound to create a revulsion, hitting both the money market and industry at large. Markets were saturated, investment was reduced and a cumulative downturn began which lasted for some years and coincided with an international depression.

The experience of 1882 confirmed the deposit banks in their caution, in the fear of immobilization of reserves and industrial investment. In the retrenchment which took place in the eighties, therefore, the investment portfolios of the banks took on the conservative form which they were to retain, on the whole, for the rest of this period; it was necessary to re-assure the rentiers. In one important sense this policy justified itself. Although there were other financial scandals, the big banking and financial houses were little affected by them or by the money market crises which marked off a number of the cyclical trends in the period in other countries as, for example, the Baring crisis of 1892 and the American panic of 1907. It seems scarcely an exaggeration to say that the pre-1914 generation of French bankers was brought up in the shadow of the 1882 crisis. They feared above all a renewed financial panic and thus sought by the conduct of their affairs to prevent an outbreak of speculation which they would be unable to control. This response was characteristic of French capitalism as a whole. It was better to place foreign loans or large public issues with the middle class savings public, collect the high fees which these services received, and then withdraw.

Banking was perhaps the most pragmatic section of French business when it might have been expected to be the most theoretically-minded.[54] It followed rather than led; although because of its influence it appeared to lead or even to dominate the economy it gave no real leadership.[55] The emphasis was upon collecting the spare funds of a conservative and unadventurous middle class, paying out the coupons of the rentiers and encouraging them to leave their takings with the bank or to accept its advice in further investment and to make their payments by cheque. The desire for liquidity and the fear of speculation reduced, if it did not preclude, long-term lending to industry. Paradoxically, much of the investment which it promoted as an alternative turned out in the long run to be much more hazardous and of doubtful benefit to the national economy.

Through this period the banking habit was spreading, although Frenchmen continued to make a large proportion of their payments in hard money, not even banknotes. It was becoming a matter of course for businesses of all types to have an account with a bank and to make use of the facilities which it offered. In this way branch banks became a feature of every town, even the smallest; another link was established between provincial France and the capital. Immense financial resources were concentrated in the control of a small number of bank boards.

No doubt some residual suspicion of banks remained; the use of the cheque, for instance, was far less widespread than in Britain. But the rise of the deposit banks was one of the most remarkable changes which the French economy underwent in this period; for the first time the whole country was endowed with modern credit facilities.

XII

The Bank of France kept pace with the development of a national system of banking by itself extending its network; from 115 branches in 1881 the number had grown to 583 by 1913. As was its practice, it discounted small bills presented by tradesmen and from 1895 the lower limit was reduced to 5 francs. It was, writes Clapham, 'pursuing a vigorous policy, extending its branches, opening deposit accounts for all comers and simplifying its formalities'.[56] Its general policy exuded prudence and conservation. Its principal function, after all, was, as a note-issuing bank, to defend the currency. This explains both its policy of building up large specie reserves and its function as a bankers' bank exercised through rediscounting for the commercial banks. The growth of the networks of deposit banks placed more emphasis on this rôle. The large stock of gold which it held could be used to cushion temporary strains on the balance of payments, arising mostly from the need for emergency grain imports in time of bad harvests. However, its influence was thrown towards the maintenance of stability rather than towards a conscious acceptance of responsibility for credit control. The discount rate was seldom changed and was not used in a deliberate manner to promote business expansion or to moderate it during booms. In this respect the practice of the bank reflected the liberal economic thinking which prevailed in financial and government circles. In any case the money market in Paris was nothing like as specialized and important as was Lombard Street so that it would not have been easy to make its rate effective. In some respects, then, the financial system still showed signs of immaturity although the circulation of credit had greatly improved since the sixties.

If the rise of national banks was the main tendency of this period in financial history, the old banking houses remained and a good deal of banking was still conducted by regional, rather than national, institutions. Despite the extension of credit facilities, many private transactions were carried on in hard money and the note was more widely used than the cheque. Much gold passed into the proverbial woollen stocking of the peasant or small saver or was hoarded by the prudent bourgeois; the historical memory of past financial excesses continued to be potent.

The stability of the monetary unit, and thus of prices, seemed to have become part of the order of nature. The paper franc had become completely convertible again by 1878. The slow downward price trend favoured savers and continued confidence in the monetary unit; there were some cries of alarm when a powerful upward trend became discernible in the years before 1914. Apart from these movements, the value of the franc appeared to the saver and investor to be something as immutable as that of the gramme or the metre: established by impersonal forces out of reach of the influence of the state.[57]

Confidence in the franc no doubt contributed to the prevailing confidence in bourgeois security and material well-being which made the 1900's *la belle époque.* Perhaps security became too much of an end in itself, to which businessmen and the rentiers adapted their habits. It underlay the investment policy of the great banking house as well as of the *père de famille*; it influenced the great industrial concerns as well as the retail draper in the small town. In the decades of devaluation and inflation which followed the First War this golden age of monetary stability was looked back to with envy and nostalgia. In practice, if it gave the middle class a sure anchor which it later felt the lack of, it also tended to confirm conservative habits and routine, to favour those in established positions and to discourage boldness and experiment; to be, in other words, the corollary of the lack of drive and initiative for which the French entrepreneur is often blamed. For the time the virtues of stability were clear enough; looking back, those impressed with the desirability of economic growth may not be so sure.

XIII

A continuous increase in the volume of savings seeking outlets, the already established connections of French financiers with foreign centres, the interest of the deposit banks in floating large loans and the activities abroad of French entrepreneurs, technicians and engineers are the main reasons for the growing export of capital in this period.

Drawing capital from France were the demands of expanding capitalist projects in all parts of the globe, the insatiable needs of governments confronted by ever rising expenditures, especially on costly modern military equipment, and the relatively greater yields which investment abroad seemed to offer over the available alternatives at home. The interest of the banks in the profits to be derived from the issuing business has already been referred to and may be taken as an important factor in the volume and character of French foreign investment.

The Paris capital market thus became second only to London as an international financial centre in this period. In particular it became the main source of loans for France's ally, Russia, from the 1890's, and more generally for the countries of Eastern Europe and the Near East.

The financial history of the period begins with the war indemnity imposed on France by the victor in the Treaty of Frankfurt. Not only did the loans floated to meet this penalty bring out the hidden reserves of patriotic Frenchmen, it also resulted in the mobilization of their foreign securities by the government and the attraction of foreign capital into holding the French *rentes.* French recovery from the financial effects of the war was rapid. From about 1873 foreign-held securities were being re-purchased by Frenchmen and a renewed demand for foreign securities came from French investors. By the end of the decade it is safe to say that the pre-war position in respect to foreign investment had been restored. From then until the First World War French holdings of foreign government stock and French-held capital abroad steadily increased; the country remained the second largest international creditor.[58] This 'rentier' position of the economy seemed to have become an established feature of French capitalism.

The measurement of French capital exports poses some exceptionally difficult problems; official figures were not compiled so that estimates have to be made from such evidence as is available. For our purposes this problem need not be discussed in detail, it is sufficient to have a general idea of the amounts involved, the annual addition to capital held abroad and the income from past investments. In addition it is useful to know what proportion of French savings went into foreign investment, whether the yield was higher than on capital invested inside the country and whether French industry was benefited or not from the flow of investment overseas. Fortunately there are useful studies which enable tentative answers to be given to these problems which are susceptible to quantitative analysis; there are others which, in the nature of things, cannot be answered accurately or which are a matter of opinion.

It is apparent from the statistics that the annual additions to French capital held abroad corresponded closely to the income from past investment. There is some difference among the authorities as to whether this income was large enough, taking one year with another, to yield a favourable balance to cover other outgoings or not. In either case it is apparent that the income which made possible the continued growth of investment abroad was generated from existing investments of French capital. Taken on a national scale, there was a continuing reinvestment of past earnings. At the same time changes took place in the holding of assets and claims to income, in the number of Frenchmen who held foreign assets and in the amounts they held. These were transactions between Frenchmen which took place on the French capital market; in the aggregate they were neutral as far as France's foreign balance was concerned. On the other hand, this market could be used by foreign governments and enterprises, private or public, or French enterprises operating abroad, as a source of long-term capital funds. They had, that is to say, access to the general pool of French savings. In turn it can be said that this pool was constituted in part from the earnings on past overseas investment.

Foreign investment must be regarded as an integral part of the structure of French capitalism in this period. In pursuit of profits with hoped-for security one-half to one-third of French savings in the period 1880 to 1914 was re-invested abroad. About 75 per cent of the investment was in government bonds; this was a measure of the search for security and also, to some extent, of the political element in international lending. The government was distinctly interested in seeing that its principal foreign allies raised the money needed on the Paris market; press comments relayed these desires to the investors, or they followed the counsels given by their banks. How far these loans benefited French industry is difficult to say; probably to a lesser extent than in the previous period. Industry, especially heavy industry, would have liked to insist that loans made abroad brought orders for French manufactures, arms and machinery. Russia, as a main borrower, used a large part of the proceeds of its loans to make purchases from other countries and her trade did not reflect the close ties which existed with France as a creditor and an ally. However, presumably Russia's trading partners directly, or at a further remove, increased their demand for goods and services from France. The strongest argument against these loans to governments was that they were unproductive in an economic sense, were made to insecure régimes and contributed to the arms race which preceded the First World War. And, in the end, the Russian and other governments simply defaulted, leaving the French rentier with nothing but worthless paper.[59]

Even the yields on foreign investment do not appear to have been strikingly higher than those obtained on investment at home. However, the existence of this foreign outlet—which, as has been seen was also a main source of capital accumulation—must have contributed to keeping up the rate of return at home. It is difficult to say conclusively whether foreign investment reduced the capital available for development at home. The State was able to raise all the funds it required. Private firms either could not, or would not attract the income accruing from past investment through stock exchange issues. Like London, the Paris market had a bias towards foreign investment. As has been seen, it meant lucrative business for the banks and had other advantages which investment in industry at home did not possess. This characteristic was stressed by White and has been confirmed by other studies. The banks were not very concerned with what happened to the loans which they promoted and what return investors received on their money. The more doubtful the credit of the borrower the higher the return for the underwriting bank and thus the temptation to paint the prospect in glowing colours. With the press often venal (and the government perhaps interested in the success of an issue) the average rentier looked in vain for a good investment counsellor and firmly believed, for example, that Russian state bonds were a gilt-edged investment. In this connection, then, the banks appeared, not as impartial advisers, but as handsomely rewarded intermediaries between financially doubtful foreign borrowers and the gullible small investor.

Foreign state bonds, like those of the French government, were exempt from tax and it was, in any case, easier to evade tax on foreign than on home issues. This may have had some influence with a public notoriously remiss about meeting its fiscal obligations and able to resist a progressive income tax through most of this period. White's calculations suggest that, taking account of defaults before 1913, yields were little higher than those on investments at home. However, if this volume of savings had also been pressing on the capital market at home the rate of return would have been lower than that actually recorded; such a hypothesis assumes a quite different structure for French capitalism than that which had been evolving since the beginning of the century.

XIV

France participated fully in the colonial expansion which characterized the latter part of the century.[60] Statesmen favourable to colonial acquisitions made great play with the economic benefits which the metropolis was likely to derive from them. However, much of the newly acquired territory was of little immediate economic consequence; heavy outlays had to be made, not only on military expeditions, but also on the building up of an infrastructure before any calculable benefits began to become apparent for the national economy.[61] In the meantime, judged as an economic enterprise of the state, financed by the taxpayer, outlays exceeded incomes and it might seem right to regard the French colonies as 'millstones' rather than money-makers.[62] Even the colonies suitable for European settlement attracted few colonists from France; many of those who settled in Algeria when the economic prospects of that country improved from the 1880's came from other Mediterranean countries.

The economic motive forces in imperialism can hardly be evaluated by a contemplation of yearly balance sheets of revenue and expenditure.[63] For one thing, even if the colonies were to be considered exclusively as economic enterprises, a considerable period of investment would have to be allowed for before mineral resources could be developed, plantations laid out or trade developed with the backward and sometimes savage inhabitants. In the nature of things, too, a governmental apparatus had to be installed and garrisons provided to defend them against predatory European rivals or the rebellious inhabitants. Imperialism was closely related to militarism and nationalism, as well as to the economy. When all the major powers were making a drive for colonies no single power which wanted to hold its political place in the world would be likely to stand aside. The costs of militarism, like those of colonial expansion, had to be met by the taxpayers and for many, if not most, the benefits derived from colonies were indeed doubtful.

As in the case of capital export, with which it was closely associated, colonial expansion offered benefits to certain economic interests. In the first place there were the contractors and entrepreneurs who supplied the expeditionary forces and then built roads, railways, harbour installations and so on at the taxpayers' expense or from the proceeds of loans. In this way colonies provided an outlet for surplus capital, although to a lesser degree than foreign countries. Special banks were founded to carry forward this process of development which was designed, of course, to serve the interests of

France. Administrators and soldiers found scope for their ambitions and made careers, looked forward to the day when they could retire quietly, still relatively young, to their native town or village.

The colonies offered privileged markets for French exporters, though the privileges which their products enjoyed in the French market may have adversely affected some agriculturalists in the mother country.[64] Later, as they were developed, and particularly as certain tropical and semi-tropical products became of increasing commercial importance, the colonies became important sources of supply. It is possible that these products were obtained on more favourable terms than would have been possible on the open market. Again, this import-export trade offered scope for French enterprise, financial as well as commercial, centred on ports like Marseilles and Bordeaux.[65]

It should be emphasized, then, that colonial policy benefited individuals and interested groups rather than the national economy as a whole. This was understood by those who opposed it at the time. But to recognize that the economic stake in colonies was not very great in absolute terms does not mean that, marginally, it may not have played a decisive rôle in shaping the nature of the economy at this time.

France, like Britain, had, in any case, its 'informal empire', notably in the Balkans and parts of the Middle East. French capital ranged quite widely over other parts of the world too. The home market for investment appeared to be too limited, the opportunities arising abroad irresistibly attractive. Capital did not pour into colonies simply because they flew the tricolor; financiers were too concerned with the balance sheet to be moved by patriotic gestures. The process of investment, after all, was cosmopolitan; international trade, if influenced by tariffs, still reasonably moderate, *was* international. It was possible for foreigners to seize opportunities in French colonies which Frenchmen overlooked or rejected as too risky. Foreign countries steadily increased their trade with French colonies without sharing in the cost of their administration and defence. But these undoubted facts do not mean that there was no reality in the concept of economic imperialism; they do not disprove the view that it arose in response to an inner compulsion in the advanced countries, of which France was one.

Not the absolute, but the marginal influence of the empire, formal and informal, was perhaps decisive. Enough capital flowed abroad to compensate for the insufficiently rapid expansion of investment opportunities at home, thus keeping up the rate of return. The empire provided that additional market for capital goods which made the difference between an encouraging rate of profit and a disappointing one for the enterprises involved. It provided an extra market for manufacturers at home which made the crucial difference in the scale of operations, especially when production was subject to increasing returns. It offered raw materials on more favourable terms than might otherwise have been obtainable. At least that is the hypothesis—and that is how it must have seemed to the many particular interests which colonial expansion brought into existence. Much of the rest was done by political legerdemain and belief in the civilizing mission of French culture.

Of course, it may be argued that most of the tangible gains of colonies could have been obtained by other means with no cost to the taxpayer at all. Abstractly considered the capital invested in colonies and foreign countries could have been employed more productively in France; but, after all, in the main it was the market which decided otherwise. The distribution of wealth, the structure of society, the nature of the capital market, the conditions of international competition all militated against a different disposition of available capital at this stage. Economic imperialism thus seems to have been in the nature of things.

It is sometimes said that the export of capital and economic imperialism testified to the 'maturity' of French capitalism. This is only so in a relative sense : the lack of outlets for capital investment and the inability of the economy to grow faster under the prevailing conditions. But 'mature' French capitalism still had an inordinately high proportion of its population in agriculture, it was insufficiently industrialized and contained regions which were still very underdeveloped with a per capita income considerably below the national average. The market gave insufficient incentive for this relative backwardness and unevenness of internal development to be overcome by a higher rate of investment at home. Bankers, financiers, investors responded to profit expectations as they saw them at the time. They did not will the consequences of having behaved in a particular way when making their investment decisions in the light of market indications. The weight of the inherited structures rather than deliberate calculations by bankers or by anybody else gave rise to a state of affairs which left crucial sectors of French industry starved of capital and public investment at a lower level than might, with hindsight, have appeared desirable.

The French economic structure did show, in some respects, signs of age, while in others it suffered, not from 'maturity' but from 'underdevelopment'. This was only to appear clearly some years after the Second World War when the continued possibilities for growth began to be exploited—and when some forms of colonial enterprise had been given up.

It has also been said that French capitalism had a 'rentier' character in this period.[66] Of course, national wealth did not depend upon tribute from colonies or income from past investment overseas to the exclusion of that generated by productive activities at home. As has been seen, this past investment represented the source of much of the annual addition made to French savings—which again found outlets outside the country. In addition, the peculiar composition of French society, and the aspirations which it inspired in its members, did give rise to a large volume of savings from a numerous body of savers. There were many rentiers, and to live on the proceeds of savings seems to have been the aspiration of the petty bourgeoisie. The habits and motives of these people, in turn, obviously contributed, not only to the make-up of the society, but also to the character and pace of economic life. Essentially their motives were not 'modern', though their savings were mobilized by men in charge of the most modern credit institutions. Even the banks were only able to modify, but not transform, the attitudes and habits of Frenchmen; they might hold bank deposits and buy Russian bonds on the advice of their bankers, but practically all their everyday transactions were made in gold or silver coins as was the way with their grandfathers. The bankers, as well as the rentiers, distrusted investment in industry, even though experience showed that the great industrial dynasties (which for the most part, of course, had their own internal sources of finance) had been able to outlive a succession of political régimes. The political uncertainties which remained after 1875, when the Republic was at last established, were of a kind likely to affect general business confidence rather than the *rentes*. Industrialists could not use capital which was not made available to them; some looked jealously at the flow of capital abroad or sought to tie foreign loans to the purchase of French goods; but it also seems agreed that they were reluctant to seek outside sources of finance, especially of equity capital. Nor should it be overlooked that the banks were in fact supplying ever larger amounts of working capital to industry and trade in the years before 1914; that tended, of course, to strengthen those in established positions, to confirm the existing structure, not to change it.

All the segments of the picture fit convincingly together. To deplore one or another aspect, or to deplore the absence of some element which could have changed it—assisted its growth, in particular—is an interesting exercise in partial equilibrium analysis which may have its uses. The task of historical explanation, of understanding why things were as they were, would not necessarily be much advanced thereby. Moreover, to assume that one element did change raises certain difficulties: that there was no endogenous factor able to cause it and that if one element changed none of the other components would have been unaffected. The economy would not then have been different in one particular; it would have been completely different. There was, on the other hand, no single root cause of the character and performance of the French economy in this period, unless we say that it was the weight of its history combined with the dynamic processes of a market economy. It is the whole of the historically-created structure which has to be examined in the closely inter-related and dialectical unity of its many interdependent and interacting parts. The lessons of this study suggest that the familiar stereotypes should be treated with suspicion, not because they may not contain some measure of truth but that they may easily stand in the way of historical explanation and further investigation. Moreover, they rest upon largely qualitative evaluation and contain an implied comparison with some ideal norm or the performance and behaviour of individuals or institutions in quite different environments.

XV

French population trends offer one possible explanation for

the performance of the French economy in the late nineteenth and early twentieth centuries. The precocious appearance of a tendency for the population to increase at a decreasing rate, with the consequence that between 1869 and 1939 population grew by only 4 per cent, might have been expected to have adverse economic consequences.[67] At least, the peculiarities of the French economy which have been noted must have been in some measure a product of this surprising population pattern. At the same time, economic forces may have had something to do with the production of this trend. We are obviously here once again on tricky ground. The economic influences on birth rates, marriage rates and death rates are difficult to disentangle from the social, cultural, religious, political, medical and other factors which were involved. It is equally difficult to discern a specifically demographic factor in the processes of economic change, or at least to isolate it from all the others with which it interacts.

A tendency towards the restriction of family size becomes discernible from the latter part of the eighteenth century. The fall in the birth rate becomes even more marked from about the middle of the following century. Population had been growing rapidly before the Revolution of 1789 and in absolute size it continued to grow at a steady rate in the first part of the next century, but there was not in that period a 'population explosion' comparable to that which took place in other European countries, especially Britain, Germany and Italy. The proportion of French people to the total European population thus declined and some observers have been tempted to ascribe the waning influence of France in many spheres, including the economic, to this apparent loss of vital force. The virtual stagnation of total population caused much concern on political and military as well as economic and social grounds. It generated exceptional interest in demographic problems among scholars and had a strong influence on policy in the twentieth century on matters such as birth control and family allowances.[68]

In some respects the trend which established itself in France only heralded what was to become characteristic of all the advanced countries. It signalized greater conscious control over procreation and over death; in the first case this was control by individuals who determined to limit the numbers of their children without thought about the outcome for society, in the latter it was medical and social action which affected individuals by increasing their chances of living to an old age. The limitation of family size appears to have arisen as part of the development of that possessive individualism which arose on the same soil as the Revolution and was given freer rein by it. The Napoleonic Code, with its insistence upon partible inheritance was, in a sense, in contradiction with it: it certainly gave it a special twist. Of course, the division of peasant lands among the heirs was a long-established custom over much of France so that the Code only gave legal effect to what would have happened in any case.[69] And, where the custom was for only one child to inherit, the practice continued despite the law. The combination of more conscious individualism with partible inheritance in a society of small property-owners for whom their land was their patrimony and the basis of economic existence, led to family limitation as the only alternative to the splitting up of land into smaller, fragmented and uneconomic holdings. *Morcellement* had been a feature of the rural landscape even before the Revolution; it would have gone much further afterwards had the peasantry not limited the number of its children so that there was a better chance of the property passing intact to one heir. Even without the Code this motive may have operated.

The growing, but not of course universal, peasant practice of family limitation found a parallel in the habits of the bourgeoisie on the same basis of possessive individualism. Aiming to rise in the social scale, to consolidate his property and constitute a patrimony the urban bourgeois was a malthusian, as it were, by nature. He was in most cases a member of a class whose property consisted largely of real estate and who carried on a trade, or practised a profession, for which at least a modest capital was required. Children were not economic assets; their social future had to be provided for—dowries for the daughters, capital to train the sons or set them up in business. Men who wanted to increase their riches, or lead a stylish urban life, did not want to encumber themselves with a large progeny. Looking at it more from the standpoint of health and wellbeing, desiring to lead a fuller social life, their wives concurred. Perhaps the lack of dynamic possibilities in the economy help to explain the contrast with Victorian England; indeed there were signs of the trend being arrested in the closing half of the Second Empire but it was not sustained.

The French family was closely bound up, among the peasantry and the bourgeoisie, with the preservation of a patrimony and its transmission, though arranged marriages, dowries and inheritance to the next generation. The opportunities had to be made by the family, rather than grasped from a dynamic environment. There was a background of social upheaval which strengthened the desire for security and led, amongst other things, to a high estimation being placed upon state employment and political influence. The urban working class family, as well as the peasant family in the less prosperous areas or those in which property continued to be transmitted to a single heir, tended to be larger; there was less thought for the future or no property to be transmitted. In industrial and mining areas children rapidly became economic assets; the environment did not favour malthusian restraints. These sections of the population, particularly the industrial working class, did not yet constitute a major segment of the population. In fact, as it grew, standards rose and outlooks changed. By the period now being considered the workers were also practising family limitation and it was being advocated by their organizations.[70] Continued urbanization acted in the same way; peasant immigrants into the city had fewer children than they probably would have had in the village.

The slow rate of French population growth arose out of a unique combination of conditions; some of these were peculiar to France at this time, others were to be found in all high-income, urbanized societies. Some of the factors which influenced family size, and thus the population pattern, found expression in other decisions of economic significance—in the investment policy of the *père de famille*, in the behaviour of the family firm, in the financial policy of the state—thus contributing to the aggregate structure of the French economy. If population restriction can be called malthusian, by an extension of the term to other spheres, 'malthusianism' became a term descriptive of restrictionism in economic life as a whole. In both cases there was a rational, individualist adjustment to a specific environment which, in turn, tended to strengthen its rigidities, but not to prevent change altogether —the dynamic forces of industrial capitalism were, after all, too strong for that. Whatever its defects, malthusianism did not prevent growth and it made possible a comfortable standard of living for a substantial minority of the population.

A population trend at one time determines the future level of population, which is then a given quantity when the future becomes the present. The habits implanted in the late eighteenth century thus determined future rates of population growth, the absolute levels of population at each stage and its age composition. In examining the economy the population factor operates in determining its development in the past and is something unalterable in its economically significant features for the period under consideration. In turn the developments in the economy will be among the forces which confirm or alter existing population trends.

In this period, then, the slow rate of population growth, and the changing age composition which accompanied it, have to be examined from the standpoint of their possible economic repercussions. Again it must be understood that it is difficult to isolate the population factor from all the other factors which operated on the economy. Take, for instance, the labour supply. A slow rate of population growth may be assumed to have limited the supply of labour. But this was combined with a strong peasant sector and a distribution of property which tended to keep many people on the land. The problem was presented, rather, as one of attracting population from the villages into the factories, mines and urban occupations in general. However, people were leaving the rural areas and there was no permanent labour scarcity in the towns as far as can be seen. But the demand for labour reflected a situation in which the population growth was slow so it may well have been that the economy would have grown faster had population increase been greater. On the demand side a larger population could have increased its aggregate size and changed its shape; various assumptions are possible about how this could have been done. If this argument is used it implies that the favourable possibilities offered by a growing population would in fact have been taken advantage of. A wider market at home would then have encouraged further specialization and investment in industry; there would have been greater economies of scale and external economies. What is called 'demographic investment'—hospitals, schools, houses in which serious deficiencies were later to stand out—would have been encouraged. As an increase in population could only have come through a growth in family size, considerable changes would have taken place in the pattern of consumption and perhaps in the amount of savings. Demand for food and basic necessities would, presumably, have increased while that for the bourgeois comforts would have decreased. A considerable difference in the financial system would have been involved, as well as in state policy, if the population increase was to have the effect of accelerating growth.

What is involved in criticism of the actual population trends is, therefore, the postulation of a different one, together with an array of assumptions to go with it. Nothing would have been the same if population growth had been maintained at a higher rate; that includes social attitudes and behaviour patterns. In short a major social shift would have been required; France would have been quite a different place from the one which history knows.

There does, then, seem to be a close and intimate relationship between the demographic trend and the socio-economic structure. At the time it is not certain that the slowing down of population growth was disadvantageous for the economy in its then form.[71] The consequences of population ageing had not yet had a marked effect. The proportion of producers was still favourable to growth; perhaps because of this, weaknesses in the French economy, which were to reveal themselves decades later, are masked in the statistics. The more evident adverse consequences of the trends established in the nineteenth century were to plague France after they had been further aggravated by the manpower losses of the First World War and the sharp fall in birth rates during the war years. Historical experience then enabled demographers to argue that unless steps were taken to reverse the trend France would have to face severe strains in the future as a result of population stagnation and ageing. In the period since the Second World War there has, indeed, been a recovery in the birth rate, population has grown both by natural increase and by immigration and there has, as a consequence, been a renewal of the lower levels of the age pyramid. This recent experience demonstrates the fact that the established trends were not irreversible; it has also revealed the inadequacy of past investment in the public sector geared to population growth.

The population problem, although attracting attention as early as the 1860's, was not to become acute until the twentieth century but its roots clearly lay in the development of a bourgeois society under the special conditions outlined in this work. The population pattern, therefore, mirrored rather well the specific characteristics of French social and economic development, its measured progress and its emphasis on material security and stability. It showed how, as each family took thought for its own future in an atomistic way, it created difficulties for the nation as a whole in the long run.

XVI

France thus conserved a demographic pattern unlike that of practically every other country in course of industrialization, a pattern which grew out of the practices and preferences of a peasant and petty bourgeois society. By the late nineteenth century, with population growing only slowly, the drift to the towns continued, but by this time it was characteristic of most urbanized environments that family limitation was moving down the social scale. The new layers of wage-earners who moved into the growing towns and mining areas of France in this period thus tended to adopt the small family standard and other habits of the prudent petty bourgeois: the savings bank account, the aspiration to early retirement and a place in the country, a daughter well-married and a son in the civil service.

That is not to say that there was not, at the same time, a deep class-consciousness which kept the classes apart. Class struggles in France had been fought as military operations in 1848 and 1871; industrial conflicts in the period 1880-1914 were often bitterly contested and accompanied by violence and bloodshed. But what the workers fought for was usually no more than a modest improvement in wages and material conditions, the 'myth of the general strike' which was to make way for a new industrial republic of worker-controlled industries was only consciously adopted by a minority, usually the more highly skilled and better paid.

Even the basic rights of trade union organization were granted belatedly and grudgingly. Not until 1884 did the legislators of the Third Republic repeal the Le Chapelier law and those sections of the penal code which outlawed combinations and strikes. When they did, however, they only recognized a state of fact, since trade unions were already in existence in a number of trades.[72] However, in the first period, but still under the shadow of repression which followed the Commune, working class aspirations mainly made themselves effective in political form; socialist parties came before trade unions.

France was behind in factory legislation and did little in the field of social security before 1914. The working class was thus fully exposed to the laws of the market. The development of industry produced a rising demand for labour while prices of basic necessities tended to be stable or falling. Although there were great diversities in working class conditions there was a general trend towards an improvement, at least in real wages, from the eighties.[73] Even in the coal-mining and textile factory towns, the most typical and depressing products of the industrial revolution, the workers were emerging from the deep misery which had been the lot of the great majority a decade or two before.[74] In these older industries, in the new technologically advanced industries, as well as in the better-paid artisan trades, a kind of labour aristocracy existed or was in process of formation. On the other hand, in the industries which employed mainly unskilled labour—newcomers from the country, immigrants—wages remained low or 'sweating' might prevail.

The diversity in this industrial structure thus meant great diversity in the wages and conditions of different sections of the working class. A notable feature of French industry was the paternalism of some employers who provided company housing and welfare schemes, including in some cases family allowances. The dispersion of some French plants made this policy necessary, and also left the workers little alternative but to accept a régime which, while giving them greater security, was designed principally to provide a stable labour force by tying the worker to the enterprise. In other cases, however, workers were able to preserve a tenacious independence accompanied by an open contempt for the ways of the bourgeois and the keeping alive of the memories of 1848 and 1871.

Little can be said in precise terms about the development of the labour market in these years. More industrial workers and miners were now of the second or third generation, a real hereditary proletariat. On the other hand, the rapid rise of new industries in some areas meant that there was still a problem of recruiting a new, raw labour force, in large part from a peasant background. There was not, then, always a reservoir of labour upon which employers could draw as in the older industrial towns or in Paris—no doubt this helped to explain the attraction of these areas for new enterprises or new industries. Where these required a high level of technical skill on the part of the workman, as they often did, he had more in common with the old type of handicraftsman than with the semi-skilled worker of machine industry.[75] And, as has been pointed out earlier, the older industrial forms still survived, with small units often employing only a few craftsmen.

Outside a few special areas, recruitment to the industrial proletariat took place on an individual or family basis and it extended over a long period. Newcomers to the towns, because they came from the ranks of a still large and vigorous peasantry, need not necessarily have broken all ties with their native village. Where a demand for wage-labour grew up in the provinces it might be met in part by worker-peasants who still lived in the country or had a plot of land. The recruits to industry belonged to families, and those families might have land to which they had some claim. Some might hope, eventually, to return to their village of origin, even when it was at a considerable distance from their place of work. Equally, newcomers, coming one by one rather than in great masses, would tend to merge into the existing social landscape, could more easily forge links with the local petty bourgeoisie, at least up to the 1860's or 1870's, and perhaps find employment in the new fields being created by the growth of public services (postmen, policemen, clerks), transport and distribution, in short, the tertiary sector. Such wage-earners, though their real earnings might not rank among the highest, would tend to be less class-conscious in a specifically working class sense. They had not been inured to the permanence of their position as people without property and sought to escape from the wage-earning class rather than to raise its position in society or bring it to power.

No doubt, alongside this trend, the growth of industry, from the seventies, did tend to increase the size and social weight of the modern-type, hereditary industrial proletariat and to separate it more trenchantly from other classes. But this was not a clear-cut development, it was still more of a regional than a national phenomenon and the industrial working class remained a minority of the total population. The French working class was in process of change; it was the basis for new political movements and a conscious minority formed militant trade unions—these organizations and their policies reflected in turn the specific features of the class of which they were a projection. The relationship between the changing composition of the working class with its different layers on the one hand, and the development of socialist and trade union organization on the other, deserves more detailed study than can be given it here.

XVII

In the economy of pre-1914 France the State played a mainly passive role.[76] It is true that part of the railway system had passed into its ownership, that it had established a monopoly in the production of tobacco and matches, and that there was a pervading tradition of state intervention which found expression in protection, in the special favours extended to shipping and in the influence exerted through public works and arms contracts.[77] Although the actual impact of the state, with its army of over 400,000 functionaries, was no doubt appreciable, the prevailing opinion was strongly against any extension of its activities. The middle class strongly resisted the imposition of an income tax; succession duties of 15 per cent were denounced as expropriation and a deterrent to saving, and even social reformers and socialists demanded a balanced budget.[78] Consciousness of the importance of economic policy hardly dawned on the leading politicians of the age. It was not a central subject of debate, apart from the controversy over the tariff which was more or less settled in the nineties, and played little part in the speeches and writings of statesmen and politicians, even those of the left. No doubt the prevailing views reflected liberal adages learned in youth, or repeated in the press, even though practice might lead to them being disregarded. Although an extending range of state activities may, therefore, be discerned it was a piecemeal and unconscious process which fell behind statist-minded Germany and the more pragmatic Britain.

The market therefore prevailed. Even the protectionists did not favour interference with its operation at home. Departures in policy in the direction of positive guidance by the state in agriculture or in industry was out of the question. Its influence in these fields was largely tangential, for example through the provision of educational facilities or information, and critics have pointed out how little it really did. In the main, then, it was the free play of market forces which determined the quality and performance of the economy. Quantitative measures, although they have numerous shortcomings, give a more or less accurate summary of results. There was steady, but not spectacular growth. At certain stages other countries grew faster. In particular French people formed a smaller proportion of the European population than they had done a century before. Aggregate production rose, but the spread of industrialization reduced the relative weight of the French contribution in the total industrial output of Europe or of the world. On the other hand, although France was overtaken by Germany, she retained her second place as a continental industrial producer and compared to Britain in the years immediately before 1914 her position may have slightly improved. Of course, output per head still remained below that in Britain; the sheer weight of the agrarian sector saw to that. In some areas France was as industrialized as any part of Europe and income per head was high; but the average level was dragged down by the low productivity of rural France, the large areas which had not changed fundamentally since the eighteenth century. It was this still excessively large agrarian sector, plus the preservation of small units and archaic methods in parts of industry and distribution, which gave the French economy its appearance of retardation, and which helped to drag it into virtual stagnation between the wars.

Qualitative appraisal of an economy's performance depends very much upon the assumptions, often implicit, of the observer and the advantages of hindsight which he possesses. There is a tendency to produce stereotypes of entrepreneurial behaviour, of the reaction of workers and peasants to economic change and of 'national character'. There is a tendency to underestimate the weight of 'objective conditions' which so largely determined the range of possibilities open to the principal economic actors. This applies especially to the strictures upon the alleged shortcomings of the French entrepreneur, or of French industry as a whole, during this period.

A number of considerations may be suggested to show the restricted validity of such generalizations or stereotypes. There were, of course, many small firms operating in France, perhaps below optimum; their behaviour may have seemed irrational from a strictly profit-and-loss point of view; but such small firms proliferated in Britain and even in Germany's industrial heart-land of the Ruhr.[79] If French exporters did not pay enough attention to customers' requirements or go into foreign markets sufficiently aggressively, the same things have frequently been said about the British entrepreneur. It is true that the French synthetic dye-stuffs industry, after a promising beginning, collapsed before the organized ingenuity of German technology and business, but so did the British.[80] French industry was not, before 1914, organized on continuous flow or mass production lines, but neither was the German. France had become dependent upon light engineering products from the U.S.A. and specialized machines and machine tools from Germany, but so had other countries, including Britain. The agrarian sector was abnormally large if compared with its diminutive rôle in Britain; it was less extraordinary by continental standards. The French peasant, largely because he lacked government assistance, failed to develop an efficient system of grading, packing and marketing to enable his produce to win a place in the export markets as producers in Denmark and Holland did—but even the British farmer did not do these things on any scale until after the First World War. If French agriculture had large backward sectors it also had some more efficient ones; by comparison with much of Europe it was individualist and advanced.

In the initial development of new techniques French technicians and entrepreneurs showed themselves able to keep up with, and sometimes lead, other countries. In the development of the pneumatic tyre, the improvement of the motor car and utility vehicle (taxis and lorries), in the use of metals and ferro-concrete in construction, in some branches of electrical engineering and chemicals, a good deal of brilliant pioneering work was done; and note that these were among the technologically most advanced branches of industry at this time.[81] In these new fields names like Michelin, Renault, Peugeot, Berliet, Eifel, Hennebique, Bréguet, Péchiney became famous throughout the world. In other cases, what was largely French enterprise was disguised behind imported names, like Dunlop and Thomson-Houston in rubber manufacture and electrical engineering respectively. To be noted is the fact that some of the new developments were taken up by old established firms or by men who came from a business background. If these expanding new industries are coupled with the remarkable rise of a modern steel and engineering industry referred to earlier then it can be seen that the broad basis had been laid for an advanced modern industry based on the technology of the twentieth century.[82] This was perhaps the outstanding economic fact of the pre-1914 years.

The principal defect of French industry, taken as a whole, was that it was not able to turn over earlier and more completely to large-scale production or to mass production methods. In any case, as some of the earlier comments show, it was part of an international system of division of labour; there was no reason why specialized machines, say in printing, should be made in France. There was no particular discredit in being dependent on Germany for synthetic dyestuffs. In return, France exported quality products or those in which her producers had a comparative cost advantage; no one thinks of criticising American industry for not being able to compete with Lyons in fine silk products or American farmers for not producing Camembert or Roquefort. It was, however, to a large extent the nature of the market, at home and abroad, which determined many of the characteristics of French industry.

For example, although France took a leading role in the production of motor cars from the early years of the twentieth century, this was still a small industry, producing a highly specialized product for a quality market. Much of the work done on cars (and on aircraft) was of the highly skilled artisan type; although the market was still small there was room for many firms using workshop methods and what amounted to a combination of the old craft skills with brilliant improvisation (France was the land of the *bricoleur*). Although some producers, like Renault, saw the advantages of producing a more standardized product, on a larger scale, the opportunities for mass production were simply not present in France, or Europe, before 1914. The French motor manufacturers did extremely well in the circumstances, but there was not yet room for a Henry Ford. In the same way, some gadgets and appliances for which there was not yet a large market in the country, such as typewriters, were still mainly imported from the U.S.A. where conditions had favoured both their earlier development and, still more important, their manufacture on a large scale with increasing returns. Thus such industries could not find a foothold in France before 1914 because the market was not large enough to justify the heavy outlay required to begin production. In time they did arise, as incomes grew, as structural changes continued and as consumption patterns moved closer to those associated with high-income urban living. In many cases it was not until after the Second World War that the conditions existed for the successful implantation of industries and practices (hire purchase, for example) of a modern type.

Only provisional answers are offered here to the questions which must be raised by students of French economic development in this period. The whole work will, it is hoped, have made clear the implicit assumptions upon which the qualitative assessment rests, and, bearing these in mind, the reader can be left to form his own judgement, or may be led to investigate more fully the many problems which have been left open or which he is entitled to feel have not been adequately dealt with. The lacunae in French economic history in this period, more than the earlier ones, perhaps, are many; many interesting fields of enquiry remain to be tilled but, however detailed research becomes and however quantitative the methods which it uses, the general hypothesis provides an indispensable starting point. If many of the conclusions and generalizations made in this chapter are found to be wanting as our knowledge advances, or as our perspective changes, no one will be less surprised, and more satisfied, than the author.

Notes and further reading

1. See the general works on economic history previously cited. There is no detailed economic history of this period in English or in French. Paul Combe, *Niveau de vie et progrès technique en France (1860-1939)* (Paris 1956) is too idiosyncratic in its assumptions, and in its approach, to be of much help to the student despite its length and its attempt to make use of quantitative methods. Like many authors, he is more interested in trying to

explain what went wrong with the French economy after 1918 than in examining the nature of the pre-1914 development, which is the main object here. For general background there are a host of political histories. Guy Chapman, *The Third Republic of France* (London 1962) covers the period up to 1894 and contains some very useful descriptive chapters on the economy. See also D. W. Brogan, *The Development of Modern France* (London 1940), especially Book VII, Chapter II, 'The Pleasant Land of France', the classic expression of a certain view of the French economy in this period. Jacques Chastenet, *Histoire de la troisième république,* 3 Vols. (Paris 1952, 1954, 1955) contains some perceptive glimpses of the economy. There is a useful chapter in C. Ambrosi and M. Tacel, *Histoire économique des grandes puissances* (Paris 1963) with the emphasis rather on the financial and institutional side.

2. Measurement of economic growth in France is particularly difficult owing to lack of statistics or their unreliability, although this has not prevented the compilation of statistical series. One student of the subject, Angus Maddison, 'Economic Growth in Western Europe', *Banca Nazionale del Lavoro Quarterly Review,* Vol. XII (Rome 1959), p. 59 note, reluctantly decided to give up the attempt. Some reserve is therefore necessary in using the figures given in Appendix A to this chapter.
3. For instance the well-known articles of D. S. Landes cited in previous chapters. Compare his characterization of British entrepreneurs in *The Cambridge Economic History of Europe,* Vol. VI, Part I (Cambridge 1965), pp. 563-4.
4. Indeed, it more properly applies to the preceding periods—why did not French industrialization move more rapidly in the initial stages?—and to the interwar period when the evidence of stagnation was very obvious—than to the one now being considered. It is therefore unsatisfactory to see this period in terms derived from other periods, for which they may have much greater validity.
5. For example, Landes and Brogan, op. cit., and some of the contributions to the volume *Modern France* (Princeton 1951), edited by E. M. Earle. Most of the writings of the late forties and early fifties were very deeply affected by visible evidences of French retardation and impressions formed in a period of economic difficulty after long years of stagnation. Historians of the 1870-1914 period have to be on their guard against assuming that the stereotypes then formed can be applied to this period without qualification.
6. But note the works by Palmade and Bouvier and the work in quantitative history now being carried out by, or under the direction of, J. Marczewski.
7. See the writings of Michel Augé-Laribé, notably *La politique agricole de la France de 1880 à 1940* (Paris 1950) and *La révolution agricole* (Paris 1955). A useful summary in M. Tracey, *Agriculture in Western Europe* (London 1964).
8. The available agricultural statistics have been critically appraised and processed by J. C. Toutain in 'Histoire quantitative de la

France', 1 and 2 in *Cahiers de l'Institut de Science Économique Appliquée*, 115, juillet, 1961, series AF Nos. 1 and 2.

9. Owing to doubts about the methods used in the compilation of statistics regarding land use and ownership precision is not possible. The enquiry of 1882 showed that 27 per cent of the cultivated land was farmed by tenants and 13 per cent by *métayers.* Almost all the remainder would be cultivated by peasant proprietors. Augé-Laribé, *La politique agricole,* p. 93. The probably more accurate survey of 1929 showed the following position:
   2,728,981 owner occupied holdings;
   728,131 farms;
   198,783 *métayage* holdings. Combe, op. cit., u. 207.
10. As Chapman puts it, op. cit., p. 109, 'A close look at the evidence of the standard of existence of the French peasant in the last quarter of the nineteenth century showed burdened men struggling to provide the means of life for themselves and their families, often in debt and nearly always without reserves except a few acres of land'.
11. Men with peasant backgrounds often made for white collar jobs, perhaps not only for the greater security they were supposed to have; in turn manual work on the land came to have a stigma attached to it and more might desert the land because of that. This is characteristic of the hilly and less fertile areas of southern and central France and Corsica.
12. This has been argued persuasively by Augé-Laribé, op. cit.
13. For the problems of the wine-growers see Charles K. Warden, *The Wine-growers of France and the Government since 1873* (New York 1961).
14. See Appendix.
15. See Toutain, op. cit., p. 209.
16. Rural wage-earners approximately equalled in number, over the country as a whole, the number of independent cultivators. Many of these belonged to peasant families and would probably become cultivators; others were engaged in rural crafts or were simply wage-labourers. They were the most likely to swell the rural exodus.
17. Peasants who had sampled another kind of life while serving with the army, for instance, might never return permanently to the village.
18. The standard work is E. O. Golob, *The Méline Tariff: French Agriculture and Nationalist Economic Policy* (New York 1944). He is indulgent towards the tariff and its chief architect. 'It is hardly an exaggeration to say', he writes, 'that it was part of the fundamental economic law of the Third Republic, and the life preserver of France', p. 8. The claim that the tariff saved agriculture is not very convincing. Compare Augé-Laribé, who regards Méline as a spokesman for the cotton spinners of the Vosges and the tariff as of no use to the peasants. Even so, Augé-Laribé cannot permit himself to admit that economic health required a very considerable shrinkage in the number engaged in agriculture and in its relative weight in the economy.

19. Some have lamented that this was not done to a much greater extent and make an unfavourable comparison with England and Germany. See Boudet, op. cit., p. 555 (contribution by E. Beau de Loménie).
20. Agriculture's percentage share of Gross physical product at current prices: annual averages

	at current prices	*at constant (1905-13) prices*
1865-74:	54	62
1875-84	50	54
1885-94	45	49
1895-1904	42	45
1905-13	41	41

from J. Marczewski, 'Some Aspects of the Economic Growth of France', *Economic Development and Cultural Change,* April, 1961.
21. According to Levasseur, *Histoire du Commerce de la France,* Vol. II (Paris 1912), p. 674, of four recent *cours* of political economy, one was protectionist, one did not take a stand one way or another and the other two were 'liberal' while admitting the need for moderately protectionist duties. Few economists or politicians espoused full free trade and the opposition to the tariff of 1892 was based upon leaving things as they were. On the other hand, some economists were now putting forward an openly protectionist position; Cauwès was the most prominent, see Golob, op. cit.
22. On tariffs, in addition to works already cited in this and earlier chapters, see P. W. L. Ashley, *Modern Tariff History* (3rd Ed., London 1920) and especially *Histoire du Commerce,* Vol. V, ed. Jacques Lacour-Gayet (Paris 1952), Le Commerce depuis le milieu du XIX siécle, by M. Beaumont.
23. This was important in a period of falling prices since it tended to increase the protective effect of duties.
24. As Golob, who inclines to such a view, admits, op. cit., p. 244.
25. It also became involved in costly tariff wars with Italy, which began before the Méline tariff and did not come to an end until 1898, and with Switzerland (1893-5).
26. There were also some bounties on export, and on production, of certain primary products in this period, but they were not of great significance compared with the role they were to play after 1918.
27. Harry D. White, *The French International Accounts, 1880-1913* (Cambridge, Mass. 1933), remains the most imposing study of the French balance of payments in this period. Some of his assumptions and computations are open to question, see the critique and alternative figures in Cameron, op. cit., Appendix B.
28. White, op. cit., Ch. IV passim.
29. This weakness can be exemplified by the following figures: in 1913 French shipping tonnage was less than 10 per cent of that of the registered British tonnage; 38 per cent of it was still in sail; only 30 per cent of seaborne trade was carried in French ships.

30. The earnings from foreign investments, the largest single item in the credit balance, are the main source of difficulty. Since this must be an estimated figure it depends upon how large these investments are computed to have been. On White's estimates, net earnings from this source were roughly equivalent to the new investments made annually overseas. Cameron, who claims that White's totals are underestimates, puts the earnings from foreign investments at a higher figure so that 'French investments abroad not only created the income from which new investments were made, but financed a portion of the commodity import surplus as well', op. cit., p. 505.
31. There is no pretence here at a description of French industrial development in this period, for which Clapham is still useful. *Le monde des affaires en France*, edited by Jacques Boudet (Paris 1952), although compiled as a reference work for the businessman or general reader, contains a good deal of interesting historical material.
32. Some suggestive pages in Claude Digeon, *La crise allemande de la pensée française* (Paris 1959), p. 476 seq. Awareness of the German threat was, however, late in appearing and was less pronounced than in Britain; as it took form, however, there was a tendency to deprecate the relative stagnation and decadence of France compared with German efficiency and dynamism.
33. There are many discussions of this point and the importance of quality production, see, e.g. the works of Brogan and Landes. G. Hanotaux puts it this way: 'Toutefois il faut noter la force de résistance de la petite industrie, expliquée par l'importance qu' a prise dans la production nationale de notre pays la qualité et le fini du produit, qui s'accomode mal du travail en série et des modèles uniformes', *Histoire de la nation française,* Vol. X, p. 449.
34. See, for example, the nostalgic remarks referring to pre-1914 rural and small-town economic life in the U.S.A. in E. Kefauver, *In a Few Hands* (London 1965).
35. Clapham, on the whole, puts the emphasis the other way; what strikes him most is the large number of small firms using little power or hired labour. From the present-day perspective what seems important is not what was dying away—however long it was to take to die—but what was struggling to be born and what is so evident to-day technologically advanced, large-scale modern industry. French self-depreciation and patronizing Anglo-Saxon enquiry have perhaps both seen the picture out of focus.
36. It was also a difference between 'a family capitalism' in textiles and consumer goods and a capitalism of large units which found its clearest expression in the producer goods industries. See C. Morazé, *La France bourgeoise* (Paris 1946).
37. The economic consequences of 'excessive' centralization have often been deplored, most forcefully by J. F. Gravier in *Décentralisation et progrès technique* (Paris 1953). It was probably not until the age of the motor car that anything like 'atrophy' in the metropolitan centre itself becomes a possibility. In France, it was rather

the lack of powerful provincial poles of attraction which could arrest the flow of capital, talent, labour and industry to the capital. See Kemp, op. cit. On the other hand, at this time, Paris was pre-eminently the place in which modern patterns of urban living were being developed with, perhaps, favourable net effects for the growth of the economy.

38. As in the case, for example, of the *Compagnie française pour l'exploitation des Procédés Thomson-Houston* established in 1893.
39. The origins of the Peugot business go back to the early eighteenth century; it turned from textiles to metallurgy and established a firm position in the market for a wide range of metal manufactures. Some were staple lines such as utensils and tools, others, like crinoline frames, it took up as opportunity afforded. In the eighties it added bicycles and in 1893 its first car; a motor car factory was opened at Sochaux in 1912. The Bréguet family business went back to the later eighteenth century when a Swiss immigrant established its reputation in the production of chronometers. It grew with industrialization, turning to the electrical construction industry in the latter part of the nineteenth century and playing a pioneer role here. Louis Bréguet, who branched out into aviation in its pioneer days, was of the fifth generation. See the brief accounts in Boudet, op. cit., pp. 675-683.
40. See Boudet, op. cit., N. J. G. Pounds and W. N. Parker, *Coal and Steel in Europe* (London 1957) and J. Levainville, *L'industrie du fer* (Paris (1932).
41. Schneider and Wendel bought the rights from a Belgian, Taskin, who had, in turn, acquired them from Thomas for £50; the price they paid for an invention which enabled them to transform their firms, was £32,000. Boudet, op. cit., p. 91. 'Nowhere was the Thomas process welcomed more warmly and adopted more speedily than in Lorraine'. Pounds and Parker, op. cit., p. 196.
42. For the early history of this and other employers' organizations see Roger Priouret, *Origines du patronat français* (Paris 1963).
43. Boudet, op. cit., p. 108.
44. A short account is given in T. H. Burnham and G. O. Hoskins, *Iron and Steel in Britain, 1817–1930* (London 1943).
45. It should be noted, too, that the leading employers in iron and steel were often of the third generation, thus suggesting caution towards the idea that men who inherited wealth necessarily showed less initiative than the self-made founder of the firm or new men. Opportunity counted for a great deal: especially the possibilities opened up in new areas, such as Lorraine, in which the landscape could be re-made and there were no historical resistances to change.
46. A vivid description in Philippe Ariès, *Histoire des populations françaises et leurs attitudes devant la vie* (Paris 1948), pp. 221 seq.
47. Clapham lays considerable emphasis on it. Kindelberger is inconclusive: 'it makes just as much sense to say that faster French economic development would have produced more coal as that more coal would have produced faster economic development',

op. cit., p. 324. See also Kemp, op. cit., p. 345 and references.

48. W. G. Hoffman, *The Growth of Industrial Economies* (trans. by W. O. Henderson and W. H. Chaloner, Manchester, 1958) gives the following figures:

All industry = 100

	Industrial employment		*Net output*		
	Consumer goods	*Capital goods*	*Consumer goods*	*Capital goods*	*Ratio*
1861-5	63.9	16.7	64.6	14.5	4.5
1896	49.9	18.1	43.8	19.7	2.3
1921	37.4	24.9	35.1	23.2	1.5

49. Jean Bouvier, *Le Crédit Lyonnais de 1863 à 1882* (Paris 1961). For banking in this period see *inter alia* Boudet and Palmade, op. cit.
50. Bouvier, op. cit., p. 374 seq. This was at the same time an episode in the decline of the French dyestuffs industry under the pressure of German competition, see John Joseph Beer, *The Emergence of the German Dye Industry* (Urbana, Illinois, 1959).
51. Cameron, op. cit. passim.
52. Cameron, 'Profit, croissance et stagnation au xixe. siècle', *Economie appliquée,* v. (Paris 1957).
53. Jean Bouvier, *Le Krach de l'Union Générale (1878-1885)* (Paris 1960) for a detailed account.
54. According to Pierre Cauboue, 'The French Money Market', *Banca Nazionale del Lavoro Quarterly Review,* Vol. VII (Rome 1955) there was only one French book—Tenel and Lejeune's *Traité des opèrations commerciales des banques*—on 'banking matters' que peuvent l'être le metre, le gramme ou le watt'.
55. To have power is not the same thing as to exercise leadership. Ever since the July monarchy the bankers had been denounced as the 'real' rulers of France.
56. Clapham, op. cit., p. 388.
57. Chastenet, op. cit., Vol. IX, p. 277, 'le franc apparait un étalon aussi invariable, aussi à l'abri de l'action des pouvoirs publics que peuvant l'être le metre, le gramme ou le watt'.
58. See H. Feis, *Europe: the World's Banker* (New Haven 1930).
59. As A. K. Cairncross puts it, *Home and Foreign Investment, 1870-1913* (Cambridge 1953). 'The French rentier—the most cautious of capitalists and the most credulous—was content with a gilt-edged return on securities in which no self-respecting gambler would have dabbled', p. 225, and see the whole analysis of French foreign investment in pp. 223-5.
60. A summary in Ambrosi and Tacel, op. cit.
61. In the case of Algeria much of this infrastructure had been laid and the demand for wine, following the phylloxera in France, as well as for minerals and agricultural products, gave this territory some economic importance from the eighties and attracted immigrants, though more from other Mediterranean countries than from France.

62. Henri Brunschwig, *Mythes et réalités de l'impérialisme colonial français* (Paris 1960), regards the economic value of colonies to the nation as 'mythical' and attributes French expansionism to the nationalist fervour which followed the events of 1870-1.
63. An attempt was made to do this by Constant Southworth, *The French Colonial Venture* (London 1931) with the conclusion that 'the French colonies, from an economic point of view, have been an unprofitable venture for France . . .', p. 131.
64. Brunschwig, Ch. 6 passim, Augé-Laribé, op. cit., first part, Ch. VI.
65. Between 1901 and 1913 trade with the colonies increased by two-thirds, or by 67.6 per cent if Algeria and Tunisia are included; but general trade grew by 84 per cent over the same period. In 1913 colonial trade amounted to 12 per cent of total trade and the colonies had a merchandise trade deficit with the rest of the world which fell on the French balance of payments.
66. The term is used both by Henry Sée in his *Histoire économique* and by Lenin in *Imperialism.*
67. If French population had grown at the same rate as the British after 1850 it would have amounted to 60 million in 1910 instead of the actual 39 million. A. Sauvy, *Thèorie générale de la population,* 2 vols: (Paris 1959), Vol. II, p. 13. See also Pierre Froment, *Démographie économique* (Paris 1947).
68. There were some family allowance schemes instituted by employers. The absence of a progressive income tax ruled out one possible form of discrimination in favour of families with children. Only the seventh or subsequent children were eligible for any state aid before 1914; the regulations applicable to conscripts also made allowances for families but could do little against the possibly unfavourable effects on the birth rate of military service itself.
69. There has been a good deal of controversy on these matters. See, for example, Louis Chevalier, *Traité de démographie* (Paris 1961), pp. 188 seq.
70. Ariès, op. cit., makes an interesting comparison of the population pattern in France and England, pp. 347 seq. As he points out, the creation of large industrial centres with a numerous proletariat of a modern type only really came in France in the latter part of the nineteenth century when factors making for family limitation were already operating among the workers. The French industrial towns, therefore, never attained the fecundity of their English counterparts of the early nineteenth century.
71. Some areas were more sharply influenced by the trend than others. According to Dudley Kirk, E. M. Earle (ed.), op. cit., p. 316, 'By 1860, 37 departments of France had net reproduction rates below the level of replacement, by 1890 more than half of the departments (49 of a total of 87) were not replacing themselves, and the deserted village was becoming a common thing in France'. It must be added, however, that it was not necessarily an undesirable situation that infertile or hilly lands should go out of cultivation. Some of the writing on decentralization seems to

imply that the benefits of modern technology can be obtained without concentration and that some kind of equality of development between areas is possible or desirable.

72. Edouard Dolléans, *Histoire du mouvement ouvrier*, Vol. II (Paris 1947), p. 25.
73. Jurgen Kuczynski, *A Short History of Labour Conditions in France 1800 to the Present Day* (London 1946) shows average real wages rising from 80 in 1879-80 to 100 in 1900, p. 128, and to 104 for 1909 to 1914, p. 162. See also Paul Louis, *La condition ouvrière en France depuis cent ans* (Paris 1950), Ch. V, is instructive on the absolute level of living of the working class, which, in most cases, meant little or no expenditure on medical care or holidays; housing conditions which had improved little if at all between the eighties and 1914 and a very tight budget for the necessary expenditure on rent, food and clothing.
74. For example, the conditions described in *Germinal* were changing by the end of the century, although the mining areas conserved many of the traits which Zola described. Wages, in money terms, had practically doubled in a period of stable or falling prices. Miners became less 'primitive', able to save, to improve the lot of their families and to form, after 1884, powerful trade unions. See Ariès, op. cit., pp. 233-241.
75. This would be true, at this stage, for example, of the motor car and aviation industries and part of the engineering industry; *le métallo* was still typically an all-round, skilled man.
76. Clapham, op. cit., p. 260, say that 'in the nineties, the government of France finally reverted to extreme forcing tactics for the maintenance and development both of her industries and of agriculture.' But this was a *tactical matter*, based mainly on tariffs and bounties in response to pressure from the producers; that it was, in strategic terms, of much value is doubtful. As for the weight of the state in the economy, public expenditure by Central and local government bodies amounted to some 16 per cent of G.N.P. in 1913 against 28 per cent in 1960; social expenditure amounted to only 2.8 per cent of G.N.P. in 1913 against 18.8 per cent in 1960. The great increase in the role of the state really came after 1944 although it had been steadily increasing between the wars.
77. The Freycinet plan probably comes in for more than its fair share of attention in histoires which are biased towards an institutional treatment of economic change. In its essentials, this 'plan' provided for further state assistance in developing the means of communication. Lines of 'local interest' which had been losing money were taken over and others were given financial assistance. A wholly new network of local lines was provided for in Algeria as well as France amounting in all to about 5,000 miles. Sums were also set aside for the modernization of canals and for roads and harbours. The finances for these projects were provided by a public loan. The law was voted in 1879 and the final convention with the railway companies, which assumed control of most of the new lines, was concluded in 1883. This, the most notable

example of state intervention in this period, thus left most of the railways in private control.

78. Thus Léon Blum: 'J'aiécrit dans un article récent, que l'équilibre du budget importe au parti socialiste plus encore qu'à tout autre groupe républican. Mais il ne nous suffit pas d'avoir un budget en équilibre; il nous faut un budget en excédent', *L'oeuvre de Leon Blum, 1891-1905* (Paris 1954), p. 510.
79. Pointed out by N. J. G. Pounds, *The Ruhr* (London 1952), pp. 118, 189-90.
80. J. J. Beer, op. cit.
81. Nothing has been said in detail here about the chemical industry, where, outside the dye-stuffs field considerable advances took place with a process of concentration into the three main firms, St. Gobain, Kuhlmann and Péchiney, nor about the electrical trades or the production of aluminium where French enterprise was by no means backward.
82. According to Kuczynski's calculations: 'The number of machines in use, which rose by about 30 per cent between 1890 and 1900, continued to rise by somewhat over 10 per cent up to 1910. . . . Between 1890 and 1900 the amount of power employed had risen by roughly 100 per cent; during the following ten years the rise amounted to about two-thirds.' Op. cit., p. 157.

APPENDIX TO CHAPTER IX

TABLE 1

Proportion of Rural Inhabitants and Proportion of Labour Force in Agriculture

Census year	*Total pop. Mn.*	*Rural pop. Mn.*	*Rural pop. % total*	*% of pop. living from agric.*	*% of active pop in agric.*
1872	36.10	24.89	58.9	51.3	49.0
1881	37.67	24.57	65.2	48.4	47.5
1891	38.34	24.03	62.2	45.5	41.4
1901	38.96	23.00	59.1	(not available)	44.2
1911	39.60	22.10	55.8	38.1	40.9

Source: Toutain, op. cit. Table 141

TABLE 2

Industrial Production per Capita–1955 = 100

	1901	1913	*% increase* 1901–1913
France	35	55	57
U.K.	63	77	22
Germany	55	77	40

Source: Parett, V., Bloch, G., Industrial Production in Western Europe and the United States 1901-1955,' Table 30, p. 294, *Banca Nazionale del Lavoro Quarterly Review* No. 39, 1956.

%shares of West European Industrial Production

	1901	1913	1955
France	19.0	20.0	14.0
U.K.	34.0	29.5	30.0
Germany	22.0	23.5	23.5

Source: ibid., Table 4, p. 192.

TABLE 3

Comparison of Coal Output per Head and Industrial Output per Head, 1913

	Coal	*Industry*
U.K.	674	180
Germany	281	157
France	100	100

On this showing, then, French industrial performance was better than her ouput of coal would suggest.

Source: Walter, F. 'Recherches sur le développement économique de la France', *Cahiers de l'Institut de Science Économique Appliquée,* March 1957, p. 40.

CHAPTER X

Epilogue

(i) *French capitalism in 1914: equilibrium or inadaptability?*

There are sound reasons why this work should conclude in 1914. The outbreak of the First World War marks the end of an era in French economic history and opens a new one of great turbulence and complexity. To examine it adequately would require another substantial volume.[1] In a sense, however, the present study can be regarded as an introduction to the history of French capitalism in the modern period. Sometimes it seems that the modern problems of the French economy are considered too much in abstraction from its antecedents, as though they only began after the First War. On the other hand, some of the characteristics of the economy which then appeared were largely novel and pre-1914 development may be wrongly appraised if this is not recognized. One of the tasks of the historian of the French economy is to distinguish the old from the new, as has been seen constantly throughout this work. Entirely new influences and problems are certainly to be found after 1918; in particular this period stands out as one of economic perturbation compared with the comparatively tranquil and expansive years of the later nineteenth and the early twentieth century. It was not surprising that, in the inter-war years, many looked back nostalgically at *la belle époque* when savings conserved their value and material progress seemed assured. Frequently, too, the symptoms of the change were taken for its cause.

In the light of what has happened, not only since 1914, but also during the period of unprecedented growth, since the mid-fifties, the whole of this modern period of French economic history from 1870 stands in need of appraisal from a new perspective. Equally, the significance of recent developments needs to be evaluated in the light of the long-run trends which begin about this time. There is no pretence at being able to perform either of these tasks here, but, although 1914 is our terminal point, it may be permitted to sum up briefly the nature of the French economy on the eve of its entry into the war and to peer into the subsequent decades of instability, stagnation and renewed expansion.

In the pre-1914 years France appeared to be prosperous and expansive. Wealth and income were steadily growing and in the last years of peace the industrial growth matched or exceeded that of Britain and Germany. Emphasis has already been laid on the fact that in this period the foundations of a technologically advanced industry of large units were being laid. And it is necessary to insist that, although, as elsewhere, there were periods of crisis and depression, when the cyclical fluctuations are smoothed out, the economy grew steadily. In the aggregate it was never stagnant, although there were large sectors which virtually stood still. Stability is not, however, the same thing as stagnation: at least to many it seemed a virtue. The still large proportion of the population committed to agriculture was taken to be a sign of equilibrium compared with the 'overindustrialization' of Britain or Germany. The old forms of artisan and small-scale industry continued to hold a strong position in the economy. There were relatively large numbers of small property-owners, besides the peasantry; a petty bourgeoisie which was more numerous and more influential than in countries which were more thoroughly industrialized or had experienced a different history. In social terms peasantry and petty bourgeoisie formed a conservative and stabilizing force, tending to grow in wealth as the economy expanded, but, at the same time, a barrier to more rapid change.

The stability of French society was always relative. Its history had been punctuated by wars and revolutions and even in this period there were some sharp social struggles. Even the peasantry, in some places, was discontented enough to riot. Some members of the lower middle class, feeling threatened by the growth of large scale industry and the influence of high finance as well as by the rise of a militant labour movement, turned to right-wing movements and anti-semitism. Anarchism found its adherents and the direct action of the syndicalists was disturbing to industrialists and property-owners. These rumbles of impending disruption, accompanied by growing international tensions, confirmed the petty bourgeoisie all the more in the need for security and stability. They sought safe outlets for their growing savings and directed their sons into the employment of the state or the respectable professions. For the owners of capital this was a period of effortless enrichment without the fear of monetary depreciation or high taxation to finance large government expenditures. For all the signs that these conditions would not be permanent, stability and security were the dominant features of the period. Prudence, moderation and provision for the future were the characteristics of the rentier mentality of the French petty bourgeois, in his business affairs as in his most intimate personal concerns. Nowhere was this more pronounced than his practice of family limitation. Children were seen as divisors for a given patrimony, rather than ends in themselves or eventual contributors to family income. The outcome of this, a slowing down of population growth almost to stability, and its possible economic effects, have already been referred to. This population pattern seemed in profound accord with the whole nature of the society which produced it.

Yet, as has also been pointed out, this was a period in which French capitalism had gone through important changes and the ground had been prepared for others. New technologies, advanced financial techniques, more complex business procedures, international competition, all tended towards large-scale organization. Businesses grew or combined into larger units; industrialists sought the economies of large-scale production; wealth accumulated on an unprecedented scale: there was a ceaseless search for investment outlets and wider markets. True, in France, these processes may have been less pronounced than elsewhere, or less openly admitted, but they were certainly present.

The new, 'high capitalism' of large units found expression, then, despite the continued prominence of the earlier forms, archaic techniques and backward-looking habits and attitudes in business circles. In the long perspective, it was the emergence of the former, rather than the persistence of much which was old and obsolescent which best distinguishes this period in economic history. It was to dominate the later history of capitalism in France, as elsewhere, only to win its final victory as late as the 1950's in the form which some were to call 'neo-capitalism' but is best seen as the working out of established trends in monopoly capitalism.

The 1914 economy, on the surface prosperous and stable, was building up pressures which were to contribute to the great upheavals of the following decades. It was, despite the weight of the backward-looking sectors, dominated by a continued trend towards industrialization and a capitalism of large units. It was growing, and its growth was rapid. It was an economy of profound contrasts and mounting contradictions; the interplay of continuity and change, of stability and growth, noted so often, provides for this, as for earlier periods, a valid framework for analysis. The picture is thus a complex one, not to be explained in terms of a simple stereotype or a few causative factors. Its understanding requires consideration of a long involved history.

France was an 'old' industrial country, in one sense; its industrialization had roots back in the eighteenth century. The long experience with machine techniques and the institutions and practices of capitalism, the reserves of capital in the hands of the property-owning classes, make it possible to speak of 'maturity'. But, as has been suggested, this term, if taken too literally, can be misleading. How could a 'mature' economy have discovered the reserves for the rapid growth of recent years? The answer is to be found rather in the incompleteness of French development which had pushed far ahead in some sectors and still remained very much behind in others. Or, to look at the problem in a different way, it was the uneven nature of its development, giving the sharp contrasts so often noted, which was one of the most pronounced features of the French economy. It was this, for example, which accounted for the abundance of savings seeking profitable employment side-by-side with an industry suffering from under-investment and the inability of the market to do anything about it. A country which, comparatively speaking, was under-urbanized—of a population of 41.5 million under 7 million lived in towns of over 50,000 inhabitants—could hardly be regarded as 'mature' in another sense. The characteristics of modern life are so closely bound up with urban-type work and the pattern of urban living that it is not surprising that, in

1914, France still conserved many of the characteristics of an underdeveloped country. Not only were whole regions underdeveloped in a literal sense, but not only then, but thirty years later, family patterns, consumption habits, commercial methods and the outlook of industrial entrepreneurs were still marked by their origins in the eighteenth century, or earlier.

The great event which had determined many of the prevailing structural characteristics of the French economy was, of course, the Revolution of 1789. The effects of the revolutionary land settlement, the family pattern intertwined with possessive individualism, and the nature of the bourgeoisie which rose to dominance as a result of it have all been referred to many times. While the Revolution ensured bourgeois dominance and a legal system attuned to the needs of a capitalist economy it created a social balance which, in other respects, was unfavourable to change and growth. Instead of a capitalism geared to the boundless pursuit of acquisition it was a capitalism more concerned with maintaining established positions. Part of the economy was still anchored to these practices while the other, dynamic and steadily more important part, was moving into the twentieth century on the same lines as in the other advanced countries. In the mid-twentieth century the tensions and conflicts springing from this clash between the old and the new were to reach their height.

In 1914, then, the French economy was very much in process of transformation. The rates of growth suggest it. The evidence of industrial change supports the view. The growing role of producer goods industries corroborates it. Even the import of machine tools seems to indicate a growing emphasis on modernization and technical change in industry. The new industries of the scientific type were attracting much interest; brilliant pioneers and entrepreneurs were pushing them on. In a qualitative sense French industry could teach as well as learn; in some fields it held the initiative. Undoubtedly the nature of the internal market and the lack of a powerful place in world markets acted as a brake on these developments, and would have done even if the war had not distorted and retarded them.

(ii) *Since 1914: strains and adjustments.*

The economic history of France after 1914 was compounded of instability, insecurity, stagnation and crisis to an extent which made the pre-1914 years stand out as a time of certainty and progress. The territory of the nation was twice invaded and was once occupied completely by the German army. The wars involved an immense waste of resources and loss of life. Industrial societies have a resilience to such disasters which seems to exceed that which they have to monetary disorders or depression. The rapid recovery from the effects of the First World War was followed by a slowing down and then a plunge into the void created by the World Economic Depression of the 1930s. A crisis of confidence seized the business and political leaders. Investment, especially industrial investment, fell sharply. Production fell away from the 1929 peaks. Industrial equipment aged; house building dropped off sharply and there was all too little renovation or expansion of basic social equipment such as schools, universities, hospitals, roads and public utilities. Population trends became even more sharply depressive and the ageing process continued; the labour force was supplemented, as in no other European country at this time, by a large foreign immigration. At least that showed that economic decline was more relative than absolute, but the prospect seemed depressing in the years before the Second World War. That sheet-anchor of the timid bourgeois, the franc itself, suffered from inflation and successive devaluations. Monetary stability had apparently gone for ever.

The working class appeared to be more permanently and completely alienated from the rest of society than at any previous period, but it was unable, as a deeply divided minority socially, as well as politically, to obtain political power. The politicians who represented it had many of the weaknesses of their rivals in the leadership of the middle class parties with whom they shared, in the main, a common background. The great social struggles of the twenties and thirties, which culminated in the unfulfilled promise of 1936 and the Popular Front, merely intensified the general crisis of confidence and exposed the lack of leadership at all levels. Certainly economic development, if slowed to a snail's pace (and it was actually negative in terms of aggregate production) did not stop entirely. France did share in the technological changes of the period, but there was no fundamental transformation. All the traits which stood for stability, and for the past, seemed to be strengthened in their inertia; the forces making for change had to make their way painfully in an unreceptive environment. The bourgeoisie looked back nostalgically at the pre-1914 epoch as a kind of golden age, when the franc stood at par and was acceptable in any part of the world. The France of those days was very much part of that world described by Keynes.[2] The France of the twenties and especially thirties seemed to be in decline and disarray, definitely to have its best days behind it.

The paralysis of will which had the politicians and business leaders in its grip was demonstrated tragically in 1940. Everything which its critics had been saying about the decay and degeneration of the Third Republic seemed to have been proved by Hitler's Panzers. The defeat and capitulation was clearly the outcome of a long-standing and deeply-rooted process. Perhaps understandably, historians have paid it less attention than later, and more creditable, episodes in recent French history. It is notable, however, that one of the best analyses, though written from passion and experience rather than from dispassionate research, is the work of one of the leading economic historians of his day.[3] There is certainly need for further enquiry into the defeat from the standpoint of social and economic history.

The Vichy régime, which has been more thoroughly studied, in its social policy and economic measures indicated a yearning for the past which was a reaction to the upheavals and calamities which had occurred practically uninterruptedly since 1914. Its supporters sought to recreate a stable social order such as they imagined had at one time existed. Their ideal was a corporate order without social conflicts, sheltered from dynamic contacts with the exigencies of modern life. Their backward-looking utopia never had a chance. The French economy continued to run down and what parts remained viable were geared to the war needs of the Wehrmacht. Allied bombing, then the activities of the Resistance and the resumption of destructive land warfare on French territory, further disrupted economic life until the end of the war.

The destruction and disruption of the war, the dislocation of ties with the world market and the problems of reconstruction and reconversion, compounded with the inherited weaknesses of an economy which had been stagnant for two decades, combined to confront the country after 1945 with problems of unprecedented scale and difficulty. Few thought that the operations of the market alone could be counted upon to restore the economy to something like working order. The rôle of the state, which had been growing, though more often to buttress established positions than to promote change, before the war, now became paramount. Nationalizations, big changes in social policy, a more active budgetary policy, state planning, were broadly accepted as inevitable. There was a large balance of payments deficit which required outside financial aid to deal with it. Social conflicts and political divisions were as sharp as ever; for some years French capitalism seemed to be on the verge of collapse or of social revolution. The discrediting or demoralization of the old leaders, the reaction from the short-lived euphoria of the Resistance period, the hardships suffered by the working class, the huge investments needs to make good wartime destruction and modernize industry, the lengthy wars in Indo-China and Algeria and their impact at home, the inability of the leaders of the Fourth Republic to compose their differences or command respect contributed to making France the 'sick man of Europe' in the late forties and early fifties.

However, partly as the French expression of a world-wide process, new long-term forces of expansion were lifting the economy forward on an ascending plane. The very need for investment resulting from wartime destruction and pre-war neglect of industrial and social equipment stimulated a boom. France was, in a sense, catching up and assimilating the new techniques which had emerged during or since the war at the same time. A new, high level of investment, a high and steady demand for labour, a growth in the home market, partly associated with the breaking of the old population trend, but also with the adoption of new methods of publicity and marketing and thus alterations in consumer habits, strengthened all the modern characteristics of the French economy while weakening the archaic survivals. In the administration, and in the top levels of the business world, new men came to the fore, more rapidly, indeed, than they could have done in the normal course of evolution. Fresh minds, conscious of French inferiority in many fields, and anxious to do something to remedy it, grappled with the technical and organizational problems. These new men were largely responsible for navigating France into the modern era and taking the risks which went with it.

The establishment of a higher rate of investment and thus the modernization of wide sections of industry and the provision of the country with a more adequate infrastructure, made possible a continuous growth in national income and in personal incomes. Consumption patterns reflected this with an expansion of demand for consumer durables, the product of sophisticated manufacturing industries, as well as for services of the kind inseparable from modern urban living. Foreign, particularly American, capital was attracted into France precisely in these expanding modern sectors which offered high profits. But capital was forthcoming in large quantities from domestic sources for private and public investment. Labour continued to flow from the agrarian sector into industry and immigration made an important contribution to the supply of unskilled and heavy manual labour. Many French workers were thus able to move up into higher grades at the same time as general job opportunities improved and real wages, over the period as a whole, steadily rose.

With the coming to power of General de Gaulle the long political crisis of the post-war years was brought, at any rate, provisionally to an end—how provisionally was shown by the 'events' of May and June, 1968. In a way, as was the case with Napoleon III, he provided the political conditions appropriate for the new stage which capitalism had reached in France and satisfied the bourgeois craving for security and stability while furthering growth and social and economic 'modernization' at the same time. In fact, growth had begun before 1958 and the measures which presumably stimulated or facilitated it had been initiated by his predecessors. But it was not simply that the new régime reaped what others had sown; it provided the essential conditions without which the harvest might not have been reaped at all. French capitalism was once again in a period when it needed a strong 'bonapartist' state and could hardly afford the luxury of parliamentarism of the old type. The new representative figure was a 'technocrat'; a businessman educated and trained to serve the big corporations, a '*grand commis*' skilled in the practices of modern administration, a highly educated scientist and technician in the field of electronics, atomic energy, aviation or engineering.

Before the onrush of the new the old France gave ground, but it has not yet disappeared. The emphasis upon the virtues of the little man, upon family enterprise, upon variety and quality still exist. There are still inefficient sectors, or enterprises which continue to exist thanks to the protection or privileges they have won from the state. Agriculture is still over-weighted in the economy. Much of the distributive apparatus is wasteful. The type of facility sometimes called 'demographic investment' still lags behind, largely because of years of neglect or because they have been low down on the schedule of priorities in the recent boom. There are still areas where the old conditions continue to prevail: the France of the small town with its rather unenterprising petty bourgeoisie to whom the old stereotypes of French entrepreneurship still largely apply. In the conflict between the old and the new, which at times in the post-war years has become open and bitter, there is no doubt that the latter has steadily gained ground. There are still signs of underdevelopment, still backward areas and serious problems arising from regional disparities, but the main line of development has clearly been towards modernization. France is now more like Britain, even more like the U.S.A., than it was twenty or fifty years ago.

The events of 1968-69 showed that the accelerated development and structural change which French capitalism had experienced since 1945, far from providing a new basis for stability, had sharpened social strains to breaking point. For the student of economic history not satisfied with surface impressions and a summary conclusion from statistical tables, the explosion should have come as no surprise. And, without attempting to prophecy, it may be concluded that the now legendary 'May-June events' were not the end of a chapter but the foretaste of things to come.

Notes and further reading

1. A longer study of the interwar period is in preparation as a companion to this volume. A detailed panorama is available in Alfred Sauvy, *Histoire économique de la France entre les deux guerres*, 2 vols. (Paris 1965, 1968). For a preliminary assessment, see Kemp, T., 'Aspects of French Capitalism between the Wars', *Science and Society*, Vol. XXXIII, No. 1, 1969.
2. In a famous passage in *The Economic Consequences of the Peace* (London 1920), Ch. II passim.
3. Marc Bloch, *Strange Defeat* (translated by Gerard Hopkins, Oxford 1949).

Index of Authors Cited

This Index refers only to the notes and further reading

General Index

This index does not refer to the notes and further reading